Thomas Middleton
Three Plays

Edited with an Introduction by
KENNETH MUIR
formerly King Alfred Professor of English Literature
University of Liverpool

DENT, LONDON
ROWMAN AND LITTLEFIELD, TOTOWA, N.J.

© J. M. Dent & Sons Ltd, 1975

All rights reserved
Made in Great Britain
at the
Aldine Press · Letchworth · Herts
for
J. M. DENT & SONS LTD
Aldine House · Albemarle Street · London
First published 1975
First published in the United States 1975
by ROWMAN AND LITTLEFIELD, Totowa, New Jersey

This book if bound as a paperback is
subject to the condition that it may not
be issued on loan or otherwise except in
its original binding
This book is set in 8 on 9 pt Times New Roman 327

Dent edition
Hardback ISBN: 0 460 10368 **7**
Paperback ISBN: 0 460 11368 **2**

Rowman and Littlefield edition
Library of Congress Cataloging in Publication Data

Middleton, Thomas, d. 1627.
 Thomas Middleton: three plays.

 (Rowman and Littlefield university library)
 Bibliography: p.
 CONTENTS: A chaste maid in Cheapside. Women beware
women. The changeling.
 I. Title.
PR2712.M8 1975   822^{1}.3   74–6889
 ISBN 0–87471–555–5
 ISBN 0–87471–556–3 (pbk.)

CONTENTS

ACKNOWLEDGMENTS

I am indebted to previous editors of separate plays of Middleton in the Revels Series (N. W. Bawcutt and R. B. Parker), in the Regents Renaissance Drama Series (G. W. Williams), in the New Mermaids (Roma Gill and Patricia Thomson) and in the Fountainwell Drama Texts (Charles Barber). I have also consulted an unpublished edition of *Women Beware Women* by R. B. Parker in the Harold Cohen Library, Liverpool University. My greatest debt is to Jane Sherman for many excellent suggestions on all three plays.

K. M.

INTRODUCTION

Thomas Middleton, the son of a builder, was born in London in April 1580. On his father's death in 1585 his mother married again. As she engaged in litigation with her second husband, Thomas Harvey, it may be assumed that the marriage was not a happy one. Middleton matriculated at Queen's College, Oxford, in 1598, but there is no record of his having graduated. In February 1601 he was reported to be 'daily accompanying the players' in London, and not long afterwards he married Mary Marbeck. He had inherited some money from his father's estate. By this time he had published three feeble poems in popular *genres*: biblical paraphrase (*The Wisdom of Solomon Paraphrased*, 1597), satire (*Micro-Cynicon*, 1599) and complaint (*The Ghost of Lucrece*, 1600).

Middleton then began to write for the stage, encouraged perhaps by his brother-in-law who was an actor. At first he was one of Henslowe's hack-writers, collaborating with Dekker, Webster and others; then he wrote for two of the children's companies [1] and thereafter as a free-lance. After 1613 he provided regular pageants for the City of London. His last play, *A Game of Chess*, a political and religious satire of extraordinary brilliance, celebrates the return of Prince Charles without a Spanish bride. It had an unprecedented success before it was banned after protests from the Spanish Ambassador. Middleton died three years later and was buried at Newington Butts on 4 July 1627.

In recent years Middleton's reputation has risen steadily, most critics now regarding him as the best of Shakespeare's successors; but his reputation still rests on a handful of plays. Everyone knows *Women Beware Women* and *The Changeling* and they have been successful on the modern stage; many enjoy *A Chaste Maid in Cheapside* and *A Trick to Catch the Old One*; and *A Game at Chess* is recognized as a remarkable *tour de force*. But Bullen's edition of the complete works has long been unobtainable except in libraries, and the projected Canadian edition is not likely to appear for some years. The useful selection in the Old Mermaid series has not been reprinted for more than a generation, and the choice of plays in the second volume was ill-advised. Middleton wrote many different kinds of play, and a fully representative selection would require three volumes the size of the present one.

---

[1] *The Phoenix* and *A Trick to Catch the Old One* were performed by 'the Children of Paules' (originally attached to the St Paul's choir school) and *A Chaste Maid* was performed by the Lady Elizabeth's servants, apparently augmented by the boys from the Queen's Revels. For the popularity of the child actors see *Hamlet* II. ii. 344 ff.

1

CITIZEN COMEDIES

Elizabethan comedy is generally romantic rather than realistic, festive rather than satirical. It is concerned with aristocratic characters in a foreign setting—Italy, France, Illyria. In the seventeenth century there was a change. Romantic comedies continued to be written but a number of dramatists, writing particularly for the children's companies and for the wealthier, more sophisticated audiences of the private theatres, began to concern themselves with contemporary city life, satirizing the citizens for their acquisitive behaviour. Jonson's contributions to the *genre* were *The Alchemist* and *Bartholomew Fair*. There were a number of collaborative works in which several dramatists were involved, including *Eastward Ho* by Marston, Chapman and Jonson. The main writer of citizen comedy, however, was Thomas Middleton, whose early work mostly belonged to this category.

After writing *The Family of Love* (c. 1602), a satirical play about an obscure religious sect, and *Your Five Gallants* (c. 1604), a cleverly constructed farce, Middleton wrote four plays on which his reputation as a comic dramatist depends: *Michaelmas Term* (1605), *A Mad World my Masters* (1605), *A Trick to Catch the Old One* (1606), and, after a curiously long interval, *A Chaste Maid in Cheapside* (1613). All except the last of these six plays were acted by one or other of the children's companies. These comedies are partly concerned with class conflict, the impoverished young gentleman outsmarting the cunning shopkeeper or lawyer, and partly with the more fundamental conflict between prodigal youth and miserly age. As in the comedy of Plautus and Terence—from which Jacobean citizen comedy is partly derived—our sympathies are enlisted on behalf of the young; but, whereas in Latin comedy the young are always victorious, in Middleton's comedies their victory is not invariable or unqualified. Follywit in *A Mad World my Masters*, after robbing his grandfather in various ingenious ways, finds that he has inadvertently married his victim's mistress.

This surprising twist in the last act is characteristic of Middleton's dramaturgy. The rascally Quomodo in *Michaelmas Term* overreaches himself by pretending to be dead and discovers that his 'widow' has immediately married the young gallant he has cheated and robbed. In *A Chaste Maid in Cheapside* the young lovers rise from their coffins and a funeral is turned into a nuptial.

These examples illustrate another characteristic of Middleton's comedies. It is often said that he is an accurate observer of the life of his time, and that he is essentially a naturalistic dramatist. It is true that there are some scenes in *Michaelmas Term* which seem like dramatizations of Robert Greene's coney-catching pamphlets, exposing the rogues of Elizabethan London. The party after the christening of Mrs Allwit's bastard in *A Chaste Maid* is convincingly real. Yet it is surely obvious, as Professor Schoenbaum pointed out, that there is a strong element of fantasy in all Middleton's comedies. The settings, details of behaviour and the dialogue itself may be naturalistic, but in plot and incident he is often extravagant. The promoters' scene in the same play, for example, begins as a sober satire of corrupt informers and ends in wild farce when they are left literally holding the baby. Sometimes indeed we cannot suspend our disbelief. It is hard to swallow Follywit's successful disguise as his grandfather's mistress when he has never set eyes on the woman.

The element of improbability may also be discerned in some of the repentances which are a common feature of the comedies. We can accept easily enough the repentance of Penitent Brothel, not merely because of his name, but because he is conscious all the time of the wickedness of his adulterous intentions. We may have little difficulty in accepting Sir Walter Whorehound's repentance when he thinks he is dying, especially as its dramatic function is to alarm the Allwits. On the other hand the speeches of repentance in jingling octosyllabic couplets at the end of *A Trick to Catch the Old One* convey the impression that they are not to be taken seriously, either by us or by the characters themselves. In other cases the speeches of repentance do not seem ironical. Middleton makes three of his unvirginal brides swear that they have reformed: Witgood's ex-mistress assures her husband that 'she that knows sin knows best how to hate sin'; Follywit's bride vows,

> What I have been is past, be that forgiven,
> And have a soul true both to thee and heaven;

and Tim's bride in *A Chaste Maid* declares that marriage has made an honest woman of her. Some critics suppose that Middleton had his tongue in his cheek; others believe that he never fully outgrew the didacticism of the adolescent who paraphrased *The Wisdom of Solomon*. At least the husbands seem content: they do not share Lucio's horror at being married to Kate Keepdown.

Middleton's attitude is not cynical; nor is it the easy tolerance with which cynicism is sometimes masked. It is rather an acceptance of the fallen state of man. He suggests that harlots are often no worse than the men they marry; and he hints that we in the audience who have applauded the rogues are worse than they since we have derided their repentance. We do not have to go to the tragedies to come face to face with damnation. The terrifying portrait of Dampit, the unrepentant dying usurer in *A Trick to Catch the Old One*, makes us realize the comparative innocence of the sexual delinquents and genial tricksters such as Follywit and Witgood.

The relationship between money and sex in these comedies may be illustrated by the importance of dowries, by Follywit's consoling himself with the thought that gold 'makes amends for vice', by the rivalry of Hoard and Lucre for the hand of a reputedly wealthy widow, by the extravagantly sordid behaviour of the Allwits, and by the frequent suggestion that there is an inverse correlation between sexual potency and wealth.

Middleton's masterpiece in the *genre* of citizen comedy is undoubtedly *A Chaste Maid in Cheapside*. It is indeed one of the greatest comedies of the period. It contains a whole series of interrelated intrigues centred on the figure of Sir Walter Whorehound: his wealth depends on the childlessness of Lady Kix; Mrs Allwit is one of his mistresses; and he hopes to marry Moll Quicksilver. He succeeds in marrying Moll's brother to his Welsh mistress, but he loses Moll to Touchwood Junior, he loses his land when the Kixes get an heir, and his repentance makes him repudiate the Allwits who are thus deprived of their main source of income. It is then a brilliantly organized play, and its dialogue is more consistently lively than that of any of the other comedies. It is not, as we have seen, a naturalistic picture of Jacobean London, any more than *Lucky Jim* gives us a photographic picture of life in a Welsh university: the fun in each case depends on the exaggeration. One has only to instance the comic complacency of the contented cuckold, Allwit, and his frantic efforts to avert Sir Walter's marriage, the satire on the puritans at the christening feast, or the endearing foolishness of the student Tim who writes in Latin to his unlettered parents and talks Latin to his Welsh bride, and provides an appropriate quotation from Cicero when he learns the truth about her:

> Come from the University
> To marry a whore in London—with my tutor too!
> *O Tempora! O Mores!*

It used to be said that this comedy touched the lowest depths of cynicism, or that it represented the neutral attitude of the detached observer. It is surely obvious now that although Middleton entertains us with his wittol, Allwit, the character is entertaining precisely because of the extraordinary way in which he sacrifices natural feeling to the acquisitive instinct. The dramatist intends that our laughter should be mingled with repulsion.

2

OTHER COMEDIES

One of Middleton's greatest qualities is his versatility. Most of his comedies are quite different in style and *genre* from those we have been discussing. *The Phoenix*, for example, is a kind of morality play in which a prince, like Vincentio in *Measure for Measure*, disguises himself to survey the sins of his subjects. *A Game at Chess*, described by Swinburne as Aristophanic, is in a class of its own. In between these plays, written at the beginning and end of his career, Middleton wrote *The Roaring Girl* in collaboration with Dekker, *A Fair Quarrel* in collaboration with Rowley, *The Old Law* with Rowley and Massinger and *The Widow* with Jonson and Fletcher.[1] All these plays have had admirers, though they are less distinctively Middleton's than either the citizen comedies or the tragedies written at the end of his career. *A Fair Quarrel*, eulogized by Lamb, is flawed by a feeble underplot and still more by the absurd behaviour of the Colonel, applauded by

---

[1] Some critics, despite the evidence of the title-pages, believe that the last two may be Middleton's unaided work. So also may *The Spanish Gipsy*, ascribed in recent years to Ford.

the authors, in offering his wealth and his sister to the man he had wronged. *The Spanish Gipsy* opens superbly and then loses itself in a complicated underplot. *The Roaring Girl*, with its pipe-smoking champion of woman's liberation, is a delightful play which, however, is more Dekker's than Middleton's. *The Widow*, despite its Italian setting, has affinities with the citizen comedies. There is an old man with a young wife, a would-be seducer who is converted to honest love on seeing what he thinks is a ghost, a widow whose hand is won by the least mercenary of her three suitors, and a girl who has run away from home, disguised as a man, to avoid marrying her father's choice. The various intrigues are interwoven in a masterly way.

Two other comedies remain to be mentioned. In *More Dissemblers Besides Women* most of the characters, of both sexes, are deceivers or self-deceivers, from the Duchess, who has vowed never to remarry, to the hypocritical Cardinal who encourages her to keep her vow until his nephew appears to be her choice of a husband. The nephew, to please his uncle, pretends to hate the female sex, but has seduced one woman and jilts a second when he thinks the Duchess is in love with him. His first victim disguises herself as a page, the second as a gipsy. Only a General, the real object of the Duchess's love, is not a dissembler. The Cardinal's nephew, Lactantio, is a study worthy of Molière, the whole play is a brilliant satire on hypocrisy, and several scenes are as entertaining as anything in the drama of the period; yet it has never been included in selections of Middleton's plays and critics have treated it perfunctorily.

Another play which deserves to be better known will be included, it is hoped, in a later volume. Swinburne, writing of *No Wit No Help like a Woman's*, spoke of its energetic invention and of 'the unfailing charm of a style worthy of Fletcher himself'; but such praise is liable to misfire now that Fletcher's reputation is less than it was in Swinburne's day. The play contains two plots of equal importance. The one to which the title refers is Kate's stratagem to recover her fortune from Lady Goldenfleece by dressing as a man and going through a form of marriage with her. The other plot is based on Della Porta's *La Sorella*; but the tone of Middleton's scenes is quite different from that of the source. He was fully aware of the improbability of the story, of Philip's staggering heartlessness, and of the doting imbecility of the mother, but he deliberately accentuated these characteristics of *La Sorella*. Indeed Philip repents only because Savorwit persuades him it is the best policy. Savorwit probably derives from the rascally servants of Latin comedy: his ingenious tricks to extricate himself from the failure of previous ones provide some amusing situations. Weatherwise's astrological obsessions could also be effective on the stage. Kate too is admirably conceived. In Middleton's world the virtuous have to be wiser than serpents and harmless as doves. Kate, it may be said, is what a Shakespearian heroine might have become if she had been transported from the world of romance to the corrupt world of Jacobean London. The neglect of the play may be due partly to insufficient annotation, partly because the verse is workmanlike rather than distinguished, but mostly because readers have not known how to respond to the anti-hero, Philip.

Yet the play represents a side of Middleton's work which deserves to be better known.

3
THE CHANGELING

The Changeling was written in collaboration with William Rowley. It is generally thought that Middleton was responsible for the Beatrice plot and that Rowley's share was the less-admired underplot; but the dramatists must have worked closely together since the idea of the changeling is a feature of both plots (see e.g. III. iv. 143–6, V. iii. 199 ff). There are, moreover, traces of Rowley's style, as Bawcutt demonstrates in his edition, in some scenes of the main plot. The lesser partner may deserve more praise than he is usually given.

A number of modern critics have shown that there are links between the two plots. Apart from the theme embodied in the title there are resemblances between the situations in which Beatrice and Isabella find themselves, but Beatrice puts herself in the power of Deflores by employing him to commit murder and Isabella extricates herself from Lollio's attempts to seduce her by threatening to get Antonio to murder him as the price of enjoying her. Isabella is faithful to her foolish husband, Beatrice is faithless both to fiancé and husband. Such links, interesting as they are, do not themselves justify the sub-plot, although it is rather more interesting, and could be more effective in the theatre, than is generally allowed. It has to be recognized that members of a Jacobean audience, accustomed to visit Bedlam for entertainment, would react differently from a modern audience to scenes set in an asylum. The main weakness of the underplot, as Richard Levin has shown,[1] is that a vital scene appears to be missing at the beginning of the last act, presumably lost between performance and publication. The scene would have shown the wedding masque, Antonio and Franciscus would be unmasked and arrested for the murder of Alonzo, and Alibius would repent of his folly. As Mr Levin says,

> the perfunctory confession of the 'changes' in the closing lines of the play is certainly no substitute for the dramatization of them, and in fact seems to look back to such a dramatization.

In any case everyone is mainly interested in the Beatrice scenes. The two chief alterations made by Middleton in the story he found in Reynolds's *God's Revenge against Murther* were to make Deflores hideously, and emblematically, ugly and to make him, and not Alsemero, the killer of Beatrice.

The dramatic power of the central scenes of the play has often been analysed. In the scene in which Beatrice incites the eager Deflores to murder her betrothed, almost every speech is fraught with double, and sometimes triple, irony: it means different things to Beatrice, to Deflores and to the spectator. To make sure that the audience is fully aware of what

[1] *The Multiple Plot in English Renaissance Drama* (1971).

the two characters are thinking, Middleton gives them a remarkable number of asides. Beatrice imagines that she is ridding herself of two inveterate loathings at one stroke, but the audience is aware that she is trapped. Beatrice tells Deflores that his reward will be precious, and the audience guesses what that reward will be.

The expected meeting between the two after the murder is deliberately postponed by the insertion of a long scene in the asylum. When the meeting does take place, the effect is overwhelming. Beatrice is slowly made to realize the price she has to pay. There are a number of famous touches, as when she naïvely exclaims that Deflores cannot be so wicked as

> To make his death the murderer of my honour;

or when her feeling of social and even moral superiority is shattered by the proof that she is now his equal—'You are the deed's creature'; or when he finally silences her pleading with the words:

> Can you weep Fate from its determin'd purpose?
> So soon may you weep me.

Beatrice comes horribly to appreciate Deflores. When he arranges a second murder for her sake, she exclaims:

> How heartily he serves me! his face loathes one;
> But look upon his care, who would not love him?
> The east is not more beauteous than his service . . .
> Here's a man worth loving!

It was passages such as this that made T. S. Eliot say in his famous and influential essay

> What constitutes the essence of the tragedy is the habituation of Beatrice to her sin; it becomes no longer sin but merely custom. . . . The tragedy of Beatrice is not that she has lost Alsemero . . . it is that she has won De Flores.

These sentences are nevertheless somewhat misleading. No doubt Beatrice finds sexual relations with Deflores less intolerable than at first; but these relations are not her sin—they are more in the nature of a punishment. Her real sin is her involvement in two murders and she hardly seems aware of her guilt. She does not appreciate that the murder of Alonzo is a sin until she knows the price she must pay; when she sees his ghost she is not greatly perturbed, and soon afterwards remarks that the night has been tedious; and she anticipates with revengeful satisfaction the murder of Diaphanta. It has often been noticed, indeed, that Beatrice's sense of values is strangely perverted. Her pleading with Deflores to spare her reveals that she thinks of herself as a pure young girl; she is genuinely surprised when Alsemero is horrified by a murder committed for love of him; she confesses to the murder but swears again and again that she is true to his bed; and, in her last speech to her father, she fears to defile him, not because she is a murderess but because she has lost her sexual 'honour'.

If *The Changeling* is not the highest kind of tragedy, this is because its heroine is lacking in self-awareness and never quite comes to a recognition of the truth about herself. Deflores, on the other hand, is fully aware. He is driven to murder and blackmail by his lust, knowing all the time that he is courting damnation. Evil as he is, it is his tragedy as well as Beatrice's. His lust leads him to murder; the murder puts him into spirit—excites him sexually; and in the last scene, when Alsemero makes him enter the closet where Beatrice is imprisoned, ostensibly to 'rehearse again' their 'scene of lust', the murder of Beatrice serves as lust's substitute:

> It was so sweet to me,
> That I have drunk up all, left none behind
> For any man to pledge me.

It is difficult to praise too highly Middleton's psychological realism with regard to the main characters.

It is arguable that it is better to be conscious of damnation, as Deflores is, than morally obtuse. Beatrice is a spoilt child who has come to assume that her will is law; and to the egotism of beauty is added the pride of birth. She falls in love with Alsemero and therefore Alonzo must be got rid of; she dislikes Deflores' face and so she insults him every time he comes into her presence. It is therefore appropriate that Deflores should be the one to humiliate her, his lust being aroused by her loathing. The fair murderess is made one with the foul villain, paired with him, and it is useless for her to brag of her birth, 'the distance that creation set' between her blood and his.

4

WOMEN BEWARE WOMEN

Women Beware Women is wholly Middleton's work, and perhaps his greatest. Like most of his plays, it is flawed; not, as many critics believe, by the slaughter in the final scene, but by the feebleness of the comic relief provided by the Ward. He has to be simple-minded, retarded and coarse, so that we may sympathize with Isabella; but in both the productions I have witnessed there have been stretches of boredom in all the scenes in which he appears.

The most important character in both plots is Livia who lures Bianca to her house so that the Duke can seduce her and, more cunningly, persuades Isabella to return Hippolito's love. Livia's character and motives have been much discussed. Lamb, prompted by the chess scene, remarked that she was 'such another jolly housewife as the Wife of Bath', although of course her kindly welcome of her poor neighbour is hypocritical. Her motives with regard to the deception of Isabella have been attributed to sisterly affection for Hippolito, pure or incestuous, to a desire to corrupt innocence, to a love of power over others' destinies. These motives are not of course mutually exclusive; and for anything comparable to this kind of depravity we should have to go forward more than a century to *Les Liaisons Dangereuses*.

Bianca and Isabella are both initially innocent, but we see a rapid deterioration in both of them. At first Bianca is prepared to face poverty with the man she loves, but after her seduction she complains to her mother-in-law of the deficiencies of her house. When she has been installed as the Duke's mistress she sneers at her husband and acquiesces in his murder; and she plots the murder of the Cardinal because he has condemned her adultery. Yet, at the very end, Middleton arouses some pity for her when she realizes that with the Duke's death she is alone among enemies:

> What make I here? These are all strangers to me,
> Not known but by their malice.

She suffers some remorse for her adultery and reminds us of the title of the play:

> Oh the deadly snares
> That women set for women!

Her face is scarred by the poison and, as Professor Bradbrook has noted, this reminds us of the question she asks after her seduction:

> Yet since mine honour's leprous, why should I
> Preserve that fair that caused the leprosy?

Isabella too deteriorates from one destined to be the victim of 'the miseries of enforced marriage' and the innocent companion of her uncle to become an adulteress who plots the murder of her aunt. Before Hippolito confesses his incestuous feelings their friendship is a marriage of true minds. Isabella's deterioration is first apparent in her prompt suggestion that the marriage with the Ward should proceed, so as to cloak her relationship with Hippolito and its possible consequences.

Leantio is another deteriorating character. His love for Bianca is genuine, but even in the opening scenes of the play, as food and jewel imagery reveals, he is both uxorious and possessive, regarding his wife as his most precious possession, and stolen goods at that. Bianca's love for him is initially less flawed than his for her. After his disillusionment he becomes Livia's possession, her paid lover, and he boasts of it to Bianca. His death at the hands of Hippolito has been criticized since we would not have suspected that the latter was 'bold and sudden/In bringing forth a ruin' or that he was extremely sensitive about his family honour. But although these traits come as a surprise, they are not impossible; and Middleton, here as elsewhere, sacrificed probability to dramatic economy.

Middleton was led into a more serious weakness by the necessity of arranging for the deaths of Bianca and the Duke. The Cardinal, after condemning the Duke for marrying Bianca, suddenly agrees to an unexplained reconciliation. Its dramatic purpose is to ensure the Cardinal's presence in the last scene, so that, in attempting to poison him, Bianca kills the Duke by mistake.

The complaint is often made of the last scene that Middleton, to bring about the destruction of all the main characters, ignores psychology and probability, sacrificing tragedy to sensationalism. The complaint is not really justified. Most of the massacre is the direct result of Hippolito's killing of Leantio, which provokes Livia to reveal her brother's incest:

> Is there a reason found for the destruction
> Of our more lawful loves, and was there none
> To kill the black lust 'twixt thy niece and thee
> That has kept close so long?

All the characters are forthwith turned into avengers. Guardiano is determined to avenge himself and his Ward on Isabella and Hippolito; and, as he is apparently ignorant of Livia's guilt, he joins forces with her. Even the gentle Isabella, parting from Hippolito, determines on the murder of her aunt:

> but for her
> That durst so dally with a sin so dangerous,
> And lay a snare so spitefully for my youth,
> If the least means but favour my revenge,
> That I may practice the like cruel cunning
> Upon her life, as she has on mine honour,
> I'll act it without pity.

The actual details of the masque are not particularly important. Yet the poisoned incense may be taken as a symbol of the corruption emanating from Livia; the shower of fire which kills Isabella as a symbol of her sexual guilt; and the poisoned arrows of Livia's pages as a symbol of Hippolito's much greater guilt. Guardiano, who had boasted earlier of the snare with which he had caught Bianca, falls into the trap prepared for Hippolito. The spectators can hardly fail to realize that the slaughter is caused by the self-destructive effects of sin, the process being clearly described by the dying Hippolito:

> Lust and forgetfulness has been amongst us,
> And we are brought to nothing . . .
> Vengeance met vengeance
> Like a set match; as if the plagues of sin
> Had been agreed to meet here all together.

We hardly need the Cardinal's reinforcement of the moral.

5

It should be added that *The Revenger's Tragedy* has not been included in this selection because the verbal parallels between it and Middleton's plays, striking as some of them are, do not prove common authorship, even though the differences between it and his known work do not prove that he could not have written it. For his range, as we have shown, is remarkable. The three plays contained in this volume are generally regarded as his masterpieces—the best of his citizen comedies, the best of his tragedies, and the best of the plays he wrote in collaboration—yet these three give only a partial idea of the variety of his talents. No one reading this selection could foresee that Middleton would write the best political satire ever performed on the English stage (*A Game at Chess*). There are several masterly plays, such as *No Wit No Help Like a Woman's* and *More Dissemblers Besides Women*, in quite other *genres*; and *A Chaste Maid* is only a little better than four or five plays concerned with London life. Yet, when all is said, the popular view, however partial, is justified. The psychological realism of his two great tragedies, and particularly his insight into women's hearts as revealed in his portraits of Beatrice, Bianca, Isabella and Livia, are superb; and we never feel with him, as we sometimes do with Ford, that his portraits are designed to illustrate a psychopathological theory. The two criticisms which have been levelled at Middleton's masterpiece—the violation of realism by sensationalism and the pedestrian nature of the verse—are not really justified. The violent deaths in the last acts are satisfying to an audience, if not to a reader; and, as Eliot pointed out long ago, Middleton became a great poet when great poetry was called for. It may be said indeed that Middleton is the prime example of the poetic dramatist whose verse is hardly noticeable except when the intensity of the situation requires the accents of greatness.

FURTHER READING

(A) BOOKS DEVOTED TO MIDDLETON:

Barker, R. H. *Thomas Middleton* (N.Y., 1958).
Farr, Dorothy M. *Thomas Middleton and the Drama of Realism* (Edinburgh, 1973).
Schoenbaum, S. *Middleton's Tragedies* (N.Y., 1955).

(B) BOOKS CONTAINING CRITICISM OF MIDDLETON:

Bradbrook, M. C. *Themes and Conventions of Elizabethan Tragedy* (Cambridge, 1935).
Eliot, T. S. *Selected Essays* (1932).
Ellis-Fermor, U. M. *The Jacobean Drama* (1936).
Empson, W. *Some Versions of Pastoral* (1935).
Gibbons, B. *Jacobean City Comedy* (1968).
Leggatt, A. *Citizen Comedy in the Age of Shakespeare* (Toronto, 1973).
Ornstein, R. *The Moral Vision of Jacobean Tragedy* (Madison, 1960).

A
CHAST MAYD
IN
CHEAPE-SIDE.

A
Pleasant conceited Comedy
neuer before printed.

As it hath beene often acted at the
Swan on the Banke-side, by the
Lady ELIZABETH her
Seruants.

By THOMAS MIDELTON Gent.

LONDON,
Printed for *Francis Constable* dwelling at the
signe of the *Crane* in *Pauls*
Church-yard.
1630.

NOTE

This edition of *A Chaste Maid in Cheapside* is based on the First Quarto (1630). A facsimile has been published by the Scolar Press. Professor R. B. Parker, editor of the Revels edition (1969), collated nineteen copies of the quarto and reported that the variants were few and unimportant; five are recorded by Charles Barber in his Fountainwell edition (1969). I am indebted to both these editions. It should be noted that Middleton's verse is often irregular and that he slides easily from prose to verse: editors therefore disagree on which passages are really verse and how it should be divided.

DRAMATIS PERSONAE

SIR WALTER WHOREHOUND
SIR OLIVER KIX
TOUCHWOOD SENIOR
TOUCHWOOD JUNIOR
ALLWIT
YELLOWHAMMER, a goldsmith
TIM, his son
TUTOR to Tim
DAVY DAHUMMA, Sir Walter's poor relation
WAT
NICK } Sir Walter's sons by Mrs Allwit
Two Promoters
Parson
Porter, Watermen, Servants, Gentleman, etc.

LADY KIX
MISTRESS TOUCHWOOD, wife of Touchwood Senior
MISTRESS ALLWIT
MAUDLINE, wife of Yellowhammer
MOLL, her daughter
WELSHWOMAN, Sir Walter's mistress
SUSAN, Yellowhammer's maid
Country Girl
Midwife, Nurses, Puritans, Gossips, Maid.

SCENE—London

3

A CHASTE MAID IN CHEAPSIDE

ACT I

[Sc. 1]

Enter Maudline and Moll, a shop being discovered

MAUD. Have you play'd over all your old lessons
  O' the virginals.
MOLL.   Yes.
MAUD.   Yes? You are a dull maid alate.
  Methinks you had need to have somewhat to quicken
  Your green sickness—do you weep?—a husband!
  Had not such a piece of flesh been ordained,   5
  What had us wives been good for? To make sallets,
  Or else cried up and down for sampier.
  To see the difference of these seasons! When
  I was of your youth, I was lightsome and quick
  Two years before I was married. You fit for a knight's bed!   10
  Drowsy-brow'd, dull-ey'd, drossy-spirited!
  I hold my life you have forgot your dancing:
  When was the dancer with you?
MOLL.   The last week.
MAUD. Last week! When I was of your bord,
  He miss'd me not a night; I was kept at it;   15
  I took delight to learn and he to teach me.
  Pretty brown gentleman, he took pleasure in my company;
  But you are dull, nothing comes nimbly from you;
  You dance like a plumber's daughter and deserve
  Two thousand pound in lead to your marriage,   20
  And not in goldsmith's ware.

Enter Yellowhammer

YELL.   Now, what's the din
  Betwixt mother and daughter, ha?
MAUD.   Faith, small:
  Telling your daughter Mary of her errors.
YELL. Errors? Nay, the city cannot hold you, wife,
  But you must needs fetch words from Westminster—   25
  I ha' done, i'faith!—
  Has no attorney's clerk been here alate

---

25   fetch . . . Westminster] use gallicisms, as at the Law Courts

5

And chang'd his half-crown piece his mother sent him.
Or rather cozen'd you with a gilded twopence,
To bring the word in fashion for her faults   30
Or cracks in duty and obedience?
Term 'em e'en so, sweet wife.
As there's no woman made without a flaw,
Your purest lawns have frays and cambrics bracks.
MAUD. But 'tis a husband solders up all cracks.   35
MOLL. What, is he come, sir?
YELL.   Sir Walter's come.
He was met at Holborn bridge, and in his company
A proper fair young gentlewoman, which I guess
By her red hair and other rank descriptions
To be his landed niece brought out of Wales,   40
Which Tim our son, the Cambridge boy, must marry.
'Tis a match of Sir Walter's own making,
To bind us to him and our heirs for ever.
MAUD. We are honour'd then, if this baggage would be humble,
And kiss him with devotion when he enters.   45
I cannot get her for my life
To instruct her hand thus, before and after,
Which a knight will look for, before and after.
I have told her still, 'tis the waving of a woman
Does often move a man and prevails strongly.   50
But, sweet, ha' you sent to Cambridge? Has Tim word on't?
YELL. Had word just the day after, when you sent him
The silver spoon to eat his broth in the hall
Amongst the gentlemen commoners.
MAUD.   O, 'twas timely.

Enter Porter

YELL.   How now?
PORT. A letter from a gentleman in Cambridge.   55
YELL. O, one of Hobson's porters: thou art welcome!—
I told thee, Maudline, we should hear from Tim.
[*Reads*] *Amantissimis carissimisque ambobus parentibus patri et matri.*
MAUD. What's the matter?
YELL.   Nay, by my troth, I know not,
Ask not me: he's grown too verbal; this learning is   60
A great witch.

29   gilded twopence] i.e. so as to pass it off as a gold coin
39   rank] see Glossary
47   instruct . . . after] make an inviting gesture
48   before . . . after] before and after marriage
56   Hobson] the carrier immortalized by the proverbial 'Hobson's choice' and
        by Milton's epitaphs
58   *Amantissimis . . . matri*] To both my dearly beloved parents, father and
        mother

MAUD. Pray let me see it; I was wont to understand him.
Amantissimis carissimis: he has sent the carrier's man, he says;
ambobus parentibus: for a pair of boots; *patri et matri*: pay the
porter or it makes no matter. 65

PORT. Yes, by my faith, mistress, there's no true construction in
that. I have took a great deal of pains, and come from the Bell
sweating. Let me come to't, for I was a scholar forty years ago.
'Tis thus, I warrant you. *Matri*: it makes no matter; *ambobus
parentibus*: for a pair of boots; *patri*: pay the porter; *amantissimus* 70
carissimis: he's the carrier's man, and his name is Sims—and there
he says true, forsooth: My name is Sims indeed; I have not forgot
all my learning! A money matter! I thought I should hit on't.

YELL. Go, thou art an old fox: there's a tester for thee.

PORT. If I see your worship at Goose Fair, I have 75
A dish of birds for you.

YELL. Why, dost dwell at Bow?

PORT. All my lifetime, sir. I could ever say
Bo to a goose! Farewell to your worship. [*Exit.*

YELL. A merry porter!

MAUD. How can he choose but be so,
Coming with Cambridge letters from our son Tim? 80

YELL. What's here? [*Reads*] *Maxime diligo?* Faith,
I must to my learned counsel with this gear,
'Twill ne'er be discern'd else.

MAUD. Go to my cousin then,
At Inns of Court.

YELL. Fie, they are all for French.
They speak no Latin.

MAUD. The parson then will do't. 85

Enter a Gentleman with a chain

YELL. Nay, he disclaims it, calls Latin 'papistry';
He will not deal with it. What is't you lack, Gentleman?

GENT. Pray weigh this chain.

*While Yellowhammer weighs the chain, enter Sir Walter
Whorehound, Welsh Gentlewoman and Davy Dahumma*

SIR W. Now, wench, thou art welcome
To the heart of the city of London.

WELSH G. *Dugat a whee.*

SIR W. You can thank me in English, if you list. 90

WELSH G. I can, sir, simply.

81 *Maxime diligo*] I love the most
84 all for French] i.e. Law French
86 papistry] The parson has puritanical leanings
89 *Dugat a whee*] God be with you

SIR W.   'Twill serve to pass, wench.
'Twas strange that I should lie with thee so often
To leave thee without English, that were unnatural.
I bring thee up to turn thee into gold, wench,
And make thy fortune shine like your bright trade: 95
A goldsmith's shop sets out a city maid.
Davy Dahumma, not a word.
DAVY.   Mum, mum, sir.
SIR W. Here you must pass for a pure virgin.
DAVY. [*Aside*]   Pure Welsh virgin!
She lost her maidenhead in Brecknockshire.
SIR W. I hear you mumble, Davy.
DAVY.   I have teeth, sir: 100
I need not mumble yet this forty years.
SIR W. [*Aside*] The knave bites plaguily!
YELL. [*to Gentleman*]   What's your price, sir?
GENT. A hundred pound, sir.
YELL.   A hundred marks the utmost;
'Tis not for me else.

                                        [*Exit Gentleman.*
                What, Sir Walter Whorehound?
MOLL. O death!   [*Exit.*
YELL.   Why, daughter! Faith, the baggage!   105
A bashful girl, sir; these young things are shamefast;
Besides, you have a presence, sweet Sir Walter,
Able to daunt a maid brought up i' the city.
A brave court-spirit makes our virgins quiver,
And kiss with trembling thighs.

                     Re-enter Moll

                Yet see, she comes, sir.   110
SIR W. Why, how now, pretty mistress? Now I have caught you.
What, can you injure so your time to stray
Thus from your faithful servant?
YELL.   Pish!
Stop your words, good knight, 'twill make her blush else,
Which are wound too high for the daughters of the freedom.   115
'Honour' and 'faithful servant'! They are compliments
For the worthies of Whitehall or Greenwich;
E'en plain, sufficient, subsidy words serves us, sir.
And is this gentlewoman your worthy niece?
SIR W. You may be bold with her on these terms; 'tis she, sir,   120
Heir to some nineteen mountains.
YELL.   Bless us all!
You overwhelm me, sir, with love and riches.

  92 'Twas] It would be
  115 daughters ... freedom] daughters of tradesmen who have the freedom of
       the city

SIR W. And all as high as Paul's.
DAVY. [*Aside*]   Here's work, i'faith!
SIR W. How sayest thou, Davy?
DAVY.   Higher, sir, by far;
  You cannot see the top of 'em.
YELL.   What, man!   125
  Maudline, salute this gentlewoman; our daughter,
  If things hit right.

                Enter Touchwood Junior

TOUCH. [*Aside.*]   My Knight with a brace of footmen,
  Is come and brought up his ewe mutton
  To find a ram at London. I must hasten it,
  Or else pick a famine. Her blood's mine,   130
  And that's the surest. Well, knight, that choice spoil
  Is only kept for me. [*Whispers to Moll.*
MOLL.   Sir?
TOUCH.   Turn not to me
  Till thou mayst lawfully; it but whets
  My stomach, which is too sharp-set already.
  Read that note carefully;   135
  Keep me from suspicion still, nor know
  My zeal but in thy heart. Read and send but
  Thy liking in three words: I'll be at hand
  To take it.
YELL. [*to Sir Walter*] O, Tim, sir, Tim!
  A poor plain boy, an university man,   140
  Proceeds next Lent to a bachelor of art.
  He will be call'd Sir Yellowhammer then
  Over all Cambridge, and that's half a knight.
MAUD. Please you draw near
  And taste the welcome of the city, sir.   145
YELL. Come, good Sir Walter, and your virtuous niece here.
SIR W. 'Tis manners to take kindness.
YELL.   Lead 'em in, wife.
SIR W. Your company, sir.
YELL.   I'll give't you instantly.
  [*Exeunt Maudline, Sir Walter, Welsh Gentlewoman and Davy.*
TOUCH. How strangely busy is the devil and riches!
  Pour soul, kept in too hard; her mother's eye   150
  Is cruel toward her, being kind to him.
  'Twere a good mirth now to set him a-work
  To make her wedding ring. I must about it.
  Rather than the gain should fall to a stranger,
  'Twas honesty in me to enrich my father.   155

129 hasten it] hurry   130 blood] sexual inclination
142–3 Sir . . . knight] 'Sir' translates *dominus*, a title by which a graduate was
  addressed

YELL. [*Aside*] The girl is wondrous peevish. I fear nothing
    But that she's taken with some other love!
    Then all's quite dash'd; that must be narrowly look'd to.
    We cannot be too wary in our children.
    [*To Touchwood*] What is't you lack?   160
TOUCH. [*Aside*] O, nothing now; all that I wish is present.—
    I would have a wedding ring made for a gentlewoman,
    With all speed that may be.
YELL.   Of what weight, sir?
TOUCH. Of some half ounce; to stand fair and comely
    With the spark of a diamond. Sir, 'twere pity   165
    To lose the least grace.
YELL.   Pray let's see it.
    Indeed, sir, 'tis a pure one.
TOUCH.   So is the mistress.
YELL. Have you the wideness of her finger, sir?
TOUCH. Yes, sure, I think I have her measure about me.
    Good faith, 'tis down; I cannot show't you,   170
    I must pull too many things out to be certain.
    Let me see, long and slender, and neatly jointed,
    Just such another gentlewoman that's your daughter, sir.
YELL. And therefore, sir, no gentlewoman.
TOUCH.   I protest
    I never saw two maids handed more alike;   175
    I'll ne'er seek further, if you'll give me leave, sir.
YELL. If you dare venture by her finger, sir.
TOUCH. Ay, and I'll 'bide all loss, sir.
YELL.   Say you so, sir?
    Let's see hither, girl.
TOUCH.   Shall I make bold
    With your finger, gentlewoman?
MOLL.   Your pleasure, sir.   180
TOUCH. That fits her to a hair, sir.
YELL.   What's your posy now, sir?
TOUCH. Mass, that's true. Posy? I'faith, e'en thus, sir:
    'Love that's wise, blinds parents' eyes'.
YELL. How, how! If I may speak without offence, sir,
    I hold my life—
TOUCH.   What, sir?
YELL.   Go to; you'll pardon me?   185
TOUCH. Pardon you? Ay, sir.
YELL.   Will you, i'faith?
TOUCH.   Yes, faith, I will.

156   peevish] Moll hasn't responded to Sir Walter's advances
170   down] i.e. at the bottom of his pocket
173   Just . . . daughter] a lady just like your daughter
178   'bide] abide

YELL. You'll steal away some man's daughter: am I near you?
  Do you turn aside? You gentlemen are mad wags!
  I wonder things can be so warily carried,
  And parents blinded so; but they're served right   190
  That have two eyes and wear so dull a sight.
TOUCH. [*Aside*] Thy doom take hold of thee.
YELL.   Tomorrow noon
  Shall show your ring well done.
TOUCH.   Being so, 'tis soon.
  Thanks; and your leave, sweet gentlewoman.
MOLL. Sir. you are welcome.   195

                        [*Exit Touchwood Junior.*

  [*Aside*] O, were I made of wishes, I went with thee.
YELL. Come now, we'll see how the rules go within.
MOLL. [*Aside*] That robs my joy; there I lose all I win.

                             [*Exeunt.*

[Sc. 2]

Enter Davy and Allwit severally

DAVY. Honesty wash my eyes! I have spied a wittol.
ALLW. What, Davy Dahumma? Welcome from North Wales, i'faith;
  And is Sir Walter come?
DAVY.   New come to town, sir.
ALLW. In to the maids, sweet Davy, and give order
  His chamber be made ready instantly.   5
  My wife's as great as she can wallow, Davy, and longs
  For nothing but pickled cucumbers and his coming,
  And now she shall have't, boy.
DAVY.   She's sure of them, sir.
ALLW. Thy very sight will hold my wife in pleasure,
  Till the knight come himself. Go in, in, in, Davy.   [*Exit Davy.* 10
  The founder's come to town. I am like a man
  Finding a table furnish'd to his hand,
  As mine is still to me, prays for the founder:
  'Bless the right worshipful, the good founder's life'.
  I thank him, h'as maintained my house this ten years,   15
  Not only keeps my wife, but a keeps me
  And all my family: I am at his will;
  He gets me all my children, and pays the nurse
  Monthly, or weekly, puts me to nothing,
  Rent, nor church duties, not so much as the scavenger: 20

187 am . . . you?] Have I guessed your secret?
197 rules] revels (Parker); agreements (George)
  15 h'as] he has   16 a] he
  20 church duties] work for which cash could be given as a substitute.

The happiest state that ever man was born to!
I walk out in a morning, come to breakfast,
Find excellent cheer, a good fire in winter;
Look in my coal-house about midsummer eve,
That's full, five or six chaldron new laid up;   25
Look in my back-yard, I shall find a steeple
Made up with Kentish faggots, which o'erlooks
The water-house and the windmills: I say nothing
But smile, and pin the door. When she lies in,
As now she's even upon the point of grunting,   30
A lady lies not in like her; there's her embossings,
Embroid'rings, spanglings, and I know not what,
As if she lay with all the gaudy shops
In Gresham's Burse about her; then her restoratives,
Able to set up a young 'pothecary,   35
And richly stock the foreman of a drug-shop;
Her sugar by whole loaves, her wines by rundlets.
I see these things, but like a happy man
I pay for none at all, yet fools think's mine;
I have the name, and in his gold I shine;   40
And where some merchants would in soul kiss hell
To buy a paradise for their wives and dye
Their conscience in the bloods of prodigal heirs
To deck their night-piece, yet all this being done,
Eaten with jealousy to the inmost bone,—   45
As what affliction nature more constrains
Than feed the wife plump for another's veins?
These torments stand I freed of; I am as clear
From jealousy of a wife, as from the charge:
O, two miraculous blessings! 'Tis the knight   50
Hath took that labour all out of my hands:
I may sit still and play; he's jealous for me;
Watches her steps, sets spies; I live at ease;
He has both the cost and torment; when the strings
Of his heart frets, I feed, laugh, or sing: 55
[*Sings.*] *La dildo, dildo la dildo, la dildo dildo de dildo.*

Enter two Servants

1 SERV. What! has he got a singing in his head now?
2 SERV. Now's out of work, he falls to making dildoes.
ALLW. Now, sirs, Sir Walter's come.
1 SERV.   Is our master come?
ALLW. Your master? What am I?
1 SERV.   Do not you know, sir?   60

27 o'erlooks] stands higher than
34 Gresham's Burse] The Royal Exchange, where there were market stalls
39 's] it is   46 nature . . . constrains] more violates nature
58 out of work] unemployed in bed

ALLW. Pray, am not I your master?

1 SERV.   O, you are but
Our mistress's husband.

ALLW.   *Ergo*, knave, your master.

Enter Sir Walter and Davy

1 SERV. *Negatur argumentum.*—Here comes Sir Walter.
  [*Aside to 2 Servant*] Now a stands bare as well as we; make the
                                                 most of him,
  He's but one pip above a serving man,   65
  And so much his horns make him.

SIR W.   How dost, Jack?

ALLW. Proud of your worship's health, sir.

SIR W.   How does your wife?

ALLW. E'en after your own making, sir; she's a tumbler a'faith,
  The nose and belly meets.

SIR W.   They'll part in time again.

ALLW. At the good hour they will, and please your worship.   70

SIR W. [*To Servant*] Here, sirrah, pull off my boots—
                        [*To Allwit*] Put on, put on, Jack.

ALLW. I thank your kind worship, sir.

SIR W.   Slippers! Heart,
  You are sleepy!

ALLW. [*Aside*] The game begins already.

SIR W. Pish! Put on, Jack.

ALLW. [*Aside*]   Now I must do it, or he'll be
  As angry now, as if I had put it on   75
  At first bidding. 'Tis but observing—[*Puts on hat*]
  'Tis but observing a man's humour once,
  And he may ha' him by the nose all his life.

SIR W. [*To Servant*] What entertainment has lain open here?
  No strangers in my absence?

1 SERV.   Sure, sir, not any.   80

ALLW. [*Aside*] His jealousy begins. Am not I happy now
  That can laugh inward whilst his marrow melts?

SIR W. How do you satisfy me?

1 SERV.   Good sir, be patient.

SIR W. For two months' absence I'll be satisfied.

1 SERV. No living creature enter'd—

SIR W.   Enter'd? Come, swear!   85

1 SERV. You will not hear me out, sir.

SIR W.   Yes, I'll hear't out, sir.

1 SERV. Sir, he can tell, himself.

SIR W.   Heart, he can tell!

---

64 *Negatur argumentum*] the argument is denied
69 nose . . . meets] i.e. because of her pregnancy
71 put on] put your hat on

Do you think I'll trust him?—as a usurer
With forfeited lordships. Him? O monstrous injury!
Believe him? Can the devil speak ill of darkness?   90
[*To Allwit*] What can you say, sir?

ALLW.   Of my soul and conscience, sir,
She's a wife as honest of her body to me
As any lord's proud lady can be.

SIR W. Yet, by your leave, I heard you were once off'ring
To go to bed to her.   95

ALLW.   No, I protest, sir.

SIR W. Heart, if you do, you shall take all. I'll marry.

ALLW. O, I beseech you, sir.

SIR W. [*Aside*]   That wakes the slave
And keeps his flesh in awe.

ALLW. [*Aside*]   I'll stop that gap
Where'er I find it open. I have poison'd
His hopes in marriage already—   100
Some old rich widows and some landed virgins—
And I'll fall to work still before I'll lose him,
He's yet too sweet to part from.

Enter Wat and Nick

WAT.   God-den, father.

ALLW. Ha, villain, peace!

NICK.   God-den, father.

ALLW.   Peace, bastard!
[*Aside*] Should he hear 'em! [*Aloud*] These are two foolish
                            children, 105
They do not know the gentleman that sits there.

SIR W. O, Wat! How dost, Nick? Go to school, ply your
                        books, boys, ha?

ALLW. [*Aside to boys*] Where's your legs, whoresons?
                  [*Aside*] They should kneel indeed,
If they could say their prayers.

SIR W. [*Aside*]   Let me see, stay;
How shall I dispose of these two brats now   110
When I am married? For they must not mingle
Amongst my children that I get in wedlock;
'Twill make foul work, that, and raise many storms.
I'll bind Wat prentice to a goldsmith,—
My father Yellowhammer, as fit as can be!   115
Nick with some vintner; good, goldsmith and vintner;
There will be wine in bowls, i' faith.

Enter Allwit's Wife

WIFE.   Sweet knight,

---

89 forfeited lordships] property forfeited because of failure to pay mortgage
    interest

Welcome! I have all my longings now in town;
　　Now welcome the good hour.
SIR W. How cheers my mistress?
WIFE.　　　　　　　　Made lightsome e'en by him　　　120
　　That made me heavy.
SIR W.　　　　　　Methinks she shows gallantly,
　　Like a moon at full, sir.
ALLW.　　　　　　True, and if she bear
　　A male child, there's the man in the moon, sir.
SIR W. 'Tis but the boy in the moon yet, goodman calf.
ALLW. There was a man, the boy had never been there else.　　125
SIR W. It shall be yours, sir.
ALLW.　　　　　　No, by my troth, I'll swear
　　It's none of mine. Let him that got it
　　Keep it! [*Aside*] Thus do I rid myself of fear,
　　Lie soft, sleep hard, drink wine, and eat good cheer.

　　　　　　　　　　　　　　　　　　　[*Exeunt.*

ACT II

Sc. 1]

Enter Touchwood Senior and his wife

T'S WIFE. 'Twill be so tedious, sir, to live from you,
　　But that necessity must be obeyed.
TOUCH. S. I would it might not, wife; the tediousness
　　Will be the most part mine, that understand
　　The blessings I have in thee: so to part,　　　　　　5
　　That drives the torment to a knowing heart.
　　But, as thou say'st, we must give way to need,
　　And live awhile asunder: our desires
　　Are both too fruitful for our barren fortunes.
　　How adverse runs the destiny of some creatures!　　10
　　Some only can get riches and no children;
　　We only can get children and no riches;
　　Then 'tis the prudent'st part to check our wills,
　　And, till our state rise, make our bloods lie still.
　　Life! every year a child, and some years two,　　　15
　　Besides drinkings abroad, that's never reckon'd!
　　This gear will not hold out.
T'S WIFE.　　　　　　Sir, for a time
　　I'll take the courtesy of my uncle's house,

13　wills] sexual desires
16　drinkings abroad] adulteries

If you be pleas'd to like on't, till prosperity
Look with a friendly eye upon our states.   20
TOUCH. S. Honest wife, I thank thee. I ne'er knew
The perfect treasure thou brought'st with thee, more
Than at this instant minute. A man's happy,
When he's at poorest, that has match'd his soul
As rightly as his body. Had I married   25
A sensual fool now, as 'tis hard to scape it
'Mongst gentlewomen of our time, she would ha' hang'd
About my neck, and never left her hold
Till she had kiss'd me into wanton businesses,
Which at the waking of my better judgement   30
I should have curs'd most bitterly,
And laid a thicker vengeance on my act
Than misery of the birth, which were enough,
If it were born to greatness, whereas mine
Is sure of beggary, though it were got in wine.   35
Fullness of joy sheweth the goodness in thee.
Thou art a matchless wife. Farewell, my joy.
T'S WIFE. I shall not want your sight?
TOUCH. S.   I'll see thee often,
Talk in mirth, and play at kisses with thee;
Anything, wench, but what may beget beggars.   40
There I give o'er the set, throw down the cards,
And dare not take them up.
T'S WIFE.   Your will be mine, sir.   [*Exit.*
TOUCH S. This does not only make her honesty perfect,
But her discretion, and approves her judgement.
Had her desires been wanton, they'd been blameless   45
In being lawful ever, but of all creatures
I hold that wife a most unmatched treasure,
That can unto her fortunes fix her pleasure,
And not unto her blood: this is like wedlock.
The feast of marriage is not lust but love   50
And care of the estate. When I please blood,
Merely I sing and suck out others' then;
'Tis many a wise man's fault, but of all men
I am the most unfortunate in that game
That ever pleas'd both genders: I ne'er play'd yet   55
Under a bastard; the poor wenches curse me
To the pit where'er I come ; they were ne'er served so,
But us'd to have more words than one to a bargain.
I have such a fatal finger in such business

___

55–6 I . . . bastard] I never slept with wife or mistress without making her
       conceive (and bastards are cheaper to rear than legitimate children)
58   more . . . bargain] not become pregnant without consent; or, without
       copulating more than once

I must forth with't, chiefly for country wenches,   60
For every harvest I shall hinder hay-making.

Enter a wench with a child

I had no less than seven lay in last progress,
Within three weeks of one another's time.
WENCH. O, snap-hance, have I found you?
TOUCH. S.   How snap-hance?
WENCH. Do you see your workmanship? Nay, turn not from it,   65
Nor offer to escape; for if you do,
I'll cry it through the streets and follow you.
Your name may well be called Touchwood, a pox on you!
You do but touch and take; thou hast undone me.
I was a maid before; I can bring a certificate for it   70
From both the church-wardens.
TOUCH S.   I'll have the parson's hand too,
Or I'll not yield to't.
WENCH.   Thou shalt have more, thou villain!
Nothing grieves me, but Ellen my poor cousin
In Derbyshire, thou hast crack'd her marriage quite,
She'll have a bout with thee.
TOUCH. S.   Faith, when she will,   75
I'll have a bout with her.
WENCH.   A law bout, sir, I mean.
TOUCH. S. True, lawyers use such bouts as other men do,
And if that be all thy grief, I'll tender her a husband.
I keep of purpose two or three gulls in pickle
To eat such mutton with, and she shall choose one.   80
Do but in courtesy, faith, wench, excuse me
Of this half yard of flesh, in which I think
It wants a nail or two.
WENCH.   No, thou shalt find, villain,
It hath right shape, and all the nails it should have.
TOUCH. S. Faith, I am poor. Do a charitable deed, wench;   85
I am a younger brother, and have nothing.
WENCH. Nothing! Thou hast too much, thou lying villain,
Unless thou wert more thankful.
TOUCH. S.   I have no dwelling:
I brake up house but this morning. Pray thee, pity me.
I am a good fellow, faith, have been too kind   90
To people of your gender. If I ha't
Without my belly, none of your sex shall want it.

62   progress] royal tour
64   snap-hance] flint-lock; hence a man as fertile as Touchwood
79–80   two . . . with] fools to marry my former whores
83   nail] (a) $2\frac{1}{2}$ inches (b) a finger nail—children of parents suffering from the
     pox were supposed to lack nails.
90   good fellow] (a) kind man (b) reveller

[*Aside*] That word has been of force to move a woman—
There's tricks enough to rid thy hand on't, wench:
Some rich man's porch tomorrow before day,   95
Or else anon i' the evening—twenty devices.
Here's all I have, i' faith, take purse and all—
[*Aside*] And would I were rid of all the ware i' the shop so.
WENCH. Where I find manly dealings, I am pitiful:
This shall not trouble you.
TOUCH S.   And I protest, wench,   100
The next I'll keep my self.
WENCH.   Soft, let it be got first.
[*Aside*] This is the fifth; if e'er I venture more,
Where I now go for a maid, may I ride for a whore.   [*Exit.*
TOUCH. S. What shift she'll make now with this piece of flesh
In this strict time of Lent, I cannot imagine.   105
Flesh dare not peep abroad now. I have known
This city now above this seven years,
But I protest in better state of government
I never knew it yet, nor ever heard of.
There has been more religious wholesome laws   110
In the half circle of a year erected
For common good, than memory ever knew of,

Enter Sir Oliver Kix and his Lady

Setting apart corruption of promoters
And other poisonous officers that infect
And with a venomous breath taint every goodness.   115
LADY K. O, that e'er I was begot, or bred, or born!
SIR OLIVER. Be content, sweet wife.
TOUCH S. [*Aside*]   What's here to do, now?
I hold my life she's in deep passion
For the imprisonment of veal and mutton
Now kept in garrets; weeps for some calf's head now.   120
Methinks her husband's head might serve with bacon.

Enter Touchwood Junior

LADY K. Hist!
SIR OLIVER. Patience, sweet wife!
TOUCH. J.   Brother, I have sought you
                                        strangely.

---

103 ride . . . whore] convicted prostitutes were carted through the streets.
104–5 What . . . Lent] Eating of meat was forbidden in Lent, and Touchwood
       jokingly referred to the baby as flesh. The wench, however, is successful.
       See II. ii. 129ff.
122 Hist!] Lady Kix sees Touchwood and tries to silence her husband. Dyce
       ascribed the word to Touchwood Junior, as a means of attracting his
       brother.

TOUCH. S. Why, what's the business?

TOUCH. J.   With all speed thou canst
  Procure a licence for me.

TOUCH. S.   How, a licence?

TOUCH. J. Cud's foot, she's lost else! I shall miss her ever.   125

TOUCH. S. Nay, sure, thou shalt not miss so fair a mark
  For thirteen shillings fourpence.

TOUCH. J.   Thanks, by hundreds!   [*Exit.*

SIR OLIVER. Nay, pray thee, cease; I'll be at more cost yet.
  Thou know'st we are rich enough.

LADY K.   All but in blessings,
  And there the beggar goes beyond us. O, O, O,   130
  To be seven years a wife, and not a child,
  O, not a child!

SIR OLIVER.   Sweet wife, have patience.

LADY K. Can any woman have a greater cut?

SIR OLIVER. I know 'tis great, but what of that, wife?
  I cannot do withal. There's things making,   135
  By thine own doctor's advice, at pothecaries';
  I spare for nothing, wife; no, if the price
  Were forty marks a spoonful,
  I'd give a thousand pound to purchase fruitfulness.
                       [*Exit Touchwood Senior.*

  'Tis but bating so many good works   140
  In the erecting of bridewells and spittlehouses,
  And so fetch it up again; for having none,
  I mean to make good deeds my children.

LADY K. Give me but those good deeds, and I'll find children.

SIR OLIVER. Hang thee, thou hast had too many.

LADY K.   Thou liest, brevity! 145

SIR OLIVER. O horrible! Dar'st thou call me brevity?
  Dar'st thou be so short with me?

LADY K.   Thou deservest worse:
  Think but upon the goodly lands and livings
  That's kept back through want on't.

SIR OLIVER.   Talk not on't, pray thee;
  Thou'lt make me play the woman and weep too.   150

LADY K. 'Tis our dry barrenness puffs up Sir Walter;
  None gets by your not-getting but that knight;
  He's made by th' means, and fats his fortunes shortly
  In a great dowry with a goldsmith's daughter.

SIR OLIVER. They may be all deceived; be but you patient, wife. 155

126 mark] (a) target (b) a coin
139 *Exit*] Not in Q. Barber gives it here to enable Touchwood Senior to learn
    of Sir Oliver's infertility.
142 fetch . . . again] (a) make up for the expense (b) regain sexual potency
148-9 Think . . . on't] Sir Walter inherits, if Lady Kix does not produce an
    heir.

LADY K. I've suffer'd a long time.
SIR OLIVER.   Suffer thy heart out!
  A pox suffer thee!
LADY K.   Nay thee, thou desertless slave!
SIR OLIVER. Come, come, I ha' done. You'll to the gossiping
  Of Mr Allwit's child?
LADY K.   Yes, to my much joy!
  Everyone gets before me; there's my sister   160
  Was married but at Bartholomew Eve last,
  And she can have two children at a birth.
  O, one of them, one of them would ha' serv'd my turn.
SIR OLIVER. Sorrow consume thee! Thou art still crossing me,
  And know'st my nature.

Enter a Maid

MAID.   O, mistress!   165
  [*Aside*] Weeping or railing, that's our house harmony!
LADY K. What say'st, Jug?
MAID.   The sweetest news.
LADY K.   What is't, wench?
MAID. Throw down your doctor's drugs: they're all
  But heretics; I bring certain remedy
  That has been taught, and prov'd, and never fail'd.   170
SIR OLIVER. O that, that, that, or nothing!
MAID.   There's a gentleman—
  I haply have his name too—that has got
  Nine children by one water that he useth.
  It never misses: they come so fast upon him,
  He was fain to give it over.
LADY K.   His name, sweet Jug?   175
MAID. One Master Touchwood, a fine gentleman,
  But run behindhand much with getting children.
SIR OLIVER. Is't possible?
MAID.   Why, sir, he'll undertake,
  Using that water, within fifteen year,
  For all your wealth, to make you a poor man,   180
  You shall so swarm with children.
SIR OLIVER. I'll venture that i'faith.
LADY K.   That shall you, husband.
MAID. But I must tell you first, he's very dear.
SIR OLIVER. No matter, what serves wealth for?
LADY K.   True, sweet husband.
SIR OLIVER. There's land to come. Put case his water   185

---

162 birth] As this is Lent, the children must have been conceived before the
    marriage on 23 August.
167 Jug] Joan
177 behindhand] in debt

Stands me in some five hundred pound a pint,
'Twill fetch a thousand and a kersten soul.
LADY K. And that's worth all, sweet husband.
SIR OLIVER.   I'll about it.
                                                    [*Exeunt.*

[Sc. 2]
                    Enter Allwit

ALLW. I'll go bid gossips presently myself,
   That's all the work I'll do. Nor need I stir,
   But that it is my pleasure to walk forth
   And air myself a little. I am tied
   To nothing in this business: what I do   5
   Is merely recreation, not constraint.
   Here's running to and fro, nurse upon nurse,
   Three charwomen, besides maids and neighbours' children!
   Fie, what a trouble have I rid my hands on;
   It makes me sweat to think on't.

              Enter Sir Walter Whorehound

SIR W.   How now, Jack?   10
ALLW. I am going to bid gossips for your worship's child, sir,
   A goodly girl, i'faith; give you joy on her;
   She looks as if she had two thousand pound
   To her portion, and run away with a tailor;
   A fine plump black-eyed slut; under correction, sir,   15
   I take delight to see her. Nurse!

                  Enter Dry Nurse

DRY N.   Do you call, sir?
ALLW. I call not you, I call the wet nurse hither.
   Give me the wet nurse!   [*Exit Dry Nurse.*

              Enter Wet Nurse with baby

                     Ay, 'tis thou; come hither, come hither!
   Let's see her once again; I cannot choose
   But buss her thrice an hour.
WET N.   You may be proud on't, sir;   20
   'Tis the best piece of work that e'er you did.
ALLW. Think'st thou so, Nurse? What sayest to Wat and Nick?
WET N. They're pretty children both, but here's a wench
   Will be a knocker.
ALLW. [*Holding baby*] Pup!—Say'st thou me so?—Pup!
                                     Little countess!   25

187   kersten] christened
  14   run . . . tailor] i.e. because she is so smart

Faith, sir, I thank your worship for this girl,
Ten thousand times, and upward.
SIR W.   I am glad
I have her for you, sir.
ALLW.   Here, take her in, nurse;
Wipe her, and give her spoon-meat.
WET N. [*Aside*]   Wipe your mouth, sir.

[*Exit.*

ALLW. And now about these gossips.
SIR W.   Get but two.   30
I'll stand for one myself.
ALLW.   To your own child, sir?
SIR W. The better policy, it prevents suspicion:
'Tis good to play with rumour at all weapons.
ALLW. Troth, I commend your care, sir; 'tis a thing
That I should ne'er have thought on.
SIR W. [*Aside*]   The more slave!   35
When man turns base, out goes his soul's pure flame;
The fat of ease o'erthrows the eyes of shame.
ALLW. I am studying who to get for godmother
Suitable to your worship. Now I ha' thought on't—
SIR W. I'll ease you of that care, and please myself in't.   40
[*Aside*] My love, the goldsmith's daughter; if I send,
Her father will command her. [*Calls*] Davy Dahumma!

Enter Davy

ALLW. I'll fit your worship then with a male partner.
SIR W. What is he?
ALLW.   A kind proper gentleman,
Brother to Master Touchwood.
SIR W.   I know Touchwood.   45
Has he a brother living?
ALLW.   A neat bachelor.
SIR W. Now we know him, we'll make shift with him.
Despatch, the time draws near. Come hither, Davy.

[*Exit with Davy.*

ALLW. In troth, I pity him: he ne'er stands still.
Poor knight, what pains he takes—sends this way one,   50
That way another, has not an hour's leisure;
I would not have thy toil for all thy pleasure.

Enter Two Promoters

Ha, how now? What are those that stand so close
At the street corner, pricking up their ears,
And snuffing up their noses, like rich men's dogs   55
When the first course goes in? By the mass, promoters!
'Tis so, I hold my life, and planted there
To arrest the dead corpse of poor calves and sheep,

Like ravenous creditors, that will not suffer
The bodies of their poor departed debtors   60
To go to th' grave, but e'en in death to vex
And stay the corpse with bills of Middlesex.
This Lent will fat the whoresons up with sweetbreads,
And lard their whores with lamb-stones; what their golls
Can clutch, goes presently to their Molls and Dolls.   65
The bawds will be so fat with what they earn,
Their chins will hang like udders by Easter Eve,
And, being strok'd, will give the milk of witches.
How did the mongrels hear my wife lies in?
Well, I may baffle 'em gallantly. By your favour, gentlemen,   70
I am a stranger both unto the city,
And to her carnal strictness.
1 PROM.   Good. Your will, sir?
ALLW. Pray tell me where one dwells that kills this Lent.
1 PROM. How, kills? [*Aside*] Come hither, Dick, a bird, a bird.
2 PROM. What is't that you would have?
ALLW.   Faith, any flesh;   75
But I long especially for veal and green sauce.
1 PROM. [*Aside*] Green goose, you shall be sauc'd.
ALLW.   I have half a scornful stomach;
No fish will be admitted.
1 PROM.   Not this Lent, sir?
ALLW. Lent! What cares colon here for Lent?
1 PROM.   You say well, sir.
Good reason that the colon of a gentleman,   80
As you were lately pleas'd to term your worship, sir,
Should be fulfill'd with answerable food,
To sharpen blood, delight health, and tickle nature.
Were you directed hither to this street, sir?
ALLW. That I was, ay, marry!
2 PROM.   And the butcher belike   85
Should kill, and sell close in some upper room?
ALLW. Some apple-loft, as I take it, or a coal-house;
I know not which, i'faith.
2 PROM.   Either will serve.
This butcher shall kiss Newgate, 'less he turn up
The bottom of the pocket of his apron.   90

62 bills of Middlesex] a notorious 'method of extending the jurisdiction of the
    King's Bench, by arresting the defendant to answer a fictitious trespass in
    Middlesex' (Parker)
63–4 sweetbreads . . . lamb-stones] aphrodisiacs
68 milk of witches] witches were thought to have an extra teat, sometimes in
    the chin, on which they suckled familiars.
76 veal . . . sauce] i.e. to be cheated
89 kiss Newgate] go to prison
89–90 'less . . . apron] i.e. bribe the promoters

You go to seek him?
ALLW.   Where you shall not find him.
I'll buy, walk by your noses with my flesh
Sheep-biting mongrels, hand-basket free-booters,
My wife lies in, a footra for promoters!   [*Exit.*

1 PROM. That shall not serve your turn. What a rogue's this!   95
How cunningly he came over us!

Enter a man with meat in a basket

2 PROM.   Hush't, stand close.
MAN. I have 'scaped well thus far. They say the knaves
Are wondrous hot and busy.
1 PROM.   By your leave, sir,
We must see what you have under your cloak there.
MAN. Have? I have nothing.
1 PROM.   No? Do you tell us that?   100
What makes this lump stick out then? We must see, sir.
MAN. What will you see, sir? A pair of sheets and two
Of my wife's foul smocks, going to the washers.
2 PROM. O we love that sight well! You cannot please us better.
What, do you gull us? Call you these shirts and smocks?   105
                              [*Takes meat out of basket.*
MAN. Now a pox choke you!
You have cozen'd me and five of my wife's kindred
Of a good dinner. We must make it up now
With herrings and milk-pottage.   [*Exit.*
1 PROM. 'Tis all veal!
2 PROM.   All veal? Pox, the worse luck!   110
I promis'd faithfully to send this morning
A fat quarter of lamb to a kind gentlewoman
In Turnbull street that longs, and now I'm cross'd!
1 PROM. Let's share this, and see what hap comes next then.

Enter another man with a basket

2 PROM. Agreed. Stand close again: another booty!   115
What's he?
1 PROM.   Sir, by your favour.
MAN.   Meaning me, sir?
1 PROM. Good Master Oliver, cry thee mercy, i' faith.
What hast thou there?
MAN.   A rack of mutton, sir,
And half a lamb: you know my mistress' diet.
1 PROM. Go, go, we see thee not; away, keep close!   120
Heart, let him pass: thou'lt never have the wit
To know our benefactors.
2 PROM.   I have forgot him.

94   My . . . in] and therefore was allowed meat

1 PROM. 'Tis Master Beggarland's man, the wealthy merchant
   That is in fee with us.
2 PROM.   Now I have a feeling of him.
1 PROM. You know he purchas'd the whole Lent together,   125
   Gave us ten groats apiece on Ash Wednesday.
2 PROM. True, true.

Enter a Wench with a basket, and a child in it under a loin of mutton

1 PROM.   A wench!
2 PROM.   Why then, stand close indeed.
WENCH. [*Aside*] Women had need of wit, if they'll shift here;
   And she that hath wit may shift anywhere.
1 PROM. Look, look! Poor fool, she has left the rump
                               uncover'd too,   130
   More to betray her; this is like a murd'rer
   That will outface the deed with a bloody band.
2 PROM. What time of the year is't, sister?
WENCH.   O sweet gentlemen,
   I am a poor servant: let me go.
1 PROM.   You shall, wench,
   But this must stay with us.
WENCH.   O, you undo me, sir.   135
   'Tis for a wealthy gentlewoman that takes physic, sir.
   The doctor does allow my mistress mutton.
   O, as you tender the dear life of a gentlewoman,
   I'll bring my master to you; he shall show you
   A true authority from the higher powers,   140
   And I'll run every foot.
2 PROM.   Well, leave your basket then,
   And run and spare not.
WENCH.   Will you swear then to me
   To keep it till I come?
1 PROM.   Now, by this light, I will.
WENCH. What say you, gentleman?
2 PROM.   What a strange wench 'tis!
   Would we might perish else!
WENCH.   Nay, then, I run, sir.   [*Exit.* 145
1 PROM. And ne'er return, I hope.
2 PROM.   A politic baggage!
   She makes us swear to keep it; I prithee, look
   What market she hath made.
1 PROM.   *Imprimis*, sir,
   A good fat loin of mutton. What comes next
   Under this cloth? Now for a quarter of lamb.   150
2 PROM. Now for a shoulder of mutton.
1 PROM.   Done!

127   *a wench*] presumably the wench who claimed that Touchwood Senior was
      the father of her child

2 PROM. Why, done, sir!
1 PROM.   By the mass, I feel I have lost,
'Tis of more weight, i'faith.
2 PROM.   Some loin of veal?
1 PROM. No, faith; here's a lamb's head; I feel that plainly.
Why, I'll yet win my wager.
2 PROM.   Ha?
1 PROM.   'Swounds, what's here?   155
2 PROM. A child!
1 PROM. A pox of all dissembling, cunning whores!
2 PROM. Here's an unlucky breakfast.
1 PROM.   What shall's do?
2 PROM. The quean made us swear to keep it too.
1 PROM. We might leave it else.
2 PROM.   Villainous strange!   160
'Life, had she none to gull but poor promoters
That watch hard for a living?
1 PROM.   Half our gettings
Must run in sugar-sops and nurses' wages now,
Besides many a pound of soap and tallow.
We have need to get loins of mutton still,   165
To save suet to change for candles.
2 PROM. Nothing mads me, but this was a lamb's head with you:
You felt it. She has made calves' heads of us.
1 PROM. Prithee, no more on't. There's time to get it up.
It is not come to mid-Lent Sunday yet.   170
2 PROM. I am so angry, I'll watch no more today.
1 PROM. Faith, nor I neither.
2 PROM.   Why, then, I'll make a motion.
1 PROM. Well, what is't?
2 PROM.   Let's e'en go to the Checker
At Queenhive, and roast the loin of mutton
Till young flood, then send the child to Brainford.   175

                                        [*Exeunt.*

[Sc. 3]

Enter Allwit in one of Sir Walter's suits, and Davy trussing him

ALLW. 'Tis a busy day at our house, Davy.
DAVY. Always the kursning day, sir.
ALLW.   Truss, truss me, Davy.

173 Checker] Inn with a chess-board sign
174 Queenhive] Queenhithe, a quay opposite Southwark
175 young flood] turn of tide
175 Brainford] Brentford

DAVY. [*Aside*] No matter and you were hang'd, sir.
ALLW. How does this suit fit me, Davy?
DAVY.   Excellent neatly;
  My master's things were ever fit for you, sir,   5
  E'en to a hair, you know.
ALLW.   Thou has hit it right, Davy;
  We ever jump'd in one, this ten years, Davy;
  So well said.

Enter a Servant with a box

          What art thou?
SERV.   Your comfit-maker's man, sir.
ALLW. O, sweet youth, in to the nurse, quick, quick!
  'Tis time, i'faith. Your mistress will be here?   10
SERV. She was setting forth, sir.   [*Exit.*

Enter two Puritans

ALLW.   Here comes our gossips now:
  O, I shall have such kissing work today!—
  Sweet Mistress Underman, welcome, i'faith.
1 PUR. Give you joy of your fine girl, sir;
  Grant that her education may be pure,   15
  And become one of the faithful.
ALLW. Thanks to your sisterly wishes, Mistress Underman.
2 PUR. Are any of the brethren's wives yet come?
ALLW. There are some wives within, and some at home.
1 PUR. Verily, thanks, sir.
                                    [*Exeunt Puritans.*
ALLW.   Verily, you are an ass, forsooth.   20
  I must fit all these times, or there's no music.

Enter two Gossips

  Here comes a friendly and familiar pair:
  Now I like these wenches well.
1 GOS.   How dost, sirrah?
ALLW. Faith, well, I thank you, neighbour; and how dost thou?
2 GOS. Want nothing, but such getting, sir, as thine.   25
ALLW. My gettings, wench, they are poor.
1 GOS.   Fie, that thou'lt say so!
  Th'hast as fine children as a man can get.
DAVY. [*Aside*] Ay, as a man can get, and that's my master.
ALLW. They are pretty foolish things, put to making in minutes:
  I ne'er stand long about 'em. Will you walk in, wenches?   30
                                    [*Exeunt Gossips.*

Enter Touchwood Junior and Moll

7 jump'd in one] (a) agreed together (b) shared the same woman
21 fit . . . times] alter my style of conversation to suit that of the guests

TOUCH. J. The happiest meeting that our souls could wish for!
  Here's the ring ready; I am beholding
  Unto your father's haste; h'as kept his hour.
MOLL. He never kept it better.

Enter Sir Walter Whorehound

TOUCH. J.   Back, be silent!
SIR W. Mistress and partner, I will put you both   35
  Into one cup.
DAVY. [*Aside*] Into one cup! Most proper;
  A fitting compliment for a goldsmith's daughter.
ALLW. Yes, sir, that's he must be your worship's partner
  In this day's business, Master Touchwood's brother.
SIR W. I embrace your acquaintance, sir.
TOUCH. J.   It vows your service, sir.   40
SIR W. It's near high time. Come, Master Allwit.
ALLW.   Ready, sir.
SIR W. Will't please you walk?
TOUCH. J.   Sir, I obey your time.

                                        [*Exeunt.*

[Sc. 4]

Enter Midwife with the child, five Gossips, Maudline and two Puritans
      to the Christening. Exit Midwife with child.

1 GOSS. Good Mistress Yellowhammer.
MAUDL.   In faith, I will not.
1 GOSS. Indeed it shall be yours.
MAUDL.   I have sworn, i'faith.
1 GOSS. I'll stand still then.
MAUDL.   So will you let the child
  Go without company and make me forsworn.
1 GOSS. You are such another creature!
2 GOSS.   Before me?   5
  I pray come down a little.
3 GOSS.   Not a whit;
  I hope I know my place.
2 GOSS.   Your place? Great wonder, sure!
  Are you any better than a comfit-maker's wife?
3 GOSS. And that's as good at all times as a pothecary's.
2 GOSS. Ye lie—yet I forbear you too.
1 PUR.   Come, sweet sister;   10
  We go in unity and show the fruits of peace,
  Like children of the spirit.
2 PUR.   I love lowliness.

5 You . . . creature!] proverbial, meaning 'You are a one!'

4 GOSS. True, so say I, though they strive more,
　There comes as proud behind, as goes before.
5 GOSS. Every inch, i'faith.   15

　　　　　　　　　　　　　　　　　　　[*Exeunt.*

ACT III

[Sc. 1]
　　　　　　　Enter Touchwood Junior and a Parson

TOUCH. J. O sir, if ever you felt the force of love,
　Pity it in me.
PAR.　　　　　　Yes, though I ne'er was married, sir,
　I have felt the force of love from good men's daughters,
　And some that will be maids yet three years hence.
　Have you got a licence?
TOUCH. J.　　　　　　Here, 'tis ready, sir.
PAR. That's well.   5
TOUCH. J.　　　　The ring and all things perfect.
　She'll steal hither.
PAR.　　　　　　She shall be welcome, sir.
　I'll not be long a-clapping you together.

　　　　　　Enter Moll and Touchwood Senior

TOUCH. J. O, here's she come, sir.
PAR.　　　　　　　　　What's he?
TOUCH. J.　　　　　　　　　　My honest brother.
TOUCH S. Quick! Make haste, sirs.
MOLL.　　　　　　　　You must despatch with all   10
　The speed you can, for I shall be miss'd straight.
　I made hard shift for this small time I have.
PAR. Then I'll not linger.
　Place that ring upon her finger;
　This the finger plays the part,   15
　Whose master vein shoots from the heart.
　Now join hands.
　　　　　　Enter Yellowhammer and Sir Walter

YELL.　　　　Which I will sever,
　And so ne'er again meet, never.
MOLL. O, we are betray'd!
TOUCH. J.　　　　Hard fate!
SIR W.　　　　　　　I am struck with wonder.
YELL. Was this thy politic fetch, thou mystical baggage,   20
　Thou disobedient strumpet? [*To Sir Walter*] And were you
　So wise to send for her to such an end?

SIR W. Now I disclaim the end; you'll make me mad.

YELL. And what are you, sir?

TOUCH. J.   And you cannot see
With those two glasses, put on a pair more.   25

YELL. I dream'd of anger still! [*Takes ring from Moll's finger*]
                    Here, take your ring, sir.
Ha! this! Life, 'tis the same! Abominable!
Did not I sell this ring?

TOUCH. J.   I think you did:
You receiv'd money for't.

YELL.   Heart! Hark you, knight,
Here's an inconscionable villainy!   30
Set me a-work to make the wedding ring,
And come with an intent to steal my daughter!
Did ever runaway match it?

SIR W.   'This your brother, sir?

YELL. He can tell that as well as I.

YELL. The very posy mocks me to my face: 35
      'Love that's wise
         Blinds parents' eyes.'
I thank your wisdom, sir, for blinding of us:
We have good hope to recover our sight shortly.
In the meantime, I will lock up this baggage   40
As carefully as my gold. She shall see
As little sun, if a close room or so,
Can keep her from the light on 't.

MOLL.   O sweet father,
For love's sake, pity me.

YELL.   Away!

MOLL.   Farewell, sir.
All content bless thee; and take this for comfort: 45
Though violence keep me, thou canst lose me never;
I am ever thine although we part for ever.

YELL. Ay, we shall part you, minx.

                 Exeunt Yellowhammer and Moll.

SIR W.   Your acquaintance, sir,
Came very lately, yet it came too soon.
I must hereafter know you for no friend,   50
But one that I must shun like pestilence,
Or the disease of lust.

TOUCH J.   Like enough, sir.
You ha' ta'en me at the worst time for words
That e'er ye pick'd out. Faith, do not wrong me, sir.

                 [*Exit with Parson.*

TOUCH. S. Look after him and spare not. There he walks   55

33 'This] Is this   42 so] something else
55 Look after] Beware of

That never yet receiv'd baffling. You're blest
More than e'er I knew; so take your rest.   *[Exit.*
SIR W. I pardon you; you are both losers.   *[Exit.*

[Sc. 2]

    A Bed thrust out upon the stage, Allwit's wife in it. Enter all the
Gossips, Maudline, Lady Kix, Dry Nurse with child, and the Puritans

1 GOSS. How is't, woman? We have brought you home
  A kursen soul.
WIFE.   Ay, I thank your pains.
1 PUR. And verily well kursen'd, i' the right way,
  Without idolatry or superstition,
  After the pure manner of Amsterdam.   5
WIFE. Sit down, good neighbours. Nurse!
NURSE.   At hand, forsooth.
WIFE. Look they have all low stools.
NURSE.   They have, forsooth.
2 GOSS. Bring the child hither, nurse. How say you now, gossip,
  Is't not a chopping girl, so like the father?
3 GOSS. As if it has been spit out of his mouth;   10
  Ey'd, nos'd and brow'd as like a girl can be,
  Only indeed it has the mother's mouth.
2 GOSS. The mother's mouth up and down, up and down.
3 GOSS. 'Tis a large child; she's but a little woman!
1 PUR. No, believe me,   15
  A very spiny creature, but all heart,
  Well mettled, like the faithful, to endure
  Her tribulation here, and raise up seed.
2 GOSS. She had a sore labour on't, I warrant you;
  You can tell, neighbour.
3 GOSS.   O, she had great speed.   20
  We were afraid once, but she made us all
  Have joyful hearts again. 'Tis a good soul, i' faith;
  The midwife found her a most cheerful daughter.
1 PUR. 'Tis the spirit; the sisters are all like her.

    Enter Sir Walter with two spoons and plate, and Allwit

2 GOSS. O, here comes the chief gossip, neighbours!   25
SIR W. The fatness of your wishes to you all, ladies.
3 GOSS. O dear sweet gentleman! What fine words he has!
  'The fatness of our wishes'!
2 GOSS.   Calls us all 'ladies'.
4 GOSS. I promise you, a fine gentleman and a courteous.

  5   Amsterdam] a centre of puritanism
 13   up and down] (a) entirely (b) above and below

2 GOSS. Methinks her husband shows like a clown to him.   30
3 GOSS. I would not care what clown my husband were too,
  So I had such fine children.
2 GOSS.   She's all fine children, gossip.
3 GOSS. Ay, and see how fast they come.
1 PUR.   Children are blessings,
  If they be got with zeal by the brethren,
  As I have five at home.
SIR W. [*To Mrs Allwit*]   The worst is past,   35
  I hope now, gossip.
WIFE.   So I hope too, good sir.
ALLW. Why, then, so hope I too for company;
  I have nothing to do else.
SIR W. [*giving presents*]   A poor remembrance, lady,
  To the love of the babe: I pray accept of it.
WIFE. O, you are too much at charge, sir.
2 GOSS.   Look, look!   40
  What has he given her? What is't, gossip?
3 GOSS. Now, by my faith, a fair high standing cup,
  And two great 'postle spoons, one of them gilt.
1 PUR. Sure that was Judas then with the red beard.
2 PUR. I would not feed my daughter with that spoon   45
  For all the world, for fear of colouring her hair.
  Red hair the brethren like not, it consumes them much:
  'Tis not the sisters' colour.

Enter Nurse with comfits and wine

ALLW.   Well said, nurse.
  About, about with them amongst the gossips!
  (*Aside*) Now out comes all the tassell'd handkerchers;   50
  They are spread abroad between their knees already;
  Now in goes the long fingers that are wash'd
  Some thrice a day in urine—my wife uses it.
  Now we shall have such pocketing: see how
  They lurch at the lower end.
1 PUR.   Come hither, nurse.   55
ALLW. Again! She has taken twice already.
1 PUR. [*Taking comfits*] I had forgot a sister's child that's sick.
ALLW. [*Aside*] A pox! it seems your purity loves sweet things well
  That puts in thrice together. Had this been
  All my cost now, I had been beggar'd;   60
  These women have no consciences at sweetmeats,
  Wheree'er they come; see and they have not cull'd out
  All the long plums too, they have left nothing here
  But short riggle-tail comfits, not worth mouthing.
  No mar'l I heard a citizen complain once   65

53 my . . . it] i.e. as a cosmetic

That his wife's belly only broke his back.
Mine had been all in fitters seven years since,
But for this worthy knight,
That with a prop upholds my wife and me,
And all my estate buried in Bucklersbury. 70
WIFE. [*Pledging them*] Here, Mistress Yellowhammer and neighbours,
To you all that have taken pains with me,
All the good wives at once.
1 PUR. I'll answer for them.
They wish all health and strength, and that you may
Courageously go forward, to perform 75
The like and many such, like a true sister,
With motherly bearing.
ALLW. [*Aside*] Now the cups troll about
To wet the gossips' whistles. It pours down, i'faith;
They never think of payment.
1 PUR. Fill again, nurse,
ALLW. Now, bless thee, two at once! I'll stay no longer. 80
It would kill me and if I paid for't.
[*To Sir Walter*] Will it please you
To walk down and leave the women?
SIR W. With all my heart, Jack.
ALLW. Troth, I cannot blame you.
SIR W. Sit you all merry, ladies.
ALL GOSS. Thank your worship, sir.
1 PUR. Thank your worship, sir.
ALLW. [*Aside*] A pox twice tipple ye; you are last and lowest. 85
[*Exeunt Sir Walter and Allwit.*
1 PUR. Bring hither that same cup, nurse; I would fain
Drive away this—hup!—antichristian grief.
3 GOSS. See, gossip, and she lies not in like a countess!
Would I had such a husband for my daughter!
4 GOSS. Is not she toward marriage?
3 GOSS. O no, sweet gossip. 90
4 GOSS. Why, she's nineteen!
3 GOSS. Ay, that she was last Lammas;
But she has a fault, gossip, a secret fault.
4 GOSS. A fault, what is't?
3 GOSS. I'll tell you when I have drunk.
4 GOSS. [*Aside*] Wine can do that, I see, that friendship cannot.
3 GOSS. And now I'll tell you, gossip: she's too free. 95
4 GOSS. Too free?
3 GOSS. O ay, she cannot lie dry in her bed.
4 GOSS. What, and nineteen?
3 GOSS. 'Tis as I tell you, gossip.

66   broke his back] overworked him (with sexual innuendo)
70   Bucklersbury] a turning out of Cheapside

MAUDL. Speak with me, nurse? Who is't?
NUR.   A gentleman
  From Cambridge; I think it be your son, forsooth.
MAUDL. 'Tis my son Tim, i'faith; prithee call him up   100
  Among the women; 'twill embolden him well,
  For he wants nothing but audacity.
  'Would the Welsh gentlewoman at home
  Were here now.

                                        [*Exit Nurse.*

LADY K.   Is your son come forsooth?
MAUDL. Yes, from the university forsooth.   105
LADY K. 'Tis great joy on ye.
MAUDL.   There's a great marriage
  Towards for him.
LADY K.   A marriage?
MAUDL.   Yes, sure,
  A huge heir in Wales, at least to nineteen mountains,
  Besides her goods and cattle.

                    Enter Nurse and Tim

TIM.   O, I'm betray'd!   [*Exit.*
MAUDL. What gone again? Run after him, good nurse.   110

                                        [*Exit Nurse.*

  He's so bashful, that's the spoil of youth.
  In the university they're kept still to men,
  And ne'er train'd up to women's company.
LADY K. 'Tis a great spoil of youth, indeed.

                    Enter Nurse and Tim

NUR. Your mother will have it so.
MAUDL.   Why son, why Tim?
  What, must I rise and fetch you? For shame, son!   115
TIM. Mother, you do entreat like a freshwoman.
  'Tis against the laws of the university
  For any that has answer'd under bachelor,
  To thrust 'mongst married wives.
MAUDL.   Come, we'll excuse you here.   120
TIM. Call up my tutor, mother, and I care not.
MAUDL. What, is your tutor come? Have you brought him up?
TIM. I ha' not brought him up: he stands at door.
  Negatur: there's logic to begin with you, mother.
MAUDL. Run, call the gentleman, nurse; he's my son's tutor. 125

                                        [*Exit Nurse.*

  Here, eat some plums.
TIM.   Come I from Cambridge,
  And offer me six plums?
MAUDL.   Why, how now, Tim,

124 *Negatur*] It is denied

Will not your old tricks yet be left?

TIM.   Serv'd like a child,
When I have answer'd under bachelor?

MAUDL. You'll never lin till I make your tutor whip you.   130
You know how I serv'd you once at the free school
In Paul's Churchyard?

TIM.   O monstrous absurdity!
Ne'er was the like in Cambridge since my time!
'Life, whip a bachelor? You'll be laugh'd at soundly.
Let not my tutor hear you. 'Twould be a jest   135
Through the whole university. No more words, mother.

Enter Tutor

MAUDL. Is this your tutor, Tim?

TUT.   Yes, surely, lady.
I am the man that brought him in league with logic,
And read the Dunces to him.

TIM.   That did he, mother;
But now I have 'em all in my own pate   140
And can as well read 'em to others.

TUT.   That can he, mistress,
For they flow naturally from him.

MAUDL.   I'm the more beholding
To your pains, sir.

TUT.   *Non ideo sane.*

MAUDL.   True,
He was an idiot indeed when he
Went out of London, but now he's well mended.   145
Did you receive the two goose-pies I sent you?

TUT. And eat them heartily, thanks to your worship.

MAUDL. 'Tis my son, Tim; I pray bid him welcome, gentlewomen.

TIM. Tim? Hark you: Timotheus, mother, Timotheus.

MAUDL. How! Shall I deny your name? 'Timotheus', quoth he!   150
Faith, there's a name! 'Tis my son Tim, forsooth.

LADY K. You're welcome, Master Tim.   [*Kisses him.*

TIM.   O, this is horrible!
She wets as she kisses. Your handkercher, sweet tutor,
To wipe them off as fast as they come on.

2 GOSS. Welcome from Cambridge.   [*Kisses him.*

TIM.   This is intolerable!   155
This woman has a villainous sweet breath,
Did she not stink of comfits. Help me sweet tutor,
Or I shall rub my lips off.

TUT.   I'll go kiss

139 Dunces] Schoolmen (from Duns Scotus)
142 naturally] by a quibble the word implies that Tim is half-witted, a natural.
143 *Non . . . sane*] certainly not on that account

The lower end the whilst.

TIM.   Perhaps that's the sweeter,
And we shall despatch the sooner.

1 PUR.   Let me come next.   160
Welcome from the wellspring of discipline,
That waters all the brethren.   [*She reels and falls.*

TIM.   Hoist, I beseech thee.

3 GOSS. O bless the woman! Mistress Underman.

1 PUR. 'Tis but the common affliction of the faithful;
We must embrace our falls.

TIM.   I'm glad I scap'd it;   165
It was some rotten kiss, sure; it dropp'd down
Before it came at me.

Enter Allwit and Davy

ALLW. [*Aside*]   Here's a noise!
Not parted yet? Heyday! A looking-glass!
They have drunk so hard in plate, that some of them
Had need of other vessels.[*Aloud*] Yonder's the bravest show!   170

ALL GOSS. Where? Where, sir?

ALLW.   Come along presently
By the Pissing-Conduit, with two brave drums
And a standard-bearer.

ALL GOSS.   O brave!

TIM.   Come, tutor.
          [*Exeunt Tim and Tutor.*

ALL GOSS. Farewell, sweet gossip.

WIFE.   I thank you all for your pains.
          [*Exeunt Gossips.*

1 PUR. Feed and grow strong.

          [*Exeunt all, except Allwit and Davy.*

ALLW.   You had more need to sleep than eat.   175
Go take a nap with some of the brethren; go.
And rise up a well-edified, boldified sister.
O here's a day of toil well past o'er,
Able to make a citizen hare-mad!
How hot they have made the room with their thick bums!   180
Dost not feel it, Davy?

DAVY.   Monstrous strong, sir.

ALLW. What's here under the stools?

DAVY.   Nothing but wet, sir;
Some wine spilt here belike.

ALLW.   Is't no worse, think'st thou?
Fair needle-work stools cost nothing with them, Davy.

161–2   Welcome . . . brethren] Cambridge was a puritan stronghold.
172   Pissing-Conduit] near the Royal Exchange
175   S.D.] The bed would be removed, or its curtains drawn.
179   hare-mad] Cf. mad as a March hare

DAVY. [*Aside*] Nor you neither, i'faith.
ALLW.   Look, how they have laid them, 185
  E'en as they lie themselves with their heels up!
  How they have shuffled up the rushes too, Davy,
  With their short figging little shittle-cork heels!
  These women can let nothing stand as they find it.
  But what's the secret thou'st about to tell me   190
  My honest Davy?
DAVY.   If you should disclose it, sir—
ALLW. Life! Rip my belly up to the throat then, Davy.
DAVY. My master's upon marriage.
ALLW.   Marriage, Davy!
  Send me to hanging rather.
DAVY. [*Aside*]   I have stung him.
ALLW. When, where, what is she, Davy?
DAVY.   E'en the same   195
  Was gossip, and gave the spoon.
ALLW. I have no time to stay, nor scarce can speak:
  I'll stop those wheels, or all the work will break.   [*Exit.*
DAVY. I knew 'twould prick. Thus do I fashion still
  All mine own ends by him and his rank toil: 200
  'Tis my desire to keep him still from marriage.
  Being his poor nearest kinsman, I may fare
  The better at his death; there my hopes build,
  Since my Lady Kix is dry, and hath no child.   [*Exit.*

[Sc. 3]
Enter both the Touchwoods

TOUCH. J. Y'are in the happiest way to enrich yourself
  And pleasure me, brother, as man's feet can tread in;
  For though she be lock'd up, her vow is fix'd
  Only to me. Then time shall never grieve me,
  For by that vow e'en absent I enjoy her,   5
  Assuredly confirm'd that none else shall;
  Which will make tedious years seem gameful to me.
  In the mean space lose you no time, sweet brother;
  You have the means to strike at this knight's fortunes,
  And lay him level with his bankrupt merit.   10
  Get but his wife with child; perch at tree top,
  And shake the golden fruit into her lap.
  About it, before she weep herself to a dry ground,
  And whine out all her goodness.
TOUCH. S.   Prithee, cease.

188 shittle-cork] shuttle-cock, slang for 'whore'
192 Life!] i.e. By God's life!

I find a too much aptness in my blood   15
For such a business without provocation.
You might 'well spar'd this banquet of oringoes
Artichokes, potatoes and your butter'd crab.
They were fitter kept for your own wedding dinner.
TOUCH. J. Nay, and you'll follow my suit and save my purse too,   20
Fortune dotes on me: he's in a happy case
Finds such an honest friend i' the common place.
TOUCH. S. Life, what makes thee so merry? Thou hast no cause
That I could hear of lately since thy crosses,
Unless there be news come with new additions.   25
TOUCH. J. Why, there thou hast it right; I look for her
This evening, brother.
TOUCH. S.   How's that, look for her?
TOUCH. J. I will deliver you of the wonder straight, brother.
By the firm secrecy and kind assistance
Of a good wench i' the house, who made of pity,   30
Weighing the case her own, she's led through gutters,
Strange hidden ways, which none but love could find,
Or ha' the heart to venture. I expect her
Where you would little think.
TOUCH. S.   I care not where,
So she be safe, and yours.
TOUCH. J.   Hope tells me so,   35
But from your love and time my peace must grow.
TOUCH. S. You know the worst then, brother.

                              [*Exit Touchwood Junior.*
                              Now to my Kix,
The barren he and she: they're i' the next room,
But to say which of their two humours hold them
Now at this instant, I cannot say truly.
SIR OLIV. [*Within*]   Thou liest, barrenness!   40
TOUCH. S. O, is't that time of day? Give you joy of your tongue;
There's nothing else good in you; this their life
The whole day, from eyes open to eyes shut,
Kissing or scolding, and then must be made friends;
Then rail the second part of the first fit out,   45
And then be pleas'd again, no man knows which way;
Fall out like giants, and fall in like children:
Their fruit can witness as much.

                    Enter Sir Oliver and Lady Kix

SIR OLIV.   'Tis thy fault.
LADY K. Mine, drouth and coldness?
SIR OLIV.   Thine; 'tis thou art barren.

17–18 oringoes . . . crab] aphrodisiacs
22 i' . . . place] at need   48 fruit] or rather, lack of it

LADY K. I barren? O life, that I durst but speak now   50
   In mine own justice, in mine own right! I barren!
   'Twas otherways with me when I was at Court:
   I was ne'er call'd so till I was married.
SIR OLIV. I'll be divorc'd.
LADY K.   Be hang'd! I need not wish it,
   That will come too soon to thee; I may say   55
   Marriage and hanging goes by destiny,
   For all the goodness I can find in't yet.
SIR OLIV. I'll give up house and keep some fruitful whore,
   Like an old bachelor, in a tradesman's chamber.
   She and her children shall have all.
LADY K.   Where be they?
TOUCH. S.   Pray cease;   60
   When there are friendlier courses took for you,
   To get and multiply within your house
   At your own proper costs in spite of censure,
   Methinks an honest peace might be establish'd.
SIR OLIV. What, with her? Never.
TOUCH. S.   Sweet sir—
SIR OLIV.   You work all in vain.   65
LADY K. Then he doth all like thee.
TOUCH. S.   Let me entreat, sir.
SIR OLIV. Singleness confound her!
   I took her with one smock.
LADY K.   But, indeed, you came not so single,
   When you came from shipboard.
SIR OLIV. [Aside]   Heart, she bit sore there!
   [To Touchwood] Prithee, make's friends.   70
TOUCH. S. [Aside] Is't come to that? The peal begins to cease.
SIR OLIV. [To Lady Kix] I'll sell all at an outcry.
LADY K.   Do thy worst, slave.
   [To Touchwood] Good sweet sir, bring us into love again.
TOUCH. S. [Aside] Some would think this impossible to compass.—
   Pray let this storm fly over.
SIR OLIV.   Good sir, pardon me;   75
   I'm master of this house, which I'll sell presently.
   I'll clap up bills this evening.
TOUCH. S.   Lady,—friends, come!
LADY K. If e'er ye lov'd woman, talk not on't, sir.
   What? Friends with him? Good faith, do you think I'm mad?
   With one that's scarce the hinder quarter of a man?   80
SIR OLIV. Thou art nothing of a woman.
LADY K.   Would I were

68–9 you . . . shipboard] Two explanations are suggested (a) that he was
    lousy (b) that he had a 'smock', a wench, with him.
77 clap up bills] stick up advertisements for the sale

Less than nothing!   *[Weeps.*

SIR OLIV.   Nay, prithee, what dost mean?

LADY K. I cannot please you.

SIR OLIV.   I'faith, thou art a good soul;
He lies that says it. Buss, buss, pretty rogue.

LADY K. You care not for me.   85

TOUCH. S. [*Aside*] Can any man tell now which way they came in?
By this light, I'll be hang'd then.

SIR OLIV.   Is the drink come?

TOUCH. S. [*Aside*] Here's a little vial of almond-milk
That stood me in some threepence.

SIR OLIV. I hope to see thee, wench, within these few years, 90
Circled with children, pranking up a girl,
And putting jewels in their little ears—
Fine sport, i' faith.

LADY K.   Ay, had you been ought, husband,
It had been done ere this time.

SIR OLIV.   Had I been ought!
Hang thee! Hadst thou been ought! But a cross thing 95
I ever found thee.

LADY K.   Thou art a grub to say so.

SIR OLIV. A pox on thee!

TOUCH. S. [*Aside*] By this light, they are out again
At the same door, and no man can tell which way.
Come, here's your drink, sir.

SIR OLIV.   I will not take it now, sir,
And I were sure to get three boys ere midnight. 100

LADY K. Why, there thou show'st now of what breed thou com'st,
To hinder generation. O thou villain,
Thou knows how crookedly the world goes with us
For want of heirs, yet put by all good fortune.

SIR OLIV. Hang, strumpet! I will take it now in spite. 105

TOUCH. S. Then you must ride upon't five hours.

SIR OLIV.   I mean so.
Within there!

Enter a Servant

SERV.   Sir?

SIR OLIV.   Saddle the white mare. *[Exit Servant.*
I'll take a whore along, and ride to Ware.

LADY K. Ride to the Devil.

SIR OLIV.   I'll plague you every way.
[*Drinks*] Look ye, do you see, 'tis gone.

LADY K.   A pox go with it! 110

SIR OLIV. Ay, curse and spare not now.

TOUCH. S.   Stir up and down, sir;
You must not stand.

SIR OLIV.   Nay, I'm not given to standing.

TOUCH S. So much the better, sir, for the —
SIR OLIV. I never could stand long in one place yet.
  I learn'd it of my father, ever figient. 115
  How if I cross'd this, sir?
TOUCH S.   O, passing good, sir,
  And would show well a-horseback. When you come to your inn,
  If you leap'd over a joint-stool or two,
  'Twere not amiss—[Aside] although you broke your neck, sir.
SIR OLIV. What say you to a table thus high, sir? 120
TOUCH. S. Nothing better, sir—[Aside] if it be furnish'd
  With good victuals—you remember how
  The bargain runs about this business?
SIR OLIV. Or else I had a bad head: you must receive, sir,
  Four hundred pounds of me at four several payments: 125
  One hundred pound now in hand.
TOUCH. S.   Right, that I have, sir,
SIR OLIV. Another hundred when my wife is quick;
  The third when she's brought a-bed; and the last hundred
  When the child cries, for if it should be still-born
  It doth no good, sir.
TOUCH. S.   All this is even still, 130
  A little faster, sir,
SIR OLIV.   Not a whit, sir.
  I'm in an excellent pace for any physic.

Enter a Servant

SERV. Your white mare's ready.
SIR OLIV.   I shall up presently.
  One kiss, and farewell.
LADY K.   Thou shalt have two, love.
SIR OLIV. Expect me about three.
LADY K.   With all my heart, sweet. 135
                     [*Exit Sir Oliver.*
TOUCH. S. [Aside] By this light, they have forgot their anger since,
  And are as far in again as e'er they were.
  Which way the devil came they? Heart, I saw 'em not:
  Their ways are beyond finding out. Come, sweet Lady,
LADY K. How must I take mine, sir?
TOUCH. S.   Clean contrary. 140
  Yours must be taken lying.
LADY K.   A-bed, sir?
TOUCH. S. A-bed, or where you will for your own ease:
  Your coach will serve.
LADY K.   The physic must needs please.
                       [*Exeunt.*

113 the —] possibly an obscenity has been deleted, though many have been
     retained.
114 stand . . . place] i.e. in sexual intercourse   116 cross'd] jumped over

ACT IV

[Sc. 1]

Enter Tim and Tutor

TIM. *Negatur argumentum*, tutor.

TUT. *Probo tibi*, pupil, *stultus non est animal rationale.*

TIM. *Falleris sane.*

TUT. *Quaeso ut taceas: probo tibi —*

TIM. *Quomodo probas domine?*   5

TUT. *Stultus non habet rationem, ergo non est animal rationale.*

TIM. *Sic argumentaris, domine, stultus non habet ratonem, ergo non est animal rationale, negatur argumentum* again, tutor.

TUT. *Argumentum iterum probo tibi, domine: qui non participat de ratione nullo modo potest vocari rationalibus,* but *stultus non partici-*   10
pat de ratione, ergo stultus nullo modo potest dicere rationalis.

TIM. *Participat.*

TUT. *Sic disputas: qui participat, quodmodo participat?*

TIM. *Ut homo, probabo tibi ib syllogismo.*

TUT. *Hunc proba.*   15

TIM. *Sic probo, domine: stultus est homo sicut tu et ego sumus; homo est animal rationale, sicut stultus est animal rationale.*

Enter Maudline

MAUDL. Here's nothing but disputing all the day long with 'em!

TUT. *Sic disputas: stultus est homo sicut tu et ego sumus; homo est animal rationale, sicut stultus est animal rationale.*   20

MAUDL. Your reasons are both good, whate'er they be.
Pray give them o'er. Faith, you'll tire yourselves.
What's the matter between you?

TIM.   Nothing but reasoning
About a fool, mother.

MAUDL.   About a fool, son?
Alas, what need you trouble your heads about that?   25
None of us all but knows what a fool is.

TIM. Why, what's a fool, mother? I come to you now.

MAUDL. Why, one that's married before he has wit.

TIM. 'Tis pretty, i'faith, and well-guess'd of a woman
Never brought up at the university: 30
But bring forth what fool you will, mother,
I'll prove him to be as reasonable a creature
As myself or my tutor here.

MAUDL.   Fie! 'tis impossible.

2   *Probo . . . rationale*] 'I'll prove to you, pupil, that a fool is not a rational
animal'. Tim argues that a fool is a man, that a man is a rational animal, and
that therefore a fool is a rational animal. The tutor's refutation is cut short
by the entrance of Maudline.

TUT. Nay, he shall do't forsooth.

TIM.   'Tis the easiest thing   35
  To prove a fool by logic: by logic
  I'll prove anything.

MAUDL.   What, thou wilt not!

TIM. I'll prove a whore to be an honest woman.

MAUDL. Nay, by my faith, she must prove that herself,
  Or logic will never do't.

TIM.   'Twill do't, I tell you.   40

MAUDL. Some in this street would give a thousand pounds
  That you could prove their wives so.

TIM.   Faith, I can,
  And all their daughters too, though they had three bastards.
  When comes your tailor hither?

MAUDL.   Why, what of him?

TIM. By logic I'll prove him to be a man,   45
  Let him come when he will.

MAUDL.   How hard at first
  Was learning to him! Truly, sir, I thought
  He would never 'a took the Latin tongue.
  How many accidences do you think he wore out
  Ere he came to his grammar?   50

TUT.   Some three or four.

MAUDL. Believe me, sir, some four and thirty.

TIM.   Pish!
  I made haberdins of 'em in church porches.

MAUDL. He was eight years in his grammar and stuck horribly
  At a foolish place there call'd *as in presenti*.

TIM. Pox, I have it here now.   [*taps his forehead.*

MAUDL.   He so sham'd me once   55
  Before an honest gentleman that knew me
  When I was a maid.

TIM.   These women must have all out.

MAUDL. '*Quid est grammatica?*' says the gentleman to him—
  J shall remember by a sweet, sweet token—
  But nothing could he answer.

TUT.   How now pupil, ha?   60
  Quid est grammatica?

TIM.   *Grammatica?* Ha, ha, ha!

38 I'll ... woman] Cf. Tim's predicament in Act V.
45 I'll ... man] Cf. proverb 'Nine tailors make but one man'.
49 accidences] copies of an elementary Latin text-book
52 haberdins] Apparently Tim tore up his accidences to use the paper in some
    game; possibly he acted as a Lenten scapegoat (Parker).
54 *as in presenti*] referring to the endings of Latin verbs in the first conjuga-
    tion, present tense, with a quibble on *ass*.
57 *Quid est grammatica?* 'What is grammar?' Tim is amused because of the
    schoolboy pun on *ars*/arse in the standard reply.

MAUDL. Nay, do not laugh, son, but let me hear you say it now.
   There was one word went so prettily off
   The gentleman's tongue, I shall remember it
   The longest day of my life.
TUT.   Come, *Quid est grammatica?*   65
TIM. Are you not asham'd, tutor? *Grammatica?*
   Why, *recte scribendi atque loquendi ars,*
   Sir—reverence of my mother.
MAUDL.   That was it, i'faith.
   Why now, son, I see you are a deep scholar:
   And, Master Tutor, a word I pray. [*Aside*] Let us
   Withdraw a little into my husband's chamber.   70
   I'll send in the North Wales gentlewoman to him:
   She looks for wooing; I'll put together both,
   And lock the door.
TUT.   I give great approbation
   To your conclusion.   75
                 [*Exeunt Maudline and Tutor.*
TIM. I mar'l what this gentlewoman should be
   That I should have in marriage: she's a stranger to me.
   I wonder what my parents mean, i'faith,
   To match me with a stranger so—a maid
   That's neither kiff nor kin to me. Life!   80
   Do they think I have no more care of my body
   Than to lie with one that I ne'er knew,
   A mere stranger, one that ne'er went to school
   With me neither, nor ever play-fellows together?
   They're mightily o'er-seen in't methinks.   85
   They say she has mountains to her marriage:
   She's full of cattle, some two thousand runts.
   Now what the meaning of these runts should be,
   My tutor cannot tell me. I have look'd
   In Rider's *Dictionary* for the letter R,   90
   And there I can hear no tidings of these runts neither,
   Unless they should be Romford hogs, I know them not.

Enter Welsh Gentlewoman

   And here she comes! If I know what to say to her now
   In the way of marriage, I'm no graduate.
   Methinks, i'faith, 'tis boldly done of her   95
   To come into my chamber, being but a stranger.
   She shall not say I'm so proud yet, but I'll speak to her:
   Marry as I will order it, she shall take no hold

---

67 *recte . . . ars*] 'The art of speaking and writing correctly'.
68 Sir—reverence of] 'with due respect to'—apologizing for the obscenity
86 to . . . marriage] i.e. as dowry
90 Rider's *Dictionary*] An English-Latin, Latin-English Dictionary (1509).

Of my words I'll warrant her. She looks and makes a cur'sey.
Salve tu quoque, puella pulcherrima; quid vis nescio nec   100
sane curo—Tully's own phrase to a hair.
WELSH G. [*Aside*] I know not what he means. A suitor quotha?
I hold my life he understands no English.
TIM. *Fertur, me hercule, tu virgo, Wallia ut opibus abundas maximis.*
WELSH G. [*Aside*] What's this *fertur* and *abandundis*?   105
He mocks me sure and calls me a bundle of farts.
TIM. I have no Latin word now for their runts;
I'll make some shift or other.
*Iterum dico, opibus abundas maximis montibus et fontibus et, ut
ita dicam, rontibus; attamen vero homunculus ego sum natura*   110
simul et arte baccalaureus, lecto profecto non paratus.
WELSH G. This is most strange: maybe he can speak Welsh:
Avedera a whee comrage, der due cog foginis.
TIM. [*Aside*] *Cog foggin?* I scorn to cog with her; I'll tell her so too
In a word near her own language. [*To her*] *Ego non cogo.*   115
WELSH G. *Rhegosin a whiggin harle ron corid ambre.*
TIM. By my faith, she's a good scholar: I see that already.
She has the tongues plain: I hold my life she has travell'd.
What will folks say? There goes the learned couple?
Faith, if the truth were known, she hath proceeded.   120

Enter Maudline

MAUDL. How now?
How speeds your business?
TIM.   I'm glad my mother's come
To part us.
MAUDL. How do you agree forsooth?
WELSH G. As well as e'er we did before we met.
MAUDL. How's that?   125
WELSH G. You put me to a man I understand not:
Your son's no Englishman, methinks.
MAUDL.   No Englishman?
Bless my boy! and born i' the heart of London?

100-1 *Salve . . . curo*] 'Save you, too, most lovely girl; I don't know what you
       want, and I don't greatly care'—
104   *Fertur . . . maximis*] 'It's said, maiden, by Hercules, that you've great
       riches in Wales'
109-11 *Iterum . . . paratus*] 'I say again you abound in great riches, in moun-
       tains, fountains, and "runts"; but, indeed, I'm a little chap and a
       Bachelor of Arts, so not ready for the marriage bed'. Possibly, as Parker
       suggests, this is evidence that the play was written for the Queen's Revels
       company, rather than for adult players.
113   *Avedera . . . foginis*] 'Can you speak Welsh? Is he having me on?' Middle-
       ton's Welsh is unreliable.
115   *Ego . . . cogo*] 'I don't compel you'.
116   *Rhegosin . . . ambre*] obscure

WELSH G. I ha' been long enough in the chamber with him,
   And I find neither Welsh nor English in him.   130
MAUDL. Why, Tim, how have you us'd the gentlewoman?
TIM. As well as a man might do, mother, in modest Latin.
MAUDL. Latin, fool?
TIM.   And she recoil'd in Hebrew.
MAUDL. In Hebrew, fool? 'Tis Welsh.
TIM.   All comes to one, mother.
MAUDL. She can speak English too.
TIM.   Who told me so much?   135
   Heart, and she can speak English, I'll clap to her:
   I thought you'ld marry me to a stranger.
MAUDL. You must forgive him: he's so inur'd to Latin,
   He and his tutor, that he hath quite forgot
   To use the Protestant tongue.
WELSH G.   'Tis quickly pardon'd   140
   Forsooth.
MAUDL. Tim, make amends and kiss her.
   He makes towards you forsooth.
           [Tim kisses Welsh Gentlewoman]
TIM.   O delicious!
   One may discover her country by her kissing:
   'Tis a true saying, there's nothing tastes so sweet   145
   As your Welsh mutton. It was reported you could sing.
MAUDL. O rarely, Tim! The sweetest British songs.
TIM. And 'tis my mind, I swear, before I marry,
   I would see all my wife's good parts at once,
   To view how rich I were.
MAUDL.   Thou shalt hear sweet music, Tim.   150
   [To Welsh Gentlewoman] Pray, forsooth.
    [Music and Song]
WELSH G. *Cupid is Venus' only joy,*
        But he is a wanton boy,
        A very, very wanton boy.
        He shoots at ladies' naked breasts,   155
        He is the cause of most men's crests,—
        I mean upon the forehead;
        Invisible but horrid;
        'Twas he first thought upon the way
        To keep a lady's lips in play.   160

        Why should not Venus chide her son
        For the pranks that he hath done,
        The wanton pranks that he hath done?
        He shoots his fiery darts so thick,
        They hurt poor ladies to the quick,   165

140 Protestant tongue] i.e. English

Ah me, with cruel wounding;
His darts are so confounding,
That life and sense would soon decay,
But that he keeps their lips in play.

Can there be any part of bliss   170
In a quickly fleeting kiss,
A quickly fleeting kiss?
To one's pleasure, leisures are but waste,
The slowest kiss makes too much haste . . .   175
And lose it ere we find it.
The pleasing sport they only know
That close above and close below.

TIM. I would not change my wife for a kingdom.
    I can do somewhat too in my own lodging.

Enter Yellowhammer and Allwit

YELL. Why, well said, Tim; the bells go merrily;
    I love such peals alife. Wife, lead them in awhile;   180
    Here's a strange gentleman desires private conference.
              [*Exeunt Maudline, Welsh Gentlewoman and Tim.*
    You're welcome, sir, the more for your name's sake.
    Good Master Yellowhammer, I love my name well:
    And which o' the Yellowhammers take you descent from,   185
    If I may be bold with you? which, I pray?
ALLW. The Yellowhammers in Oxfordshire, near Abingdon.
YELL. And those are the best Yellowhammers, and truest bred.
    I came from thence myself, though now a citizen.
    I will be bold with you; you are most welcome.   190
ALLW. I hope the zeal I bring with me shall deserve it.
YELL. I hope no less. What is your will, sir?
ALLW. I understand by rumours you have a daughter,
    Which my bold love shall henceforth title 'cousin'.
YELL. I thank you for her, sir.
ALLW.   I heard of her virtues   195
    And other confirm'd graces.
YELL.   A plaguy girl, sir.
ALLW. Fame set her out with richer ornaments
    Than you are pleas'd to boast of. 'Tis done modestly.
    I hear she's towards marriage.
YELL.   You hear truth, sir.
ALLW. And with a knight in town, Sir Walter Whorehound?   200
YELL. The very same, sir.
ALLW.   I am the sorrier for it.
YELL. The sorrier? Why, cousin?
ALLW.   'Tis not too far past, is't?
    It may be yet recall'd?
YELL.   Recall'd? Why, good sir?

ALLW. Resolve me in that point, ye shall hear from me.
YELL. There's no contract pass'd.
ALLW.   I am very joyful, sir.   205
YELL. But he's the man must bed her.
ALLW.   By no means, coz;
  She's quite undone then, and you'll curse the time
  That e'er you made the match. He's an arrant whoremaster;
  Consumes his time and state—[*Whispers*]
  Whom in my knowledge he hath kept this seven years;   210
  Nay, coz, another man's wife too.
YELL.   O, abominable!
ALLW. Maintains the whole house, apparels the husband,
  Pays servants' wages, not so much, but—[*Whispers*]
YELL. Worse and worse, and doth the husband know this?
ALLW. Knows? Ay and glad he may too; 'tis his living,   215
  As other trades thrive—butchers by selling flesh,
  Poulters by vending conies, or the like, coz.
YELL. What an incomparable wittol's this!
ALLW. Tush, what cares he for that? Believe me, coz,
  No more than I do.
YELL.   What a base slave's that!   220
ALLW. All's one to him; he feeds and takes his ease,
  Was ne'er the man that ever broke his sleep
  To get a child yet, by his own confession,
  And yet his wife has seven.
YELL.   What, by Sir Walter?
ALLW. Sir Walter's like to keep 'em, and maintain 'em   225
  In excellent fashion: he dares do no less, sir.
YELL. Life! has he children too?
ALLW.   Children? Boys thus high,
  In their Cato and Corderius.
YELL.   What, you jest, sir?
ALLW. Why, one can make a verse and is now at Eton College.
YELL. O, this news has cut into my heart, coz!   230
ALLW. It had eaten nearer if it had not been prevented:
  One Allwit's wife.
YELL.   Allwit? 'Foot, I have heard of him.
  He had a girl kersen'd lately?
ALLW.   Ay, that work
  Did cost the knight above a hundred mark.
YELL. I'll mark him for a knave and villain for 't.   235
  A thousand thanks and blessings, I have done with him.
ALLW. [*Aside*] Ha, ha, ha, this knight will stick by my ribs still,
  I shall not lose him yet; no wife will come:

228   Cato] *Disticha de Moribus*, a popular school book of moral precepts.
228   Corderius] Mathurin Cordier's *Colloquia Scholastica* (1564), another
     school book, approved by Puritans because Cordier taught Calvin.

Where'er he woos, I find him still at home.

Ha, ha!   [*Exit.*   240

YELL. Well, grant all this; say now his deeds are black,

Pray what serves marriage but to call him back?

I have kept a whore myself, and had a bastard

By Mistress Anne in *anno*—

I care not who knows it. He's now a jolly fellow,   245

H'as been twice warden, so may his fruit be:

They were but base begot, and so was he.

The knight is rich, he shall be my son-in-law:

No matter, so the whore he keeps be wholesome;

My daughter takes no hurt then—so let them wed: 250

I'll have him sweat well e'er they go to bed.

Enter Maudline

MAUDL. O husband, husband!

YELL.   How now, Maudline?

MAUDL.   We are all undone.

She's gone, she's gone.

YELL.   Again? Death! Which way?

MAUDL. Over the houses. Lay the waterside:

She's gone for ever, else.

YELL.   O vent'rous baggage!   255

[*Exeunt.*

[Sc. 2]

Enter Tim and Tutor

TIM. Thieves, thieves! My sister's stol'n! Some thief hath got her:

O, how miraculously did my father's plate 'scape!

'Twas all left out, tutor.

TUT.   Is't possible?

TIM. Besides three chains of pearl and a box of coral.

My sister's gone. Let's look at Trig-stairs for her.   5

My mother's gone to lay the common stairs

At Puddle-Wharf; and at the dock below

Stands my poor silly father. Run, sweet tutor, run.

[*Exeunt.*

[Sc. 3]

Enter both the Touchwoods

TOUCH. S. I had been taken, brother, by eight sergeants,

But for the honest watermen; I am bound to them;

They are the most requiteful'st people living,

251   I'll . . . bed] Sweating was thought to be a cure for V.D.

For as they get their means by gentlemen
They are still the forwardest to help gentlemen,   5
You heard how one 'scap'd out of the Blackfriars
But a while since from two or three varlets—
Came into the house with all their rapiers drawn,
As if they'd dance the sword-dance on the stage,
With candles in their hands like chandlers' ghosts,   10
Whilst the poor gentleman so pursued and banded
Was by an honest pair of oars safely landed.
TOUCH. J. I love them with my heart for 't.

Enter three or four Watermen

1 WAT.   Your first man, sir.
2 WAT. Shall I carry you, gentlemen, with a pair of oars?
TOUCH S. These be the honest fellows. Take one pair,   15
  And leave the rest for her.
TOUCH. J.   Barn Elms.
TOUCH. S.   No more, brother.
1 WAT. Your first man.
2 WAT.   Shall I carry your worship?
TOUCH. J. [*To his brother*] Go.
              [*Exit Touchwood Senior with First Waterman.*
                    And you honest watermen that stay,
Here's a French crown for you.
  There comes a maid with all speed to take water;   20
Row her lustily to Barn Elms after me.
2 WAT. To Barn Elms, good, sir? Make ready the boat, Sam:
  We'll wait below.
                              [*Exeunt Watermen.*

Enter Moll

TOUCH. J.   What made you stay so long?
MOLL. I found the way more dangerous than I look'd for.
TOUCH. J. Away, quick! There's a boat waits for you; and I'll   25
  Take water at Paul's Wharf and overtake you.
MOLL. Good sir, do; we cannot be too safe.
                              [*Exeunt.*

[Sc. 4]
              Enter Sir Walter, Yellowhammer, Tim and Tutor
SIR W. Life, call you this close keeping?
YELL.   She was kept

  6   Blackfriars] the 'private' theatre
  8   Came] who came. Presumably this incident was topical
 16   Barn Elms] a notorious resort on the South Bank, opposite Hammersmith
 19   French crown] worth four or five shillings

Under a double lock.
SIR W.   A double devil!
TIM. That's a buff sergeant, tutor; he'll ne'er wear out.
YELL. How would you have women lock'd?
TIM.   With padlocks, father.   5
   The Venetian uses it; my tutor reads it.
SIR W. Heart! If she were so lock'd up, how got she out?
YELL. There was a little hole look'd into the gutter;
   But who would have dreamt of that?
SIR W.   A wiser man would.
TIM. He says true, father; a wise man for love
   Will seek every hole: my tutor knows it.
TUT.   *Verum poeta dicit.*   10
TIM. *Dicit Virgilius*, father.
YELL. Prithee talk of thy gills somewhere else:
   She's play'd the gill with me. Where's your wise mother now?
TIM. Run mad I think. I thought she would have drown'd herself;
   She would not stay for oars, but took a smelt-boat.   15
   Sure, I think she be gone a-fishing for her.
YELL. She'll catch a goodly dish of gudgeons now
   Will serve us all to supper.

   Enter Maudline, drawing Moll by the hair, and watermen

MAUDL. I'll tug thee home by the hair.
1 WAT.   Good mistress, spare her!
MAUDL. Tend your own business.
2 WAT.   You are a cruel mother.   20
                    [*Exeunt Watermen.*

MOLL. O, my heart dies!
MAUDL.   I'll make thee an example
   For all the neighbours' daughters.
MOLL.   Farewell life!
MAUDL. You that have tricks can counterfeit.
YELL.   Hold, hold, Maudline!
MAULD. I have brought your jewel by the hair.
YELL.   She's here, Knight.
SIR W. Forbear, or I'll grow worse.
TIM.   Look on her, tutor;   25
   She hath brought her from the water like a mermaid;
   She's but half my sister now, as far as the flesh goes;
   The rest may be sold to fishwives.
MAUDL. Dissembling, cunning baggage!
YELL.   Impudent strumpet!
SIR W. Either give over both, or I'll give over.   30

10   *Verum . . . dicit*] 'The poet says truly'
11   *Virgilius*] It was, in fact, Ovid.
13   play'd . . . gill] played a gill or trick
17   catch . . . gudgeons] be made to look a fool

Why have you us'd me thus, unkind mistress?
Wherein have I deserv'd?
YELL.   You talk too fondly, sir.
We'll take another course and prevent all:
We might have done't long since; we'll lose no time now,
Nor trust to't any longer. Tomorrow morn,   35
As early as sunrise we'll have you join'd.
MOLL. O, bring me death tonight, love-pitying fates!
Let me not see tomorrow up upon the world!
YELL. Are you content, sir? Till then she shall be watch'd.
MAUDL. Baggage, you shall!

                              [*Exit Maudline with Moll.*
TIM.   Why, father, my tutor and I   40
Will both watch in armour.

                              [*Exit Yellowhammer.*
TUT.   How shall we do for weapons?
TIM. Take you no care for that. If need be, I can send
For conquering metal, tutor, ne'er lost day yet.
'Tis but at Westminster; I am acquainted
With him that keeps the monuments. I can borrow   45
Harry the Fifth's sword. 'Twill serve us both
To watch with.

                              [*Exeunt Tim and Tutor.*
SIR W.   I never was so near my wish,
As this chance makes me. Ere tomorrow noon,
I shall receive two thousand pound in gold,
And a sweet maidenhead worth forty.   50

                Enter Touchwood Junior and First Waterman

TOUCH. J. O, thy news splits me!
1 WAT.   Half drown'd, she cruelly
Tugg'd her by the hair; forc'd her disgracefully,
Not like a mother.
TOUCH. J.   Enough! Leave me, like my joys.

                              [*Exit 1 Waterman.*
Sir, saw you not a wretched maid pass this way?
Heart, villain, is it thou?
SIR W.   Yes, slave, 'tis I.   55

                              [*Both draw and fight.*
TOUCH. J. I must break through thee then; there is no stop
That checks my tongue and all my hopeful fortunes.
That breast excepted, and I must have way.
SIR W. Sir, I believe 'twill hold your life in play.

                              [*Sir Walter wounds Touchwood.*
TOUCH. J. So, you'll gain the heart in my breast at first?   60
SIR W. There is no dealing then? Think on the dowry
For two thousand pounds.

60   at first] first   61   dealing] coming to terms (by sharing the dowry)

TOUCH. J. [*wounding Sir Walter*] O, now 'tis quit, sir.
SIR W. And being of even hand, I'll play no longer.
TOUCH. J. No longer, slave?
SIR W.   I have certain things to think on,
  Before I dare go further.   [*Exit.*
TOUCH. J.   But one bout!   65
  I'll follow thee to death, but ha' 't out.   [*Exit.*

ACT V

[Sc.1]
                Enter Allwit, his wife and Davy Dahumma

WIFE. A misery of a house!
ALLW.   What shall become of us?
DAVY. I think his wound be mortal.
ALLW.   Think'st thou so, Davy?
  Then am I mortal too, but a dead man, Davy.
  This is no world for me: whene'er he goes,
  I must e'en truss up all and after him, Davy—   5
  A sheet with two knots, and away!

                Enter Sir Walter, led in by two servants

DAVY.   O see, sir,
  How faint he goes! Two of my fellows lead him.
WIFE. O me! [*faints*]
ALLW. Heyday! My wife's laid down too. Here's like to be
  A good house kept, when we are all together down.   10
  Take pains with her, good Davy: cheer her up there.
  Let me come to his worship, let me come.
SIR W. Touch me not, villain! My wound aches at thee,
  Thou poison to my heart.
ALLW.   He raves already;
  His senses are quite gone; he knows me not.   15
  Look up, an't like your worship; heave those eyes;
  Call me to mind; is your remembrance left?
  Look in my face. Who am I, an't like your worship?
SIR W. If anything be worse than slave or villain,
  Thou art the man.
ALLW.   Alas, his poor worship's weakness!   20
  He will begin to know me by little and little.
SIR W. No devil can be like thee.
ALLW.   Ah, poor gentleman!
  Methinks the pain that thou endurest—
SIR W. Thou know'st me to be wicked, for thy baseness

Kept the eyes open still on all my sins.   25
None knew the dear account my soul stood charg'd with
So well as thou; yet, like hell's flattering angel,
Would'st never tell me on't, let'st me go on
And join with death in sleep; that if I had not wak'd,
Now by chance, even by a stranger's pity,   30
I had everlastingly slept out all hope
Of grace and mercy.

ALLW.   Now he is worse and worse.
    Wife! to him, wife! Thou wast wont to do good on him.
WIFE. How is't with you, sir?
SIR W.   Not as with you,
Thou loathsome strumpet. Some good pitying man,   35
Remove my sins out of my sight a little.
I tremble to behold her: she keeps back
All comfort while she stays. Is this a time,
Unconscionable woman, to see thee?
Art thou so cruel to the peace of man,   40
Not to give liberty now? The devil himself
Shows a far fairer reverence and respect
To goodness than thy self. He dares not do this,
But parts in time of penitence, hides his face:
When man withdraws from him, he leaves the place.   45
Hast thou less manners and more impudence
Than thy instructor? Prithee, show thy modesty,
If the least grain be left, and get thee from me.
Thou shouldst be rather lock'd many rooms hence
From the poor miserable sight of me,   50
If either love or grace had part in thee.
WIFE. He is lost for ever.
ALLW.   Run, sweet Davy, quickly
And fetch the children hither. Sight of them
Will make him cheerful straight.

                                              [Exit Davy.

SIR W. [To Mrs Allwit]   O Death! Is this
A place for you to weep? What tears are those?   55
Get you away with them: I shall fare the worse
As long as they are a-weeping, they work against me.
There's nothing but thy appetite in that sorrow;
Thou weep'st for lust; I feel it in the slackness
Of comforts coming towards me. I was well   60
Till thou began'st to undo me. This shows like
The fruitless sorrow of a careless mother
That brings her son with dalliance to the gallows,
And then stands by, and weeps to see him suffer.

                    Enter Davy with the Children

59 slackness] slowness

DAVY. There are the children, sir, an't like your worship.   65
  Your last fine girl: in troth, she smiles:
  Look, look, in faith, sir.
SIR W.   O, my vengeance!
  Let me for ever hide my cursed face
  From sight of those that darkens all my hopes,
  And stands between me and the sight of heaven!   70
  Who sees me now, her too, and those so near me,
  May rightly say I am o'ergrown with sin.
  O, how my offences wrestle with my repentance!
  It hath scarce breath;
  Still my adulterous guilt hovers aloft,   75
  And with her black wings beats down all my prayers,
  Ere they be half way up. What's he knows now
  How long I have to live? O, what comes then?
  My taste grows bitter, the round world all gall now;
  Her pleasing pleasures now hath poison'd me,   80
  Which I exchang'd my soul for.
  Make way a hundred sighs at once for me!
ALLW. Speak to him, Nick.
NICK.   I dare not. I am afraid.
ALLW. Tell him he hurts his wounds, Wat, with making moan.
SIR W. Wretch, death of seven!   Come, let's be talking   85
  Somewhat to keep him alive. Ah, sirrah Wat,
  And did my lord bestow that jewel on thee
  For an epistle that thou mad'st in Latin?
  Thou art a good forward boy: there's great joy on thee.
SIR W. O sorrow!
ALLW. [Aside]   Heart! Will nothing comfort him?   90
  If he be so far gone, 'tis time to moan.—
  Here's pen and ink, and paper, and all things ready:
  Will't please your worship for to make your will?
SIR W. My will? Yes, yes, what else? Who writes apace now?
ALLW. That can your man Davy, an't like your worship,   95
  A fair, fast, legible hand.
SIR W.   Set it down then.
  Imprimis, I bequeath to yonder wittol
  Three times his weight in curses.
ALLW.   How!
SIR W.   All plagues
  Of body and of mind.
ALLW.   Write them not down, Davy.
DAVY. It is his will, I must.
SIR W.   Together also,   100
  With such a sickness, ten days ere his death.

---

85   death of seven!] referring to his bastards, the fruit of his sins

ALLW. [*Aside*] There's a sweet legacy: I am almost choked with't.
SIR W. Next I bequeath to that foul whore, his wife,
    All barrenness of joy, a drouth of virtue,
    And dearth of all repentance. For her end,   105
    The common misery of an English strumpet,
    In French and Dutch, beholding ere she dies
    Confusion of her brats before her eyes,
    And never shed a tear for it.

Enter a Servant

SERV.   Where's the knight?
    O sir, the gentleman you wounded is   110
    Newly departed.
SIR W.   Dead? Lift, lift! who helps me?
ALLW. Let the law lift you now, that must have all!
    I have done lifting on you, and my wife too.
SERV. [*To Sir Walter*] You were best lock yourself close.
ALLW.   Not in my house, sir:
    I'll harbour no such persons as men-slayers.   115
    Lock yourself where you will.
SIR W.   What's this?
WIFE.   Why, husband!
ALLW. I know what I do, wife.
WIFE.   You cannot tell yet:
    For having kill'd the man in his defence,
    Neither his life nor estate will be touch'd, husband.
ALLW. Away, wife! Hear a fool! His lands will hang him.   120
SIR W. Am I denied a chamber? What say you forsooth?
WIFE. Alas, sir, I am one that would have all well,
    But must obey my husband. Prithee, love,
    Let the poor gentleman stay, being so sore wounded.
    There's a close chamber at one end of the garret   125
    We never use: let him have that, I prithee.
ALLW. We never use? You forget sickness then
    And physic times. Is't not a place for easement?

Enter Second Servant

SIR W. O Death! Do I hear this with part
    Of former life in me? What's the news now?   130
2 SERV. Troth, worse and worse: you're like to lose your land—
    If the law save your life, sir, or the surgeon.
ALLW. Hark you there, wife.
SIR W.   Why, how, sir?
2 SERV. Sir Oliver Kix's wife is new quicken'd:

107 In . . . Dutch] Venereal diseases
108 Confusion . . . brats] Incest (Parker)
112 lift] hang
113 lifting] (a) raising (b) arousing sexually   128 place . . . easement] privy

That child undoes you, sir.

SIR W. All ill at once. 135

ALLW. I wonder what he makes here with his consorts?
Cannot our house be private to ourselves,
But we must have such guests? I pray, depart, sirs,
And take your murderer along with you.
Good he were apprehended ere he go: 140
H'as killed some honest gentleman. Send for officers.

SIR W. I'll soon save you that labour.

ALLW. I must tell you, sir,
You have been somewat bolder in my house
Than I could well like of; I suffer'd you
Till it struck here at my heart. I tell you truly 145
I thought you had been familiar with my wife once.

WIFE. With me? I'll see him hang'd first. I defy him
And all such gentlemen in the like extremity.

SIR W. If ever eyes were open, these are they:
Gamesters, farewell, I have nothing left to play. 150

[*Exit with Servants.*

ALLW. And therefore get you gone, sir.

DAVY. Of all wittols
Be thou the head; thou the grand whore of spittles. [*Exit.*

ALLW. So, since he's like now to be rid of all,
I am right glad I am so well rid of him.

WIFE. I knew he durst not stay, when you nam'd officers. 155

ALLW. That stopp'd his spirits straight. What shall we do now, wife?

WIFE. As we were wont to do.

ALLW. We are richly furnish'd, wife
With household stuff.

WIFE. Let's let out lodgings then,
And take a house in the Strand.

ALLW. In troth, a match, wench.
We are simply stock'd with cloth of tissue cushions 160
To furnish out bay-windows: Push! What not
That's quaint and costly from the top to the bottom!
Life, for furniture, we may lodge a countess!
There's a close-stool of tawny velvet too,
Now I think on't, Wife.

WIFE. There's that should be, sir; 165
Your nose must be in everything.

ALLW. I have done, wench;
And let this stand in every gallant's chamber:
'There's no gamester like a politic sinner
For whoe'er games, the box is sure a winner.' [*Exeunt.*

150 Gamesters] (a) gamblers (b) lechers
168–9 'There's . . . winner'] The box is the bank in a gambling game, so that
the couplet warns careful fornicators, such as Sir Walter, that they are
playing a losing game.

[Sc. 2]

Enter Yellowhammer and Maudline

MAUDL. O husband, husband, she will die, she will die.
　There is no sign but death.
YELL.　　　　　　　　'Twill be our shame then.
MAUDL. O, how she's changed in compass of an hour!
YELL. Ah, my poor girl! Good faith, thou wert too cruel
　To drag her by the hair.
MAUDL.　　　　　　　You would have done as much, sir.　　5
　To curb her of her humour.
YELL.　　　　　　　'Tis curb'd sweetly!
　She catch'd her bane o'th'water.

Enter Tim

MAUDL.　　　　　　　How now, Tim?
TIM. Faith, busy, mother, about an epitaph
　Upon my sister's death.
MAUDL.　　　　　　Death! She is not dead, I hope?
TIM. No, but she means to be, and that's as good,　　　　10
　And when a thing's done, 'tis done. You
　Taught me that, mother.
YELL.　　　　　　What is your tutor doing?
TIM. Making one too in principal, pure Latin,
　Cull'd out of Ovid his *De Tristibus.*
YELL. How does your sister look? Is she not chang'd?　　15
TIM. Chang'd? Gold into white money has never so chang'd
　As is my sister's colour into paleness.

Enter Moll, attended

YELL. O, here she's brought! See how she looks like death!
TIM. Looks she like death, and ne'er a word made yet?
　I must go beat my brains against a bed-post,　　　　20
　And get before my tutor.
YELL.　　　　　　Speak, how dost thou?
MOLL. I hope I shall be well, for I am as sick
　At heart as I can be.
YELL.　　　　　　'Las, my poor girl!
　The doctor's making a most sovereign drink for thee;
　The worst ingredience dissolv'd pearl and amber:　　25
　We spare no cost, girl.
MOLL.　　　　　　Your love comes too late.
　Yet timely thanks reward it. What is comfort
　When the poor patient's heart is past relief?
　It is no doctor's art can cure my grief.
YELL. All is cast away then. Prithee look　　　　　　30

16   white money] silver

Upon me cheerfully.

MAUDL.   Sing but a strain or two,
Thou wilt not think how 'twill revive thy spirits.
Strive with thy fit, prithee, sweet Moll.

MOLL.   You shall have
My good will, mother.

MAUDL.   Why, well said, wench.

MOLL. [*Sings*] *Weep eyes, break heart;*   35
      My love and I must part.
      Cruel fates true love do soonest sever,
      O, I shall see thee, never, never, never.
      O, happy is the maid whose life takes end,
      Ere it knows parents' frown, or loss of friend.   40
      Weep eyes, break heart;
      My love and I must part.

       Enter Touchwood Senior with a letter

MAUDL. O, I could die with music! Well sung, girl.

MOLL. If you call it so, it was.

YELL.   She plays the swan
And sings herself to death.

TOUCH. S.   By your leave, sir.   45

YELL. What are you, sir? Or what's your business, pray?

TOUCH. S. I may be now admitted, though the brother
Of him your hate pursued: it spreads no further.
Your malice sets in death, does it not, sir?

YELL. In death?

TOUCH. S.   He's dead: 'twas a dear love to him: 50
It cost him but his life, that was all, sir.
He paid enough, poor gentleman, for his love.

YELL. There's all our ill remov'd, if she were well now.
Impute not, sir, his end to any hate
That sprung from us: he had a fair wound brought that.   55

TOUCH. S. That help'd him forward, I must needs confess;
But the restraint of love and your unkindness,
Those were the wounds that from his heart drew blood;
But, being past help, let words forget it too.
Scarcely three minutes ere his eyelids clos'd   60
And took eternal leave of this world's light,
He wrote this letter, which by oath he bound me
To give to her own hands—that's all my business.

YELL. You may perform it then: there she sits.

TOUCH. S. O, with a following look!

YELL.   Ay, trust me, sir,   65
I think she'll follow him quickly.

TOUCH S.   Here's some gold,
He will'd me to distribute faithfully

65 following] ready to follow her lover

Amongst your servants.
YELL.   'Las, what doth he mean, sir?
TOUCH. S. How cheer you, mistress?
MOLL.   I must learn of you, sir.
TOUCH. S. Here's a letter from a friend of yours,   70
  And where that fails in satisfaction,
  I have a sad tongue ready to supply.
MOLL. How does he, ere I look on't?
TOUCH. S.   Seldom better.
  H'as a contented health now.
MOLL.   I am most glad on't.
MAUDL. [*Aside to Yellowhammer*] Dead, sir?
YELL.   He is. Now wife, let's but get the girl   75
  Upon her legs again, and to church roundly with her.
MOLL. O, sick to death, he tells me. How does he after this?
TOUCH. S. Faith, feels no pain at all. He's dead, sweet mistress.
MOLL. Peace, close mine eyes. [*faints*]
YELL.   The girl! Look to the girl, wife.
MAUDL. Moll, daughter, sweet girl, speak! Look but once up,   80
  Thou shalt have all the wishes of thy heart
  That wealth can purchase.
YELL.   O, she's gone for ever!
  That letter broke her heart.
TOUCH. S.   As good now, then,
  As let her lie in torment and then break it.

Enter Susan

MAUDL. O Susan, she thou loved'st so dear is gone.   85
SUS. O sweet maid!
TOUCH. S.   This is she that help'd her still:
  I've a reward for thee.
YELL.   Take her in:
  Remove her from our sight, our shame, and sorrow.
TOUCH. S. Stay, let me help thee: 'tis the last cold kindness
  I can perform for my sweet brother's sake.   90
      [*Exeunt Touchwood Senior, Susan, and servants, carrying Moll.*
YELL. All the whole street will hate us, and the world
  Point me out cruel. It is our best course, wife,
  After we have given order for the funeral,
  To absent ourselves, till she be laid in ground.
MAUDL. Where shall we spend that time?
YELL.   I'll tell thee where, wench.   95
  Go to some private church and marry Tim
  To the rich Brecknock gentlewoman.
MAUDL.   Mass, a match!
  We'll not lose all at once; somewhat we'll catch.
                                        [*Exeunt.*

[Sc. 3]

Enter Sir Oliver Kix and four Servants

SIR OLIV. Ho! My wife's quicken'd! I am a man for ever.
  I think I have bestirr'd my stumps, i'faith:
  Run, get your fellows altogether instantly,
  Then to the Parish Church and ring the bells.
I SERV. It shall be done, sir.   *[Exit.*
SIR OLIV.   Upon my love,   5
  I charge you, villain, that you make a bonfire
  Before the door at night.
2 SERV.   A bonfire, sir?
SIR OLIV. A thwacking one, I charge you.
2 SERV. [*Aside*]   This is monstrous.
                                        [Exit.

SIR OLIV. Run, tell a hundred pound out for the gentleman
  That gave my wife the drink, the first thing you do.   10
3 SERV. A hundred pounds, sir?
SIR OLIV.   A bargain! As our joy grows,
  We must remember still from whence it flows,
  Or else we prove ungrateful multipliers.   *[Exit 3 Servant.*
  The child is coming, and the land comes after;
  The news of this will make a poor Sir Walter.   15
  I have struck it home, i'faith.
4 SERV.   That you have, marry, sir;
  But will not your worship go to the funeral
  Of both these lovers?
SIR OLIV.   Both? Go both together?
4 SERV. Ay sir; the gentleman's brother will have it so.
  'Twill be the pitifullest sight. There's such running,   20
  Such rumours, and such throngs, a pair of lovers
  Had never more spectators, more men's pities,
  Or women's wet eyes.
SIR OLIV.   My wife helps the number then?
4 SERV. There's such drawing out of handkerchers,
  And those that have no handkerchers lift up aprons.   25
SIR OLIV. Her parents may have joyful hearts at this!
  I would not have my cruelty so talk'd on
  To any child of mine, for a monopoly.
4 SERV. I believe you, sir.
  'Tis cast so too that both their coffins meet,   30
  Which will be lamentable.
SIR OLIV.   Come, we'll see it.
                                        [Exeunt.

[Sc. 4]

> *Recorders dolefully playing: Enter at one door the coffin of the gentleman,*
> *solemnly decked, his sword upon it, attended by many in black, his*
> *brother being the chief mourner. At the other door, the coffin of the virgin,*
> *with a garland of flowers, with epitaphs pinned on't, attended by maids and*
> *women. Then set them down one right over against the other; while all the*
> *company seem to weep and mourn, there is a sad song in the music-room.*
> *The Company includes Sir Oliver and Lady Kix, Allwit and his wife, a*
> *Parson and Susan.*

TOUCH. S. Never could death boast of a richer prize
  From the first parent: let the world bring forth
  A pair of truer hearts. To speak but truth
  Of this departed gentleman, in a brother
  Might by hard censure be call'd flattery;   5
  Which makes me rather silent in his right,
  Than so to be deliver'd to the thoughts
  Of any envious hearer, starv'd in virtue,
  And therefore pining to hear others thrive.
  But for this maid, whom envy cannot hurt   10
  With all her poisons, having left to ages
  The true, chaste monument of her living name
  Which no time can deface, I say of her
  The full truth freely, without fear of censure;
  What nature could there shine, that might redeem   15
  Perfection home to woman, but in her
  Was fully glorious? Beauty set in goodness
  Speaks what she was, that jewel so infix'd,
  There was no want of any thing of life
  To make these virtuous precedents man and wife.   20
ALLW. Great pity of their deaths!
ALL.   Ne'er more pity!
LADY K. It makes a hundred weeping eyes, sweet gossip.
TOUCH. S. I cannot think there's any one amongst you
  In this full fair assembly, maid, man or wife,
  Whose heart would not have sprung with joy and gladness,   25
  To have seen their marriage day?
ALL.   It would have made
  A thousand joyful hearts.
TOUCH. S.   Up then apace,
  And take your fortunes; make these joyful hearts;
  Here's none but friends.
       [Touchwood Junior and Moll rise from their coffins]
ALL.   Alive, sir? O sweet, dear couple!

S.D. *music-room]* above the stage

TOUCH. S. Nay, do not hinder 'em now, stand from about 'em.   30
  If she be caught again, and have this time,
  I'll ne'er plot further for 'em, nor this honest chambermaid
  That help'd all at a push.
TOUCH. J. [*To Parson*]   Good sir, apace!
PARS. Hands join now, but hearts for ever,
  Which no parents' mood shall sever.   35
    [*To Touchwood Junior*] You shall forsake all widows, wives
                                              and maids.
    [*To Moll*] You, lords, knights, gentlemen and men of trades.
  And if in haste any article misses,
  Go interline it with a brace of kisses.
TOUCH. S. Here's a thing troll'd nimbly! Give you joy, brother.   40
  Were't not better thou shouldst have her
  Than the maid should die?
WIFE.   To you, sweet mistress bride.
ALL. Joy, joy to you both.
TOUCH. S.   Here be your wedding sheets
  You brought along with you: you may both go to bed
  When you please to.
TOUCH. J.   My joy wants utterance.   45
TOUCH. S. Utter all at night then, brother.
MOLL.   I am
  Silent with delight.
TOUCH. S.   Sister, delight will silence
  Any woman; but you'll find your tongue again
  Among maid-servants, now you keep house, sister.
ALL. Never was hour so fill'd with joy and wonder.   50
TOUCH. S. To tell you the full story of this chamber-maid,
  And of her kindness in this business to us,
  'Twould ask an hour's discourse. In brief, 'twas she
  That wrought it to this purpose cunningly.
ALL. We shall all love her for 't.

Enter Yellowhammer and Maudline

ALLW.   See who comes here now.   55
TOUCH. S. A storm, a storm! But we are shelter'd for it.
YELL. I will prevent you all, and mock you thus,
  You and your expectations. I stand happy
  Both in your lives, and your hearts' combination.
TOUCH. S. Here's a strange day again.
YELL.   The knight's proved villain.   60
  All's come out now; his niece an arrant baggage;
  My poor boy Tim is cast away this morning,
  Even before breakfast—married a whore

31 time] opportunity
34–5 Hands . . . sever] The Parson continues the interrupted ceremony in III. i.

Next to his heart.

ALL.   A whore?

YELL.   His niece, forsooth!

ALLW. I think we rid our hands in good time of him.   65

WIFE. I knew he was past the best when I gave him over.
  [*To Yellowhammer*] What is become of him, pray sir?

YELL.   Who? The knight?
  He lies i' th' knight's ward. [*To Lady Kix*] Now your belly, Lady,
  Begins to blossom, there's no peace for him,
  His creditors are so greedy.

SIR OLIV.   Master Touchwood,   70
  Hear'st thou this news? I am so endear'd to thee
  For my wife's fruitfulness, that I charge you both,
  Your wife and thee, to live no more asunder
  For the world's frowns. I have purse and bed and board for you.
  Be not afraid to go to your business roundly: 75
  Get children, and I'll keep them.

TOUCH. S.   Say you so, sir?

SIR OLIV. Prove me, with three at a birth, and thou dar'st now.

TOUCH. S. Take heed how you dare a man, while you live, sir,
  That has good skill at his weapon.

Enter Tim with Welsh Gentlewoman and Tutor

SIR OLIV.   'Foot, I dare you, sir.

YELL. Look gentlemen, if ever you say the picture   80
  Of the unfortunate marriage, yonder 'tis.

WELSH G. Nay, good sweet Tim.

TIM.   Come from the University
  To marry a whore in London, with my tutor too!
  O Tempora! O Mores!

TUT.   Prithee, Tim,
  Be patient.

TIM.   I bought a jade at Cambridge.   85
  I'll let her out to execution, tutor,
  For eighteen pence a day, or Brainford horse-races;
  She'll serve to carry seven miles out of town well.
  Where be these mountains? I was promis'd mountains,
  But there's such a mist, I can see none of 'em.   90
  What are become of those two thousand runts?
  Let's have a bout with them in the meantime.
  A vengeance runt thee!

MAUDL.   Good sweet Tim, have patience.

TIM. *Flectere si nequeo superos, Acheronta movebo*, mother.

80   say] saw
84   *O . . . Mores!*] Cicero on Catiline's conspiracy
92   runt] berate
92   *Flectere . . . movebo*] Virgil, *Aeneid* VII. 312

MAUDL. I think you have married her in logic, Tim.
   You told me once, by logic you would prove   95
   A whore an honest woman. Prove her so, Tim,
   And take her for thy labour.
TIM.   Troth, I thank you.
   I grant you I may prove another man's wife so,
   But not mine own.
MAUDL.   There's no remedy now, Tim.   100
   You must prove her so as well as you may.
TIM. Why, then, my tutor and I will about her
   As well as we can.
   Uxor non est meretrix, ergo falleris.
WELSH G. Sir, if your logic cannot prove me honest,   105
   There's a thing called marriage, and that makes me honest.
MAUDL. O, there's a trick beyond your logic, Tim.
TIM. I perceive then a woman may be honest
   According to the English print, when she is
   A whore in the Latin. So much for marriage and logic.   110
   I'll love her for her wit, I'll pick out my runts there;
   And for my mountains, I'll mount upon —
YELL. So Fortune seldom deals two marriages
   With one hand, and both lucky. The best is,
   One feast will serve them both. Marry, for room,   115
   I'll have the dinner kept in Goldsmiths' Hall,
   To which, kind gallants, I invite you all.
                                [*Exeunt.*

102   *Uxor . . . falleris*] A wife is not a whore, so you're wrong.
110   upon —] the rhyme would be obscene.
114   Goldsmiths' Hall] Yellowhammer would be a member of the guild and
     entitled to hire the hall.

WOMEN
BEWARE
WOMEN.

A
TRAGEDY,
BY
Tho. Middleton, Gent.

LONDON:
Printed for *Humphrey Moseley,* 1657.

NOTE

Women Beware Women, published in 1657 along with *More Dissemblers Besides Women*, under the title of *Two New Playes*, was probably written towards the end of Middleton's career, though some critics date it earlier. The Bianca plot is based on the story of a Bianca Capello who became the mistress of Francesco de' Medici, and later his wife. They died of fever in 1587. Middleton makes Leantio of a lower social status than Bianca's actual husband. The Isabella plot is to be found in the *Histoire Veritable . . . d'Hypolite et d'Isabella* (1597). It should be added that in the 1657 Octavo, Bianca is called Brancha throughout. As this spelling leads to some stumbling lines, and as it conflicts with that of the story that served as a source, I have, like most editors, corrected it. R. B. Parker lists forty-seven variants in different copies of the first edition. All of them are concerned merely with spelling and punctuation.

DRAMATIS PERSONAE

DUKE OF FLORENCE
LORD CARDINAL, his brother
FABRITIO
HIPPOLITO, his brother
GUARDIANO
THE WARD, his nephew
LEANTIO, a factor
SORDIDO, servant to the Ward
   Cardinals, Knights, Nobles, Citizens, Servants
LIVIA, Fabritio's sister
ISABELLA, Fabritio's daughter
BIANCA, Leantio's wife
MOTHER of Leantio
   Ladies

Scene—Florence

WOMEN BEWARE WOMEN

ACT I

[Sc. 1]

Enter Leantio with Bianca, and Mother

MOTHER. Thy sight was never yet more precious to me;
  Welcome with all the affection of a mother,
  That comfort can express from natural love:
  Since thy birth-joy—a mother's chiefest gladness
  After sh'as undergone her curse of sorrows—   5
  Thou wast not more dear to me than this hour
  Presents thee to my heart. Welcome again!
LEANT. [*Aside*] 'Las, poor affectionate soul, how her joys speak to me!
  I have observ'd it often, and I know it is
  The fortune commonly of knavish children   10
  To have the loving'st mothers.
MOTH.   What's this gentlewoman?
LEANT. O, you have nam'd the most unvalued'st purchase
  That youth of man had ever knowledge of.
  As often as I look upon that treasure,
  And know it to be mine—there lies the blessing—   15
  It joys me that I ever was ordain'd
  To have a being, and to live 'mongst men;
  Which is a fearful living, and a poor one,
  Let a man truly think on't,
  To have the toil and griefs of fourscore years   20
  Put up in a white sheet, tied with two knots.
  Methinks it should strike earthquakes in adulterers,
  When ev'n the very sheets they commit sin in
  May prove, for ought they know, all their last garments.
  O, what a mark were there for women then!   25
  But beauty able to content a conqueror
  Whom earth could scarce content, keeps me in compass;
  I find no wish in me bent sinfully
  To this man's sister, or to that man's wife:
  In love's name let 'em keep their honesties,   30
  And cleave to their own husbands—'tis their duties.
  Now when I go to church, I can pray handsomely,

---

21 white . . . knots] a shroud
23–4 When . . . garments] This idea is reversed at the end of *A Chaste Maid in Cheapside*

71

Not come like gallants only to see faces.
As if Lust went to market still on Sundays.
I must confess I am guilty of one sin, mother,   35
More than I brought into the world with me;
But that I glory in: 'tis theft, but noble,
As ever greatness yet shot up withal.
MOTH. How's that?
LEANT.   Never to be repented, mother,
Though sin be death: I had died if I had not sinn'd;   40
And here's my masterpiece. Do you now behold her!
Look on her well, she's mine; look on her better:
Now say, if't be not the best piece of theft
That ever was committed; and I have my pardon for't:
'Tis seal'd from Heaven by marriage.
MOTH.   Married to her!   45
LEANT. You must keep counsel, mother; I am undone else.
If it be known I have lost her; do but think now
What that loss is; life's but a trifle to't.
From Venice her consent and I have brought her
From parents great in wealth, more now in rage.   50
But let storms spend their furies; now we have got
A shelter o'er our quiet innocent loves,
We are contented. Little money sh'as brought me:
View but her face, you may see all her dowry,
Save that which lies lock'd up in hidden virtues,   55
Like jewels kept in cabinets.
MOTH.   Y'are too blame,
If your obedience will give way to a check,
To wrong such a perfection.
LEANT.   How?
MOTH.   Such a creature,
To draw her from her fortune, which no doubt,
At the full time, might have prov'd rich and noble.   60
You know not what you have done; my life can give you
But little helps, and my death lesser hopes;
And hitherto your own means has but made shift
To keep you single, and that hardly too.
What ableness have you to do her right then   65
In maintenance fitting her birth and virtues?
Which ev'ry woman of necessity looks for,
And most to go above it, not confin'd
By their conditions, virtues, bloods, or births,
But flowing to affections, wills and humours.   70
LEANT. Speak low, sweet mother: you are able to spoil as many

---

32 Now] Barber suggests that Leantio is contrasting his former church-going
56 too blame] Middleton and some of his contemporaries took *blame* to mean
    'blameworthy'.

As come within the hearing. If it be not
Your fortune to mar all, I have much marvel.
I pray do not you teach her to rebel
When she's in a good way to obedience, 75
To rise with other women in commotion
Against their husbands, for six gowns a year,
And so maintain their cause, when they're once up.
In all things else that require cost enough.
They are all of 'em a kind of spirits soon rais'd 80
But not so soon laid, mother; as for example,
A woman's belly is got up in a trice,
A simple charge ere it be laid down again:
So ever in all their quarrels and their courses;
And I'm a proud man, I hear nothing of 'em; 85
They're very still, I thank my happiness,
And sound asleep; pray let not your tongue wake 'em.
If you can but rest quiet, she's contented
With all conditions that my fortunes bring her to;
To keep close as a wife that loves her husband; 90
To go after the rate of my ability,
Not the licentious swinge of her own will,
Like some of her old school-fellows. She intends
To take out other works in a new sampler
And frame the fashion of an honest love 95
Which knows no wants but, mocking poverty,
Brings forth more children to make rich men wonder
At divine providence that feeds mouths of infants
And sends them none to feed, but stuffs their rooms
With fruitful bags, their beds with barren wombs. 100
Good mother, make not you things worse than they are
Out of your too much openness; pray take heed on't;
Nor imitate the envy of old people,
That strive to mar good sport, because they are perfect.
I would have you more pitiful to youth, 105
Especially to your own flesh and blood.
I'll prove an excellent husband, here's my hand,
Lay in provision, follow my business roundly,
And make you a grandmother in forty weeks.
Go, pray salute her, bid her welcome cheerfully. 110
MOTH. [*Kissing her*] Gentlewoman, thus much is a debt of courtesy
Which fashionable strangers pay each other
At a kind meeting; then there's more than one
Due to the knowledge I have of your nearness; [*Kisses again.*
I am bold to come again, and now salute you 115
By th' name of daughter, which may challenge more

83 A simple charge] sheer expense (Barber)
107 Here's my hand] as a token of his promise

Than ordinary respect. [*Kisses her again.*
LEANT. [*Aside*]   Why, this is well now,
And I think few mothers of threescore will mend it.
MOTH. What I can bid you welcome to, is mean,
  But make it all your own; we are full of wants,   120
  And cannot welcome worth.
LEANT. [*Aside*]   Now this is scurvy,
  And spake as if a woman lack'd her teeth.
  These old folks talk of nothing but defects,
  Because they grow so full of 'em themselves.
BIANCA. Kind mother, there is nothing can be wanting   125
  To her that does enjoy all her desires.
  Heaven send a quiet peace with this man's love,
  And I am as rich as virtue can be poor;
  Which were enough after the rate of mind
  To erect temples for content plac'd here;   130
  I have forsook friends, fortunes, and my country,
  And hourly I rejoice in't. Here's my friends,
  And few is the good number; thy successes,
  Howe'er they look, I will still name my fortunes:
  Hopeful or spiteful, they shall all be welcome.   135
  Who invites many guests has of all sorts,
  As he that traffics much drinks of all fortunes,
  Yet they must all be welcome, and us'd well.
  I'll call this place the place of my birth now,
  And rightly too; for here my love was born,   140
  And that's the birthday of a woman's joys.
  [*To Leantio*] You have not bid me welcome since I came.
LEANT. That I did questionless.
BIANCA.   No sure, how was't?
  I have quite forgot it.
LEANT.   Thus. [*Kissing her.*
BIANCA.   Oh sir, 'tis true:
  Now I remember well. I have done thee wrong.   145
  Pray take't again, sir. [*Kissing him.*
LEANT.   How many of these wrongs
  Could I put up in an hour? and turn up the glass
  For twice as many more. [*Kissing her again.*
MOTH. Will't please you to walk in, daughter?
BIANCA.   Thanks, sweet mother;
  The voice of her that bare me is not more pleasing.   150
                         [*Exeunt Mother and Bianca.*
LEANT. Though my own care and my rich master's trust
  Lay their commands both on my factorship,
  This day and night, I'll know no other business
  But here and her dear welcome. 'Tis a bitterness
  To think upon tomorrow, that I must leave her   155
  Still to the sweet hopes of the week's end.

That pleasure should be so restrain'd and curb'd,
After the course of a rich workmaster
That never pays till Saturday night! Marry,
It comes together in a round sum then,   160
And does more good, you'll say. O fair-ey'd Florence!
Didst thou but know what a most matchless jewel
Thou now art mistress of, a pride would take thee,
Able to shoot destruction through the bloods
Of all thy youthful sons; but 'tis great policy   165
To keep choice treasures in obscurest places:
Should we show thieves our wealth, 'twould make 'em bolder;
Temptation is a devil will not stick
To fasten upon a saint; take heed of that;
The jewel is cas'd up from all men's eyes.   170
Who could imagine now a gem were kept
Of that great value under this plain roof?
But how in times of absence? What assurance
Of this restraint then? Yes, yes, there's one with her:
Old mothers know the world; and such as these,   175
When sons lock chests, are good to look to keys.   [*Exit.*

[Sc. 2]

Enter Guardiano, Fabritio, and Livia

GUARD. What, has your daughter seen him yet? know you that?
FAB. No matter; she shall love him.
GUARD.   Nay, let's have fair play.
  He has been now my ward some fifteen year,
  And 'tis my purpose (as time calls upon me)
  By custom seconded and such moral virtues,   5
  To tender him a wife. Now, sir, this wife
  I'ld fain elect out of a daughter of yours.
  You see my meaning's fair: if now this daughter,
  So tender'd,—let me come to your own phrase, sir—
  Should offer to refuse him, I were hansell'd.   10
  [*Aside*] Thus am I fain to calculate all my words
  For the meridian of a foolish old man,
  To take his understanding. What do you answer, sir?
FAB. I say still, she shall love him.
GUARD.   Yet again?
  And shall she have no reason for this love?   15
FAB. Why, do you think that women love with reason?

162–76 Didst . . . keys] Leantio's possessiveness contrasts with Bianca's less
    questionable love
  5 By . . . virtues] It is characteristic of Guardiano that he should confuse
    custom and virtue.

GUARD. [*Aside*] I perceive fools are not at all hours foolish,
  No more than wise men wise.

FAB.   I had a wife,
  She ran mad for me; she had no reason for't,
  For aught I could perceive. What think you, lady sister?   20

GUARD. [*Aside*] 'Twas a fit match that,
  Being both out of their wits! A loving wife, it seem'd
  She strove to come as near you as she could.

FAB. And if her daughter prove not mad for love too,
  She takes not after her, nor after me,   25
  If she prefer reason before my pleasure.
  You're an experienc'd widow, lady sister;
  I pray let your opinion come amongst us.

LIV. I must offend you then, if truth will do't,
  And take my niece's part; and call't injustice   30
  To force her love to one she never saw.
  Maids should both see, and like, all little enough;
  If they love truly after that, 'tis well.
  Counting the time, she takes one man till death.
  That's a hard task, I tell you; but one may   35
  Enquire at three years' end amongst young wives,
  And mark how the game goes.

FAB.   Why, is not man
  Tied to the same observance, lady sister,
  And in one woman?

LIV.   'Tis enough for him;
  Besides he tastes of many sundry dishes   40
  That we poor wretches never lay our lips to,
  As obedience forsooth, subjection, duty and such kickshaws,
  All of our making, but serv'd in to them;
  And if we lick a finger, then sometimes
  We are not too blame: your best cooks use it.   45

FAB. Th'art a sweet lady, sister, and a witty—

LIV. A witty! O, the bud of commendation
  Fit for a girl of sixteen! I am blown, man;
  I should be wise by this time; and, for instance,
  I have buried my two husbands in good fashion,   50
  And never mean more to marry.

GUARD.   No? Why so, lady?

LIV. Because the third shall never bury me,
  I think I am more than witty. How think you, sir?

FAB. I have paid often fees to a counsellor
  Has had a weaker brain.

LIV.   Then I must tell you,   55
  Your money was soon parted.

GUARD. [*Aside*]   Like enow.

LIV.   Brother,
  Where is my niece? Let her be sent for straight.

If you have any hope 'twill prove a wedding,
'Tis fit, i'faith, she should have one sight of him,
And stop upon't, and not be join'd in haste,   60
As if they went to stock a new-found land.

FAB. Look out her uncle and y'are sure of her:
Those two are nev'r asunder; they've been heard
In argument at midnight; moonshine nights
Are noondays with them; they walk out their sleeps;   65
Or rather, at those hours appear like those
That walk in 'em, for so they did to me.
Look you, I told you truth. They're like a chain:
Draw but one link, all follows.

Enter Hippolito and Isabella

GUARD.   O affinity,
What piece of excellent workmanship art thou!   70
'Tis work clean wrought, for there's no lust, but love in't,
And that abundantly: when in stranger things
There is no love at all but what lust brings.

FAB. On with your mask, for 'tis your part to see now
And not be seen. Go to, make use of your time;   75
See what you mean to like, nay, and I charge you,
Like what you see. Do you hear me? There's no dallying.
The gentleman's almost twenty, and 'tis time
He were getting lawful heirs, and you a-breeding on 'em.

ISAB. Good father!

FAB.   Tell not me of tongues and rumours.   80
You'll say the gentleman is somewhat simple:
The better for a husband, were you wise;
For those that marry fools live ladies' lives.
On with the mask! I'll hear no more, he's rich:
The fool's hid under bushels.

LIV.   Not so hid neither!   85
But here's a foul great piece of him, methinks.
What will he be, when he comes altogether?

Enter the Ward, with a trap-stick, and Sordido, his man

WARD. Beat him?
I beat him out o' th' field with his own cat-stick;
Yet gave him the first hand.

SORD.   Oh strange!

WARD.   I did it,   90
Then he set jacks on me.

SORD.   What! my lady's tailor?

---

72 stranger things] relationships between those who are not kin. Guardiano's
praise of the purity of the relationship between Isabella and Hippolito
proves to be dramatically ironical.

WARD. Ay, and I beat him too.

SORD.   Nay, that's no wonder;
He's us'd to beating.

WARD.   Nay, I tickl'd him,
When I came once to my tippings.

SORD.   Now you talk on 'em,
There was a poulterer's wife made a great complaint of you last   95
night to your guardianer, that you struck a bump in her child's
head, as big as an egg.

WARD. An egg may prove a chicken then in time; the poulterer's
wife will get by't. When I am in game, I am furious; came my
mother's eyes in my way, I would not lose a fair end. No, were she   100
alive, but with one tooth in her head, I should venture the striking
out of that. I think of nobody when I am in play, I am so
earnest. Coads me, my guardianer! Prithee lay up my cat and cat-
stick safe.

SORD. Where, sir? i'th'chimney-corner?

WARD.   Chimney-corner?   105

SORD. Yes, sir, your cats are always safe i'th' chimney-corner,
Unless they burn their coats.

WARD.   Marry, that I'm afraid on.

SORD. Why then, I will bestow your cat i'th' gutter,
And there's she safe I'm sure.

WARD.   If I but live
To keep a house, I'll make thee a great man,   110
If meat and drink can do't. I can stoop gallantly,
And pitch out when I list: I'm a dog at a hole.
I mar'l my guardianer does not seek a wife for me;
I protest I'll have a bout with the maids else,
Or contract myself at midnight to the larder-woman   115
In presence of a Fool, or a sack-posset.

GUARD.   Ward!

WARD. I feel myself after any exercise
Horribly prone. Let me but ride, I'm lusty,
A cock-horse straight, i'faith.

GUARD.   Why, ward, I say!

WARD. I'll forswear eating eggs in moonshine nights;   120
There's nev'r a one I eat but turns into a cock
In four and twenty hours; if my hot blood
Be not took down in time, sure 'twill crow shortly.

GUARD. Do you hear, sir? Follow me; I must new school you.

WARD. School me? I scorn that now, I am past schooling.   125
I am not so base to learn to write and read:

106–7 your cats . . . coats] possibly quibbling on 'cats' (whores) and venereal
       disease (Gill)
112   dog . . . hole] The Ward, as usual, is boasting of his sexual prowess.
120–3 eggs . . . shortly] Eggs were thought to be aphrodisiac.

I was born to better fortunes in my cradle.

                    [Exeunt Ward, Sordido and Guardiano.

FAB. How do you like him, girl? This is your husband.
  Like him, or like him not, wench, you shall have him,
  And you shall love him.   130
LIV. Oh, soft there, brother! though you be a justice,
  Your warrant cannot be serv'd out of your liberty.
  You may compel out of the power of father
  Things merely harsh to a maid's flesh and blood;
  But when you come to love, there the soil alters: 135
  Y'are in another country, where your laws
  Are no more set by than the cacklings of geese
  In Rome's great Capitol.
FAB.   Marry him she shall then:
  Let her agree upon love afterwards.   *[Exit.*
LIV. You speak now, brother, like an honest mortal   140
  That walks upon th'earth with a staff; you were
  Up i'th'clouds before, you'ld command love,
  And so do most old folks that go without it.
  [*To Hippolito*] My best and dearest brother, I could dwell here.

                     [Kisses him]

  There is not such another seat on earth,   145
  Where all good parts better express themselves.
HIP. You'll make me blush anon.
LIV. 'Tis but like saying grace before a feast, then,
  And that's most comely; thou art all a feast,
  And she that has thee a most happy guest.   150
  Prithee cheer up thy niece with special counsel.   *[Exit.*
HIP. [*Aside*] I would 'twere fit to speak to her what I would; but
  'Twas not a thing ordain'd, Heaven has forbid it,
  And 'tis most meet that I should rather perish
  Than the decree divine receive least blemish.   155
  Feed inward, you my sorrows, make no noise;
  Consume me silent, let me be stark dead
  Ere the world know I'm sick. You see my honesty;
  If you befriend me, so.
ISAB. [*Aside*]   Marry a fool!
  Can there be greater misery to a woman   160
  That means to keep her days true to her husband,
  And know no other man? So virtue wills it.
  Why, how can I obey and honour him,
  But I must needs commit idolatry?
  A fool is but the image of a man,   165

132   liberty] jurisdiction (Barber).
137   geese] The cackling of geese warned of a suprise attack by the Gauls.
158–9 You . . . so] He is addressing his sorrows, hoping he will die of grief
    without revealing its cause.

And that but ill-made neither. Oh the heart-breakings
Of miserable maids, where love's enforc'd!
The best condition is but bad enough:
When women have their choices, commonly
They do but buy their thraldoms, and bring great portions   170
To men, to keep 'em in subjection,
As if a fearful prisoner should bribe
The keeper to be good to him, yet lies in still,
And glad of a good usage, a good look
Sometimes, by'r Lady. No misery surmounts a woman's.   175
Men buy their slaves, but women buy their masters;
Yet honesty and love makes all this happy,
And next to angels' the most blest estate.
That Providence that has made ev'ry poison
Good for some use, and sets four warring elements   180
At peace in man, can make a harmony
In things that are most strange to human reason.
Oh but this marriage!—What, are you sad too, uncle?
Faith, then there's a whole household down together!
Where shall I go to seek my comfort now   185
When my best friend's distress'd? What is't afflicts you, sir?
HIP. Faith, nothing but one grief that will not leave me,
    And now 'tis welcome; ev'ry man has something
    To bring him to his end, and this will serve,
    Join'd with your father's cruelty to you,   190
    That helps it forward.
ISAB.   Oh, be cheer'd, sweet uncle!
    How long has't been upon you, I nev'r spied it?
    What a dull sight have I! How long, I pray, sir?
HIP. Since I first saw you, niece, and left Bologna.
ISAB. And could you deal so unkindly with my heart,   195
    To keep it up so long hid from my pity?
    Alas, how shall I trust your love hereafter?
    Have we pass'd through so many arguments,
    And miss'd of that still, the most needful one?
    Walk'd out whole nights together in discourses,   200
    And the main point forgot? We are too blame both;
    This is an obstinate wilful forgetfulness,
    And faulty on both parts: let's lose no time now;
    Begin, good uncle, you that feel 't. What is it?
HIP. You of all creatures, niece, must never hear on't: 205
    'Tis not a thing ordain'd for you to know.
ISAB. Not I, sir! All my joys that word cuts off.
    You made profession once you lov'd me best:

179–80   poison . . . use] cf. Friar Lawrence in *R.J.* II. 3.
180   warring elements] cf. *No Wit, No Help*, IV. ii. 168.

'Twas but profession!
HIP.   Yes, I do't too truly
   And fear I shall be chid for't. Know the worst then: 210
   I love thee dearlier than an uncle can.
ISAB. Why, so you ever said, and I believed it.
HIP. [*Aside*] So simple is the goodness of her thoughts,
   They understand not yet th' unhallow'd language
   Of a near sinner: I must yet be forc'd   215
   (Though blushes be my venture) to come nearer.
   [*Aloud*] As a man loves his wife, so love I thee.
ISAB. What's that? Methought I heard ill news come toward me,
   Which commonly we understand too soon,
   Than over-quick at hearing. I'll prevent it,   220
   Though my joys fare the harder, welcome it:
   It shall nev'r come so near mine ear again.
   Farewell all friendly solaces and discourses,
   I'll learn to live without ye, for your dangers
   Are greater than your comforts; what's become   225
   Of truth in love, if such we cannot trust.
   When blood that should be love is mix'd with lust?   [*Exit.*
HIP. The worst can be but death, and let it come;
   He that lives joyless, ev'ry day's his doom.   [*Exit.*

[Sc. 3]
Enter Leantio alone

LEANT. Methinks I'm ev'n as dull now at departure
   As men observe great gallants the next day
   After a revels: you shall see 'em look
   Much of my fashion, if you mark 'em well.
   'Tis ev'n a second hell to part from pleasure,   5
   When man has got a smack on't; as many holidays
   Coming together makes your poor heads idle
   A great while after, and are said to stick
   Fast in their fingers' ends; ev'n so does game
   In a new-married couple: for the time   10
   It spoils all thrift, and indeed lies a-bed
   To invent all the new ways for great expenses.

Enter Bianca and Mother above

   See, and she be not got on purpose now
   Into the window to look after me.
   I have no power to go now, and I should be hang'd.   15
   Farewell all business; I desire no more
   Than I see yonder; let the goods at quay
   Look to themselves; why should I toil my youth out?

It is but begging two or three year sooner,
And stay with her continually; is't a match?   20
O fie, what a religion have I leap'd into!
Get out again for shame; the man loves best
When his care's most; that shows his zeal to love.
Fondness is but the idiot to affection
That plays at hot-cockles with rich merchants' wives;   25
Good to make sport withal when the chest's full
And the long warehouse cracks. 'Tis time of day
For us to be more wise; 'tis early with us,
And if they lose the morning of their affairs,
They commonly lose the best part of the day.   30
Those that are wealthy and have got enough,
'Tis after sunset with 'em; they may rest,
Grow fat with ease, banquet, and toy and play,
When such as I enter the heat o' th' day;
And I'll do't cheerfully.

BIAN. [*Above*]   I perceive, sir   35
Y'are not gone yet: I have good hope you'll stay now.

LEANT. Farewell, I must not.

BIAN.   Come, come; pray return!
Tomorrow, adding but a little care more,
Will dispatch all as well; believe me, 'twill, sir.

LEANT. I could well wish myself where you would have me,   40
But love that's wanton must be rul'd awhile
By that that's careful, or all goes to ruin.
As fitting is a government in love
As in a kingdom; where 'tis all mere lust,
'Tis like an insurrection in the people,   45
That rais'd in self-will wars against all reason:
But love that is respective for increase
Is like a good king, that keeps all in peace.
Once more farewell.

BIAN.   But this one night, I prithee.

LEANT. Alas, I'm in for twenty if I stay,   50
And then for forty more. I have such luck to flesh,
I never bought a horse but he bore double.
If I stay any longer, I shall turn
An everlasting spendthrift; as you love
To be maintain'd well, do not call me again,   55
For then I shall not care which end goes forward.
Again farewell to thee.   [*Exit.*

BIAN.   Since it must, farewell too.

MOTH. 'Faith, daughter, y'are too blame; you take the course
To make him an ill husband, troth you do!
And that disease is catching, I can tell you;   60

24   to] compared to

Ay, and soon taken by a young man's blood,
And that with little urging. Nay fie, see now,
What cause have you to weep? Would I had no more,
That have liv'd threescore years; there were a cause,
And 'twere well thought on; trust me y'are too blame; 65
His absence cannot last five days at utmost.
Why should those tears be fetch'd forth? Cannot love
Be ev'n as well express'd in a good look
But it must see her face still in a fountain?
It shows like a country maid dressing her head 70
By a dish of water. Come, 'tis an old custom
To weep for love.

Enter two or three boys, and a citizen or two, with an apprentice

BOYS. Now they come, now they come!
2 BOY.   The Duke!
3 BOY.   The state!
CIT. How near, boy?
1 BOY.   I' th' next street, sir, hard at hand.
CIT. You sirrah, get a standing for your mistress, 75
    The best in all the city.
APPREN.   I have't for her, sir,
    'Twas a thing I provided for her overnight:
    'Tis ready at her pleasure.
CIT.   Fetch her to't then; away, sir.
BIAN. What's the meaning of this hurry?
    Can you tell, mother?
MOTH.   What a memory 80
    Have I! I see by that years come upon me.
    Why, 'tis a yearly custom and solemnity,
    Religiously observ'd by th' Duke and State
    To St. Mark's Temple, the fifteenth of April.
    See if my dull brains had not quite forgot it. 85
    'Twas happily question'd of thee; I had gone down else,
    Sat like a drone below, and never thought on't.
    I would not to be ten years younger again,
    That you had lost the sight. Now you shall see
    Our Duke, a goodly gentleman of his years. 90
BIAN. Is he old then?
MOTH.   About some fifty-five.
BIAN. That's no great age in man; he's then at best
    For wisdom, and for judgement.
MOTH.   The Lord Cardinal
    His noble brother, there's a comely gentleman,
    And greater in devotion than in blood. 95
BIAN. He's worthy to be mark'd.

70–1 dressing . . . water] i.e. using the water as a mirror

MOTH. You shall behold
  All our chief states of Florence; you came fortunately
  Against this solemn day.
BIAN. I hope so always. [*Music.*
MOTH. I hear 'em near us now. Do you stand easily?
BIAN. Exceeding well, good mother.
MOTH. Take this stool. 100
BIAN. I need it not, I thank you.
MOTH. Use your will then.

*Enter in great solemnity six knights bare-headed, then two cardinals,
and then the Lord Cardinal, then the Duke, who looks up at Bianca;
after him the States of Florence by two and two, with variety of music
and song. Then exeunt.*

MOTH. How like you, daughter?
BIAN. 'Tis a noble state!
  Methinks my soul could dwell upon the reverence
  Of such a solemn and most worthy custom.
  Did not the Duke look up? Methought he saw us. 105
MOTH. That's ev'ry one's conceit that sees a duke:
  If he looks steadfastly, he looks straight at them,
  When he perhaps, good careful gentleman,
  Never minds any; but the look he casts
  Is at his own intentions, and his object 110
  Only the public good.
BIAN. Most likely so.
MOTH. Come come, we'll end this argument below.

[*Exeunt.*

ACT II

[Sc. 1]

Enter Hippolito and Livia

LIV. A strange affection, brother, when I think on't!
  I wonder how thou cam'st by't.
HIP. Ev'n as easily
  As man comes by destruction, which oft-times
  He wears in his own bosom.
LIV. Is the world
  So populous in women, and creation 5
  So prodigal in beauty, and so various,
  Yet does love turn thy point to thine own blood?
  'Tis somewhat too unkindly. Must thy eye
  Dwell evilly on the fairness of thy kindred,

And seek not where it should? It is confin'd   10
Now in a narrower prison than was made for't.
It is allow'd a stranger, and where bounty
Is made the great man's honour, 'tis ill husbandry
To spare, and servants shall have small thanks for't.
So he Heaven's bounty seems to scorn and mock   15
That spares free means, and spends of his own stock.

HIP. Never was man's misery so soon sew'd up,
  Counting how truly.

LIV.   Nay, I love you so
  That I shall venture much to keep a change from you
So fearful as this grief will bring upon you.   20
Faith, it even kills me, when I see you faint
Under a reprehension, and I'll leave it,
Though I know nothing can be better for you.
Prithee, sweet brother, let not passion waste
The goodness of thy time, and of thy fortune: 25
Thou keep'st the treasure of that life I love
As dearly as mine own; and if you think
My former words too bitter, which were minister'd
By truth and zeal, 'tis but a hazarding
Of grace and virtue, and I can bring forth   30
As pleasant fruits as sensuality wishes
In all her teeming longings: this I can do.

HIP. Oh, nothing that can make my wishes perfect!

LIV. I would that love of yours were pawn'd to't, brother,
  And as soon lost that way as I could win.   35
Sir, I could give as shrewd a lift to chastity
As any she that wears a tongue in Florence.
Sh'ad need be a good horse-woman, and sit fast,
Whom my strong argument could not fling at last.
Prithee take courage, man; though I should counsel   40
Another to despair, yet I am pitiful
To thy afflictions, and will venture hard;
I will not name for what, 'tis not handsome;
Find you the proof, and praise me.

HIP.   Then I fear me
  I shall not praise you in haste.

LIV.   This is the comfort;   45
  You are not the first, brother, has attempted
Things more forbidden than this seems to be:
I'll minister all cordials now to you,
Because I'll cheer you up, sir.

HIP.   I am past hope.

LIV. Love, thou shalt see me do a strange cure then,   50

17 sew'd] sewn
18 counting] recounting (Barber)

As e'er was wrought on a disease so mortal,
And near akin to shame. When shall you see her?
HIP. Never in comfort more.
LIV.   Y'are so impatient too.
HIP. Will you believe, 'death, sh'has forsworn my company
And seal'd it with a blush.
LIV.   So, I perceive   55
All lies upon my hands then; well, the more glory
When the work's finish'd.

Enter Servant

                    How now, sir, the news?
SERV. Madam, your niece, the virtuous Isabella,
Is lighted now to see you.
LIV.   That's great fortune.
Sir, your stars bless you simply. [*To Servant*] Lead her in.   60
                                        [*Exit Servant.*
HIP. What's this to me?
LIV.   Your absence, gentle brother!
I must bestir my wits for you.
HIP.   Ay, to great purpose!
                                        [*Exit Hippolito.*
LIV. Beshrew you, would I lov'd you not so well.
I'll go to bed, and leave this deed undone.
I am the fondest where I once affect,   65
The carefull'st of their healths, and of their ease forsooth,
That I look still but slenderly to mine own.
I take a course to pity him so much now,
That I have none left for modesty and my self.
This 'tis to grow so liberal: y'have few sisters   70
That love their brother's ease 'bove their own honesties:
But if you question my affections,
That will be found my fault.

Enter Isabella

                    Niece, your love's welcome.
Alas, what draws that paleness to thy cheeks?
This enforc'd marriage towards?
ISAB.   It helps, good aunt,   75
Amongst some other griefs; but those I'll keep
Lock'd up in modest silence, for they're sorrows
Would shame the tongue more than they grieve the thought.
LIV. Indeed the Ward is simple.
ISAB.   Simple! that were well.
Why one might make good shift with such a husband.   80

60   bless . . . Lead (Gill); bless; you simple, lead (1657)
70-3   This . . . fault] probably addressed to the audience
70   liberal] (a) generous (b) permissive

But he's a fool entail'd; he halts downright in't.

LIV. And knowing this, I hope 'tis at your choice
To take or refuse, niece.

ISAB.   You see it is not.
I loathe him more than beauty can hate death,
Or age, her spiteful neighbour.

LIV.   Let't appear then.   85

ISAB. How can I, being born with that obedience
That must submit unto a father's will?
If he command, I must of force consent.

LIV. Alas, poor soul! Be not offended, prithee,
If I set by the name of niece awhile,   90
And bring in pity in a stranger fashion:
It lies here in this breast would cross this match.

ISAB. How? Cross it, aunt?

LIV.   Ay, and give thee more liberty
Than thou hast reason yet to apprehend.

ISAB. Sweet aunt, in goodness keep not hid from me   95
What may befriend my life.

LIV.   Yes, yes, I must.
When I return to reputation
And think upon the solemn vow I made
To your dead mother, my most loving sister,
As long as I have her memory 'twixt mine eyelids   100
Look for no pity now.

ISAB.   Kind, sweet, dear aunt—

LIV. No, 'twas a secret I have took special care of,
Deliver'd by your mother on her death bed;
That's nine years now, and I'll not part from't yet,
Though nev'r was fitter time, nor greater cause for't.   105

ISAB. As you desire the praises of a virgin—

LIV. Good sorrow! I would do thee any kindness,
Not wronging secrecy or reputation.

ISAB. Neither of which (as I have hope of fruitfulness)
Shall receive wrong from me.

LIV.   Nay, 'twould be your own wrong,   110
As much as any's, should it come to that once.

ISAB. I need no better means to work persuasion then.

LIV. Let it suffice, you may refuse this fool,
Or you may take him, as you see occasion
For your advantage; the best wits will do't.   115
Y'have liberty enough in your own will,
You cannot be enforc'd; there grows the flower,
If you could pick it out, makes whole life sweet to you.

91   stranger] As a disinterested observer, rather than as a relative
109 as . . . fruitfulness] words which suggest the naturalness of Isabella's
     desires.

That which you call your father's command's nothing;
Then your obedience must needs be as little.   120
If you can make shift here to taste your happiness,
Or pick out aught that likes you, much good do you.
You see your cheer, I'll make you no set dinner.
ISAB. And trust me, I may starve for all the good
I can find yet in this: sweet aunt, deal plainlier.   125
LIV. Say I should trust you now upon an oath
And give you in a secret that would start you,
How am I sure of you in faith and silence?
ISAB. Equal assurance may I find in mercy,
As you for that in me.
LIV.   It shall suffice.   130
Then know, however custom has made good,
For reputation's sake, the names of niece
And aunt 'twixt you and I, w'are nothing less.
ISAB. How's that?
LIV.   I told you I should start your blood.
You are no more allied to any of us,   135
Save what the courtesy of opinion casts
Upon your mother's memory and your name,
Than the mere'st stranger is, or one begot
At Naples, when the husband lies at Rome:
There's so much odds betwixt us. Since your knowledge   140
Wish'd more instruction, and I have your oath
In pledge for silence, it makes me talk the freelier.
Did never the report of that fam'd Spaniard,
Marquess of Coria, since your time was ripe
For understanding, fill your ear with wonder?   145
ISAB. Yes, what of him? I have heard his deeds of honour
Often related when we liv'd in Naples.
LIV. You heard the praises of your father then.
ISAB. My father?
LIV.   That was he. But all the business
So carefully and so discreetly carried   150
That fame receiv'd no spot by't, not a blemish;
Your mother was so wary to her end,
None knew it, but her conscience and her friend,
Till penitent confession made it mine,
And now my pity, yours. It had been long else,   155
And I hope care and love alike in you,
Made good by oath, will see it take no wrong now.
How weak his commands now, whom you call father!
How vain all his enforcements, your obedience!
And what a largeness in your will and liberty   160
To take, or to reject, or to do both!

133   nothing less] Livia means *something* less.

For fools will serve to father wise men's children.
All this y'have time to think on. O my wench!
Nothing o'erthrows our sex but indiscretion!
We might do well else of a brittle people   165
As any under the great canopy.
I pray forget not but to call me Aunt still;
Take heed of that, it may be mark'd in time else,
But keep your thoughts to yourself, from all the world,
Kindred, or dearest friend, nay, I entreat you,   170
From him that all this while you have call'd Uncle,
And though you love him dearly, as I know
His deserts claim as much ev'n from a stranger,
Yet let not him know this, I prithee do not,
As ever thou hast hope of second pity   175
If thou should'st stand in need on't, do not do't.

ISAB. Believe my oath, I will not.

LIV.   Why, well said!
    [*Aside*] Who shows more craft t'undo a maidenhead,
    I'll resign my part to her.

Enter Hippolito

            She's thine own, go.   [*Exit.*

HIP. [*Aside*] Alas! fair flattery cannot cure my sorrows.   180

ISAB. [*Aside*] Have I pass'd so much time in ignorance,
    And never had the means to know myself
    Till this blest hour? Thanks to her virtuous pity
    That brought it now to light. Would I had known it
    But one day sooner, he had then receiv'd   185
    In favours, what, poor gentleman, he took
    In bitter words; a slight and harsh reward
    For one of his deserts.

HIP. [*Aside*]   There seems to me now
    More anger and distraction in her looks.
    I'm gone; I'll not endure a second storm: 190
    The memory of the first is not past yet.

ISAB. [*Aside*] Are you return'd, you comforts of my life?
    In this man's presence, I will keep you fast now
    And sooner part eternally from the world
    Than my good joys in you. [*Aloud*] Prithee, forgive me;   195
    I did but chide in jest; the best loves use it
    Sometimes; it sets an edge upon affection.
    When we invite our best friends to a feast,
    'Tis not all sweetmeats that we set before them.
    There's somewhat sharp and salt, both to whet appetite,   200
    And make 'em taste their wine well: so methinks,
    After a friendly, sharp and savoury chiding,

166   great canopy] the sky

A kiss tastes wondrous well, and full o' th' grape. [*Kisses him.*
  How think'st thou, does't not?
HIP.   'Tis so excellent,
  I know not how to praise it, what to say to't.   205
ISAB. This marriage shall go forward.
HIP.   With the Ward?
  Are you in earnest?
ISAB.   'Twould be ill for us else.
HIP. [*Aside*] For us? How means she that?
ISAB.   Troth, I begin
  To be so well, methinks, within this hour,
  For all this match able to kill one's heart.   210
  Nothing can pull me down now; should my father
  Provide a worse fool yet (which I should think
  Were a hard thing to compass) I'ld have him either;
  The worse the better; none can come amiss now,
  If he want wit enough. So discretion love me.   215
  Desert and judgement, I have content sufficient.
  She that comes once to be a house-keeper
  Must not look every day to fare well, sir,
  Like a young waiting-gentlewoman in service,
  For she feeds commonly as her lady does;   220
  No good bit passes her, but she gets a taste on't:
  But when she comes to keep house for herself
  She's glad of some choice cates then once a week,
  Or twice at most, and glad if she can get 'em:
  So must affection learn to fare with thankfulness.   225
  Pray make your love no stranger, sir; that's all.
  [*Aside*] Though you be one yourself, and know not on't
  And I have sworn you must not.   [*Exit.*
HIP.   This is beyond me!
  Never came joys so unexpectedly
  To meet desires in man. How came she thus?   230
  What has she done to her, can any tell?
  'Tis beyond sorcery this, drugs or love-powders;
  Some art that has no name, sure; strange to me
  Of all the wonders I e'er met withal
  Throughout my ten years' travels, but I'm thankful for't.   235
  This marriage now must of necessity forward;
  It is the only veil wit can devise
  To keep our acts hid from sin-piercing eyes.   [*Exit.*

[Sc. 2]

Enter Guardiano and Livia

LIV. How, sir? A gentlewoman, so young, so fair,
  As you set forth, spied from the widow's window!

GUARD. She!
LIV.   Our Sunday-dinner woman?
GUARD. And Thursday-supper woman, the same still.
  I know not how she came by her, but I'll swear   5
  She's the prime gallant for a face in Florence;
  And no doubt other parts follow their leader.
  The Duke himself first spied her at the window;
  Then in a rapture, as if admiration
  Were poor when it were single, beckon'd me   10
  And pointed to the wonder warily,
  As one that fear'd she would draw in her splendour
  Too soon, if too much gaz'd at; I nev'r knew him
  So infinitely taken with a woman,
  Nor can I blame his appetite, or tax   15
  His raptures of slight folly: she's a creature
  Able to draw a state from serious business,
  And make it their best piece to do her service.
  What course shall we devise? H'as spoke twice now.
LIV. Twice?
GUARD.   'Tis beyond your apprehension   20
  How strangely that one look has catch'd his heart!
  'Twould prove but too much worth in wealth and favour
  To those should work his peace.
LIV.   And if I do't not,
  Or at least come as near it,—if your art
  Will take a little pains, and second me—   25
  As any wench in Florence of my standing,
  I'll quite give o'er, and shut up shop in cunning.
GUARD. 'Tis for the Duke, and if I fail your purpose,
  All means to come, by riches or advancement,
  Miss me, and skip me over.
LIV.   Let the old woman then   30
  Be sent for with all speed, then I'll begin.
GUARD. A good conclusion follow, and a sweet one
  After this stale beginning with old ware. [*Calls*] Within there!

Enter Servant

SERV. Sir, do you call?
GUARD.   Come near: list hither.
LIV. [*Aside*] I long myself to see this absolute creature   35
  That wins the heart of love and praise so much.
GUARD. Go sir, make haste.
LIV.   Say I entreat her company;
  Do you hear, sir?
SERV.   Yes, madam.   [*Exit.*
LIV.   That brings her quickly.

33 After . . . ware] after these dull preparations

GUARD. I would 'twere done; the Duke waits the good hour,
And I wait the good fortune that may spring from't.   40
I have had a lucky hand these fifteen year
At such court passage, with three dice in a dish.

Enter Fabritio

Signior Fabritio!
FAB. Oh sir, I bring an alteration in my mouth now.
GUARD. [*Aside*] An alteration! No wise speech, I hope.   45
He means not to talk wisely, does he trow?
[*Aloud*] Good! what's the change, I pray sir?
FAB.   A new change.
GUARD. Another yet! 'faith there's enough already.
FAB. My daughter loves him now.
GUARD.   What, does she, sir?
FAB. Affects him beyond thought, who but the Ward forsooth!   50
No talk but of the Ward; she would have him
To choose 'bove all the men she ever saw.
My will goes not so fast, as her consent now;
Her duty gets before my command still.
GUARD. Why then, sir, if you'll have me speak my thoughts,   55
I smell 'twill be a match.
FAB.   Ay, and a sweet young couple.
If I have any judgement.
GUARD. [*Aside*]   Faith, that's little.
[*Aloud*] Let her be sent tomorrow before noon,
And handsomely trick'd up; for 'bout that time
I mean to bring her in, and tender her to him.   60
FAB. I warrant you for handsome; I will see
Her things laid ready, every one in order
And have some part of her trick'd up tonight.
GUARD. Why, well said.
FAB.   'Twas a use her mother had,
When she was invited to an early wedding;   65
She'ld dress her head o'ernight, sponge up herself,
And give her neck three lathers.
GUARD. [*Aside*]   Ne'er a halter?
FAB. On with her chain of pearl, her ruby bracelets;
Lay ready all her tricks and jiggambobs.
GUARD. So must your daughter.
FAB.   I'll about it straight, sir.   [*Exit.*   70
LIV. How he sweats in the foolish zeal of fatherhood,
After six ounces an hour, and seems

---

4   at ... dish] 'Passage' was a game played with three dice; but the quibble
     on the word, and the obscene meaning of 'dish' imply that Guardiano has
     acted as the Duke's pander on previous occasions.
67 halter] quibbling on leather/lather
72 After] at the rate of

To toil as much as if his cares were wise ones!
GUARD. Y'have let his folly blood in the right vein, lady.
LIV. And here comes his sweet son-in-law that shall be.   75
    They're both allied in wit before the marriage;
    What will they be hereafter, when they are nearer?
    Yet they can go no further than the Fool:
    There's the world's end in both of 'em.

Enter Ward and Sordido, one with a shuttlecock, the other a battledore

GUARD.   Now, young heir!
WARD. What's the next business after shittlecock now?   80
GUARD. Tomorrow you shall see the gentlewoman
    Must be your wife.
WARD.   There's ev'n another thing too
    Must be kept up with a pair of battledores.
    My wife? What can she do?
GUARD.   Nay, that's a question
    You should ask yourself, Ward, when y'are alone together.   85
WARD. That's as I list!
    A wife's to be ask'd anywhere, I hope:
    I'll ask her in a congregation,
    If I have a mind to't, and so save a licence.
    [*Aside*] My guardiner has no more wit than an herb-woman   90
    That sells away all her sweet herbs and nosegays,
    And keeps a stinking breath for her own pottage.
SORD. Let me be at the choosing of your beloved,
    If you desire a woman of good parts.
WARD. Thou shalt, sweet Sordido.
SORD.   I have a plaguey guess.   95
    Let me alone to see what she is.
    If I but look upon her, why! I know all
    The faults to a hair that you may refuse her for.
WARD. Dost thou? I prithee let me hear 'em, Sordido.
SORD. Well, mark 'em then; I have 'em all in rhyme.   100
    The wife your guardiner ought to tender,
    Should be pretty, straight and slender;
    Her hair not short, her foot not long,
    Her hand not huge, nor too too loud her tongue;
    No pearl in eye, nor ruby in her nose,   105
    No burn or cut, but what the catalogue shows.
    She must have teeth, and that no black ones,
    And kiss most sweet when she does smack once:
    Her skin must be both white and plumpt,
    Her body straight, not hopper-rump'd,   110
    Or wriggle sideways like a crab.

79   world's end] the absolute limit
105 pearl] a white spot, caused by some diseases

She must be neither slut nor drab,
Nor go too splay-foot with her shoes
To make her smock lick up the dews.
And two things more which I forgot to tell ye: 115
She neither must have bump in back nor belly.
These are the faults that will not make her pass.
WARD. And if I spy not these, I am a rank ass.
SORD. Nay more; by right, sir, you should see her naked,
For that's the ancient order.
WARD.   See her naked?   120
That were good sport, i'faith: I'll have the books turn'd over,
And if I find her naked on record,
She shall not have a rag on. But stay, stay!
How if she should desire to see me so too?
I were in a sweet case then—such a foul skin!   125
SORD. But y'have a clean shirt, and that makes amends, sir.
WARD. I will not see her naked for that trick, though.   [*Exit.*
SORD. Then take her with all faults, with her clothes on.
And they may hide a number with a bum-roll.
'Faith, choosing of a wench in a huge farthingale   130
Is like the buying of ware under a great penthouse:
What with the deceit of one and the false light
Of th'other—mark my speeches—
He may have a diseas'd wench in's bed,
And rotten stuff in's breeches.   [*Exit.* 135
GUARD. It may take handsomely.
LIV.   I see small hindrance.
How now, so soon returned?

Enter Servant and Mother

GUARD.   She's come.
LIV.   That's well.
Widow, come, come; I have a great quarrel to you.
Faith, I must chide you, that you must be sent for!
You make yourself so strange, never come at us,   140
And yet so near a neighbour, and so unkind.
Troth, y'are too blame, you cannot be more welcome
To any house in Florence, that I'll tell you.
MOTH. My thanks must needs acknowledge so much, madam.
LIV. How can you be so strange then? I sit here   145
Sometimes whole days together without company,
When business draws this gentleman from home,
And should be happy in society
Which I so well affect as that of yours.

---

122   naked . . . record] in the record that she ought to be naked
127   *Exit*] If this is correct, Sordido's next speech could be addressed to the
      audience.

I know y'are alone too. Why should not we   150
Like two kind neighbours then supply the wants
Of one another, having tongue-discourse,
Experience in the world, and such kind helps
To laugh down time, and meet age merrily?
MOTH. Age, madam? You speak mir_h; 'tis at my door,   155
But a long journey from your ladyship yet.
LIV. My faith, I'm nine and thirty, ev'ry stroke, wench.
And 'tis a general observation
'Mongst knights, wives, or widows, we accompt
Ourselves then old, when young men's eyes leave looking at's. 160
'Tis a true rule amongst us, and ne'er fail'd yet
In any but in one, that I remember.
Indeed, she had a friend at nine and forty;
Marry, she paid well for him, and in th'end
He kept a quean or two with her own money,   165
That robb'd her of her plate, and cut her throat.
MOTH. She had her punishment in this world, madam,
And a fair warning to all other women
That they live chaste at fifty.
LIV.   Ay, or never, wench.
Come, now I have thy company I'll not part with't   170
Till after supper.
MOTH.   Yes, I must crave pardon, madam.
LIV. I swear you shall stay supper. We have no strangers, woman,
None but my sojourners and I; this gentleman
And the young heir, his ward. You know our company.
MOTH. Some other time I will make bold with you, madam.   175
GUARD. Nay, pray stay, widow.
LIV.   'Faith, she shall not go.
Do you think I'll be forsworn?
MOTH.   'Tis a great while
Till supper time. I'll take my leave then now, madam,
And come again i' th' evening, since your ladyship
Will have it so.
LIV.   I' th' evening? By my troth, wench,   180
I'll keep you while I have you; you have great business, sure,
To sit alone at home: I wonder strangely
What pleasure you take in't! Were't to me now,
I should be ever at one neighbour's house
Or other all day long. Having no charge,   185
Or none to chide you if you go or stay,
Who may live merrier, ay, or more at hearts-ease?
Come, we'll to chess or draughts; there are an hundred tricks
To drive out time till supper, never fear't, wench.
MOTH. I'll but make one step home, and return straight, madam. 190

163   friend] lover

LIV. Come, I'll not trust you; you use more excuses
  To your kind friends than ever I knew any.
  What business can you have, if you be sure
  Y'have lock'd the doors? and that being all you have,
  I know y'are careful on't. One afternoon   195
  So much to spend here! Say I should entreat you now
  To lie a night or two, or a week with me,
  Or leave your own house for a month together,
  It were a kindness that long neighbourhood
  And friendship might well hope to prevail in: 200
  Would you deny such a request? I'faith,
  Speak truth, and freely.
MOTH.   I were then uncivil, madam.
LIV. Go to, then; set your men; we'll have whole nights
  Of mirth together, ere we be much older, wench.
MOTH. [*Aside*] As good now tell her then, for she will know't: 205
  I have always found her a most friendly lady.
LIV. Why, widow, where's your mind?
MOTH.   Troth, ev'n at home, madam.
  To tell you truth, I left a gentlewoman
  Ev'n sitting all alone, which is uncomfortable,
  Especially to young bloods.
LIV.   Another excuse!   210
MOTH. No, as I hope for health, madam, that's a truth;
  Please you to send and see.
LIV.   What gentlewoman? Pish!
MOTH. Wife to my son indeed, but not known, madam,
  To any but yourself.
LIV.   Now I beshrew you!
  Could you be so unkind to her and me,   215
  To come and not bring her? Faith, 'tis not friendly.
MOTH. I fear'd to be too bold.
LIV.   Too bold? Oh, what's become
  Of the true hearty love was wont to be
  'Mongst neighbours in old time?
MOTH.   And she's a stranger, madam.
LIV. The more should be her welcome; when is courtesy   220
  In better practice than when 'tis employ'd
  In entertaining strangers? I could chide, i'faith.
  Leave her behind, poor gentlewoman, alone too!
  Make some amends, and send for her betimes. Go!
MOTH. Please you command one of your servants, madam.   225
LIV. Within there!

Enter Servant

SERV.   Madam?
LIV.   Attend the gentlewoman.

195   on't] of it

MOTH. [*Aside*] It must be carried wondrous privately
   From my son's knowledge; he'll break out in storms else.
   Hark you, sir. [*Converses with Servant, who goes out.*
LIV.   Now comes in the heat of your part.
GUARD. True; I know it, lady, and if I be out,   230
   May the Duke banish me from all employments,
   Wanton, or serious.
LIV.   So, have you sent, widow?
MOTH. Yes, madam, he's almost at home by this.
LIV. And, 'faith, let me entreat you, that henceforward
   All such unkind faults may be swept from friendship,   235
   Which does but dim the lustre; and think thus much:
   It is a wrong to me, that have ability
   To bid friends welcome, when you keep 'em from me.
   You cannot set greater dishonour near me;
   For bounty is the credit and the glory   240
   Of those that have enough. I see y'are sorry,
   And the good 'mends is made by't.
MOTH.   Here she's, madam.

Enter Bianca and Servant

BIAN. [*Aside*] I wonder, how she comes to send for me now?
                        [*Exit Servant.*
LIV. Gentlewoman, y'are most welcome; trust me, y'are,
   As courtesy can make one, or respect   245
   Due to the presence of you.
BIAN.   I give you thanks, lady.
LIV. I heard you were alone, and't had appear'd
   An ill condition in me, though I knew you not,
   Nor ever saw you,—yet humanity
   Thinks ev'ry case her own—to have kept your company   250
   Here from you, and left you all solitary:
   I rather ventur'd upon boldness then
   As the least fault, and wish'd your presence here;
   A thing most happily motion'd of that gentleman
   Whom I request you, for his care and pity,   255
   To honour and reward with your acquaintance
   A gentleman that ladies' rights stands for—
   That's his profession.
BIAN.   'Tis a noble one,
   And honours my acquaintance.
GUARD.   All my intentions
   Are servants to such mistresses.
BIAN.   'Tis your modesty,   260
   It seems, that makes your deserts speak so low, sir.
LIV. Come, widow. Look you, lady, here's our business;
   Are we not well employ'd, think you? An old quarrel
   Between us, that will never be at an end.

BIAN. No, and methinks there's men enough to part you, lady.   265
LIV. Ho! but they set us on, let us come off
  As well as we can, poor souls; men care no farther.
  I pray sit down, forsooth, if you have the patience
  To look upon two weak and tedious gamesters.
GUARD. Faith, madam, set these by till evening: 270
  You'll have enough on't then. The gentlewoman,
  Being a stranger, would take more delight
  To see your rooms and pictures.
LIV.   Marry, good sir,
  And well remember'd! I beseech you show 'em her:
  That will beguile time well. Pray heartily do, sir;   275
  I'll do as much for you. Here take these keys.
  Show her the monument too, and that's a thing
  Every one sees not—you can witness that, widow.
MOTH. And that's worth sight indeed, madam.
BIAN.   Kind lady,
  I fear I came to be a trouble to you.   280
LIV. Oh, nothing less, forsooth.
BIAN.   And to this courteous gentleman,
  That wears a kindness in his breast so noble,
  And bounteous to the welcome of a stranger.
GUARD. If you but give acceptance to my service,
  You do the greatest grace and honour to me   285
  That courtesy can merit.
BIAN.   I were too blame else,
  And out of fashion much. I pray you lead, sir.
LIV. After a game or two, w'are for you, gentlefolks.
GUARD. We wish no better seconds in society
  Than your discourses, madam, and your partner's there.   290
MOTH. I thank your praise; I listen'd to you, sir,
  Though when you spoke there came a paltry rook
  Full in my way, and chokes up all my game.
                              [Exit Guardiano with Bianca.
LIV. Alas, poor widow, I shall be too hard for thee.
MOTH. Y'are cunning at the game, I'll be sworn, madam.   295
LIV. It will be found so ere I give you over:
  She that can place her man well—
MOTH.   As you do, madam.
LIV. As I shall, wench, can never lose her game.
  Nay, nay, the black king's mine.
MOTH.   Cry you mercy, madam.
LIV. And this my queen.
MOTH.   I see't now.
LIV.   Here's a duke   300

297 she ... well] referring to the placing of the Duke of Florence as well as of
    the chess piece

Will strike a sure stroke for the game anon;
Your pawn cannot come back to relieve itself.
MOTH. I know that, madam.
LIV.   You play well the whilst.
[*Aside*] How she belies her skill!—I hold two ducats
I give you check and mate to your white king,   305
Simplicity itself, your saintish king there.
MOTH. Well, ere now, lady,
I have seen the fall of subtlety: jest on.
LIV. Ay, but simplicity receives two for one.
MOTH. What remedy but patience!

Enter Guardiano and Bianca above

BIAN.   Trust me, sir,   310
Mine eye nev'r met with fairer ornaments.
GUARD. Nay, livelier, I'm persuaded, neither Florence
Nor Venice can produce.
BIAN.   Sir, my opinion
Takes your part highly.
GUARD.   There's a better piece
Yet than all these.
BIAN.   Not possible, sir.
GUARD.   Believe it,   315
You'll say so when you see't. Turn but your eye now,
Y'are upon't presently.
[*Draws a curtain, discovers the Duke, and exit.*
BIAN.   Oh, sir!
DUKE.   He's gone, beauty!
Pish! look not after him. He's but a vapour,
That, when the sun appears, is seen no more.
BIAN. Oh, treachery to honour!
DUKE.   Prithee tremble not;   320
I feel thy breast shake, like a turtle panting
Under a loving hand that makes much on't.
Why art so fearful? As I'm friend to brightness,
There's nothing but respect and honour near thee:
You know me, you have seen me; here's a heart   325
Can witness I have seen thee.
BIAN.   The more's my danger.
DUKE. The more's thy happiness. Pish, strive not, sweet!
This strength were excellent employ'd in love now,
But here 'tis spent amiss; strive not to seek
Thy liberty, and keep me still in prison.   330
I'faith you shall not out, till I'm releas'd now;
We'll be both freed together, or stay still by't;
So is captivity pleasant.
BIAN.   O my lord!

309 simplicity ... one] i.e. obtains odds

DUKE. I am not here in vain: have but the leisure
 To think on that, and thou'lt be soon resolv'd. 335
 The lifting of thy voice is but like one
 That does exalt his enemy, who proving high,
 Lays all the plots to confound him that rais'd him.
 Take warning, I beseech thee; thou seem'st to me
 A creature so compos'd of gentleness, 340
 And delicate meekness, such as bless the faces
 Of figures that are drawn for goddesses
 And makes Art proud to look upon her work.
 I should be sorry the least force should lay
 An unkind touch upon thee.
BIAN.   Oh, my extremity! 345
 My lord, what seek you?
DUKE.   Love.
BIAN.   'Tis gone already.
 I have a husband.
DUKE.   That's a single comfort:
 Take a friend to him.
BIAN.   That's a double mischief,
 Or else there's no religion.
DUKE.   Do not tremble
 At fears of thine own making.
BIAN.   Nor, great lord, 350
 Make me not bold with death and deeds of ruin
 Because they fear not you; me they must fright;
 Then am I best in health. Should thunder speak
 And none regard it, it had lost the name,
 And were as good be still. I'm not like those 355
 That take their soundest sleeps in greatest tempests:
 Then wake I most, the weather fearfullest,
 And call for strength to virtue.
DUKE.   Sure, I think
 Thou know'st the way to please me. I affect
 A passionate pleading 'bove an easy yielding, 360
 But never pitied any: they deserve none
 That will not pity me. I can command:
 Think upon that; yet if thou truly knewest
 The infinite pleasure my affection takes
 In gentle, fair entreatings, when love's businesses 365
 Are carried courteously 'twixt heart and heart,
 You'ld make more haste to please me.
BIAN.   Why should you seek, sir,
 To take away that you can never give?
DUKE. But I give better in exchange—wealth, honour.
 She that is fortunate in a Duke's favour 370

336–9 The . . . him] If you cry out, I'll use violence.

Lights on a tree that bears all women's wishes:
If your own mother saw you pluck fruit there,
She would commend your wit, and praise the time
Of your nativity. Take hold of glory.
Do not I know y'have cast away your life   375
Upon necessities, means merely doubtful,
To keep you in indifferent health and fashion—
A thing I heard too lately, and soon pitied—
And can you be so much your beauty's enemy,
To kiss away a month or two in wedlock   380
And weep whole years in wants for ever after?
Come, play the wise wench, and provide for ever.
Let storms come when they list, they find thee shelter'd.
Should any doubt arise, let nothing trouble thee;
Put trust in our love for the managing   385
Of all to thy heart's peace. We'll walk together,
And show a thankful joy for both our fortunes.
                              [*Exeunt Duke and Bianca above.*
LIV. Did not I say my duke would fetch you over, widow?
MOTH. I think you spoke in earnest when you said it, madam.
LIV. And my black king makes all the haste he can too.   390
MOTH. Well, madam, we may meet with him in time yet.
LIV. I have given thee blind mate twice.
MOTH.   You may see, madam,
My eyes begin to fail.
LIV.   I'll swear they do, wench.

Enter Guardiano

GUARD. [*Aside*] I can but smile as often as I think on't.
How prettily the poor fool was beguil'd,   395
How unexpectedly! it's a witty age:
Never were finer snares for women's honesties
Than are devis'd in these days; no spider's web
Made of a daintier thread than are now practis'd
To catch love's flesh-fly by the silver wing.   400
Yet to prepare her stomach by degrees
To Cupid's feast, because I saw 'twas queasy,
I showed her naked pictures by the way,
A bit to stay the appetite. Well, advancement,
I venture hard to find thee! If thou com'st   405
With a greater title set upon thy crest,
I'll take that first cross patiently, and wait

385 our] my
392 blind mate] when a player does not see that he has checkmated his
     opponent; but here Livia means that the Mother does not realize she has
     been tricked.
406 greater title] i.e. pander

    Until some other comes greater than that.
    I'll endure all.
LIV. The game's ev'n at the best now; you may see, widow,   410
    How all things draw to an end.
MOTH.   Ev'n so do I, madam.
LIV. I pray take some of your neighbours along with you.
MOTH. They must be those are almost twice your years then,
    If they be chose fit matches for my time, madam.
LIV. Has not my duke bestirr'd himself?
MOTH.   Yes, faith, madam: 415
    H'as done me all the mischief in this game.
LIV. H'as show'd himself in's kind.
MOTH.   In's kind, call you it?
    I may swear that.
LIV.   Yes, 'faith, and keep your oath.
GUARD. Hark, list, there's somebody coming down: 'tis she.

               Enter Bianca

BIAN. [*Aside*] Now bless me from a blasting! I saw that now,   420
    Fearful for any woman's eye to look on.
    Infectious mists and mildews hang at's eyes!
    The weather of a doomsday dwells upon him.
    Yet since mine honour's leprous, why should I
    Preserve that fair that caus'd the leprosy?   425
    Come poison all at once! [*To Guardiano*] Thou in whose baseness
    The bane of virtue broods, I'm bound in soul
    Eternally to curse thy smooth-brow'd treachery,
    That wore the fair veil of a friendly welcome,
    And I a stranger; think upon't, 'tis worth it.   430
    Murders pil'd up upon a guilty spirit
    At his last breath will not lie heavier
    Than this betraying act upon thy conscience.
    Beware of off'ring the first fruits to sin;
    His weight is deadly who commits with strumpets   435
    After they have been abas'd and made for use;
    If they offend to th'death, as wise men know,
    How much more they then that first make 'em so?
    I give thee that to feed on; I'm made bold now,
    I thank thy treachery; sin and I'm acquainted,   440
    No couple greater; and I'm like that great one,
    Who making politic use of a base villain,
    'He likes the treason well, but hates the traitor.'
    So I hate thee, slave.
GUARD.   Well, so the Duke love me,
    I fare not much amiss then; two great feasts   445

412 I . . . you] i.e. I, too, am nearing my end.
415 duke] rook; but with reference to the Duke of Florence.

Do seldom come together in one day;
We must not look for 'em.
BIAN.   What! at it still, mother?
MOTH. You see we sit by't; are you so soon return'd?
LIV. [*Aside*] So lively, and so cheerful— a good sign that.
MOTH. You have not seen all since, sure.
BIAN.   That have I, mother;   450
The monument and all. I'm so beholding
To this kind, honest, courteous gentleman,
You'ld little think it, mother; show'd me all,
Had me from place to place, so fashionably.
The kindness of some people, how't exceeds!   455
'Faith, I have seen that I little thought to see
I'th' morning when I rose.
MOTH.   Nay, so I told you,
Before you saw't, it would prove worth your sight.
I give you great thanks for my daughter, sir,
And all your kindness towards her.
GUARD.   O good widow!   460
[*Aside*] Much good may't do her! forty weeks hence, i'faith.

                    Enter Servant

LIV. Now sir?
SERV.   May't please you, madam, to walk in?
Supper's upon the table.
LIV.   Yes, we come.
Will't please you, gentlewoman?
BIAN.   Thanks, virtuous lady.
[*Aside to Livia*] Y'are a damn'd bawd! I'll follow you forsooth;   465
Pray take my mother in—an old ass go with you!
This gentleman and I vow not to part.
LIV. Then get you both before.
BIAN.   There lies his art.
                    [*Exeunt Guardiano and Bianca.*
LIV. Widow, I'll follow you.   [*Exit Mother.*
                Is't so, 'damn'd bawd'?
Are you so bitter? 'Tis but want of use;   470
Her tender modesty is sea-sick a little,
Being not accustomed to the breaking billow
Of woman's wavering faith, blown with temptations.
'Tis but a qualm of honour, 'twill away,
A little bitter for the time, but lasts not.   475
Sin tastes at the first draught like wormwood water;
But drunk again, 'tis nectar ever after.   [*Exit.*

466   old ass] referring to her mother-in-law.

ACT III

[Sc. 1]

Enter Mother

MOTH. I would my son would either keep at home,
    Or I were in my grave.
    She was but one day abroad, but ever since
    She's grown so cutted, there's no speaking to her.
    Whether the sight of great cheer at my Lady's,   5
    And such mean fare at home, work discontent in her,
    I know not; but I'm sure she's strangely alter'd.
    I'll nev'r keep daughter-in-law i' th' house with me
    Again, if I had an hundred. When read I of any
    That agreed long together, but she and her mother   10
    Fell out in the first quarter! nay, sometime
    A grudging of a scolding the first week, by'r Lady:
    So takes the new disease methinks in my house;
    I'm weary of my part, there's nothing likes her;
    I know not how to please her here a-late;   15
    And here she comes.

Enter Bianca

BIAN.   This is the strangest house
    For all defects, as ever gentlewoman
    Made shift withal, to pass away her love in.
    Why is there not a cushion-cloth of drawn work,
    Or some fair cut-work pinn'd up in my bed-chamber?   20
    A silver and gilt casting-bottle hung by't?
    Nay, since I am content to be so kind to you,
    To spare you for a silver basin and ewer,
    Which one of my fashion looks for of duty;
    She's never offer'd under, where she sleeps.   25
MOTH. [*Aside*] She talks of things here my whole state's not worth.
BIAN. Never a green silk quilt is there i' th' house, mother,
    To cast upon my bed?
MOTH.   No, by my troth is there,
    Nor orange tawny neither.
BIAN.   Here's a house
    For a young gentlewoman to be got with child in!   30
MOTH. Yes, simple though you make it, there has been three
    Got in a year in't, since you move me to't;
    And all as sweet-fac'd children, and as lovely
    As you'll be mother of. I will not spare you!
    What! cannot children be begot, think you,   35
    Without gilt casting-bottles? Yes, and as sweet ones.
    The miller's daughter brings forth as white boys

As she that bathes herself with milk and bean-flower.
'Tis an old saying: 'One may keep good cheer
In a mean house'; so may true love affect   40
After the rate of princes, in a cottage.
BIAN. Troth, you speak wondrous well for your old house here;
'Twill shortly fall down at your feet to thank you,
Or stoop when you go to bed, like a good child,
To ask you blessing. Must I live in want   45
Because my fortune match'd me with your son?
Wives do not give away themselves to husbands
To the end to be quite cast away; they look
To be the better us'd and tender'd rather,
Highlier respected, and maintain'd the richer;   50
They're well rewarded else for the free gift
Of their whole life to a husband. I ask less now
Then what I had at home when I was a maid
And at my father's house; kept short of that
Which a wife knows she must have, nay, and will;   55
Will, mother, if she be not a fool born;
And report went of me that I could wrangle
For what I wanted when I was two hours old,
And, by that copy, this land still I hold.
You hear me, mother.   [*Exit.*
MOTH.   Ay, too plain, methinks!   60
And were I somewhat deafer when you spake,
'Twere nev'r a whit the worse for my quietness.
'Tis the most sudden'st, strangest alteration
And the most subtilest that ev'r wit at threescore
Was puzzled to find out. I know no cause for't; but   65
She's no more like the gentlewoman at first
Than I am like her that nev'r lay with man yet,
And she's a very young thing, where'er she be.
When she first lighted here, I told her then
How mean she should find all things; she was pleas'd, forsooth, 70
None better. I laid open all defects to her:
She was contented still: but the Devil's in her;
Nothing contents her now. Tonight my son
Promis'd to be at home: would he were come once,
For I'm weary of my charge, and life too.   75
She'ld be serv'd all in silver by her good will,
By night and day; she hates the name of pewterer,
More than sick men the noise, or diseas'd bones
That quake at fall o' th' hammer, seeming to have

59   copy] copyhold; i.e. she has a permanent right to it.
74   once] once for all
77   pewterer] Because she hates drinking from pewter
78   noise] sounds heard before death

A fellow-feeling with't at every blow.   80
What course shall I think on? She frets me so.   [*Retires.*

Enter Leantio

LEAN. How near am I now to a happiness
  That earth exceeds not! Not another like it;
  The treasures of the deep are not so precious,
  As are the conceal'd comforts of a man   85
  Lock'd up in woman's love. I scent the air
  Of blessings when I come but near the house.
  What a delicious breath marriage sends forth!
  The violet-bed's not sweeter. Honest wedlock
  Is like a banqueting-house built in a garden,   90
  On which the spring's chaste flowers take delight
  To cast their modest odours; when base lust
  With all her powders, paintings, and best pride,
  Is but a fair house built by a ditch side.
  When I behold a glorious, dangerous strumpet,   95
  Sparkling in beauty and destruction too,
  Both at a twinkling, I do liken straight
  Her beautifi'd body to a goodly temple
  That's built on vaults where carcasses lie rotting,
  And so by little and little I shrink back again,   100
  And quench desire with a cool meditation;
  And I'm as well, methinks. Now for a welcome
  Able to draw men's envies upon man:
  A kiss now that will hang upon my lip.
  As sweet as morning dew upon a rose,   105
  And full as long; after a five days' fast
  She'll be so greedy now, and cling about me,
  I take care how I shall be rid of her—
  And here't begins.

Enter Bianca; Mother comes forward

BIAN.   Oh, sir, y'are welcome home.
MOTH. Oh, is he come? I'm glad on't.
LEAN. [*Aside*]   Is that all?   110
  Why this? As dreadful now as sudden death
  To some rich man that flatters all his sins
  With promise of repentance, when he's old,
  And dies in the midway before he comes to't.
  [*Aloud*] Sure y'are not well, Bianca! How dost, prithee? 115
BIAN. I have been better than I am at this time.
LEAN. Alas, I thought so.
BIAN.   Nay, I have been worse too,
  Than now you see me, sir.
LEAN.   I'm glad thou mend'st yet:

94   ditch] which would stink of sewage

I feel my heart mend too. How came it to thee?
Has any thing dislik'd thee in my absence?   120
BIAN. No certain, I have had the best content
    That Florence can afford.
LEAN.   Thou makest the best on't.
    Speak, mother, what's the cause? You must needs know.
MOTH. Troth, I know none, son; let her speak herself;
    Unless it be the same gave Lucifer   125
    A tumbling-cast—that's pride.
BIAN. Methinks this house stands nothing to my mind.
    I'ld have some pleasant lodging i' th' high street, sir;
    Or if 'twere near the court, sir, that were much better.
    'Tis a sweet recreation for a gentlewoman   130
    To stand in a bay-window, and see gallants.
LEAN. Now I have another temper, a mere stranger
    To that of yours, it seems; I should delight
    To see none but yourself.
BIAN.   I praise not that.
    Too fond is as unseemly as too churlish.   135
    I would not have a husband of that proneness,
    To kiss me before company, for a world.
    Beside, 'tis tedious to see one thing still, sir,
    Be it the best that ever heart affected;
    Nay, were't yourself, whose love had power, you know,   140
    To bring me from my friends, I would not stand thus
    And gaze upon you always, troth, I could not, sir.
    As good be blind and have no use of sight,
    As look on one thing still. What's the eyes' treasure,
    But change of objects? You are learned, sir,   145
    And know I speak not ill; 'tis full as virtuous
    For woman's eye to look on several men,
    As for her heart, sir, to be fix'd on one.
LEAN. Now thou com'st home to me; a kiss for that word.
BIAN. No matter for a kiss, sir, let it pass;   150
    'Tis but a toy, we'll not so much as mind it;
    Let's talk of other business and forget it.
    What news now of the pirates, any stirring?
    Prithee, discourse a little.
MOTH.   I am glad he's here yet
    To see her tricks himself. I had lied monst'rously   155
    If I had told 'em first.
LEAN.   Speak, what's the humour, sweet,
    You make your lip so strange? This was not wont.
BIAN. Is there no kindness betwixt man and wife
    Unless they make a pigeon-house of friendship
    And be still billing? 'Tis the idlest fondness   160

122 Florence] (a) the town (b) the Duke

That ever was invented, and 'tis pity
It's grown a fashion for poor gentlewomen:
There's many a disease kiss'd in a year by't.
And a French curtsey made to't. Alas, sir,
Think of the world, how we shall live; grow serious: 165
We have been married a whole fortnight now.
LEAN. How? a whole fortnight! Why, is that so long?
BIAN. 'Tis time to leave off dalliance; 'tis a doctrine
Of your own teaching, if you be rememb'red,
And I was bound to obey it.
MOTH. [*Aside*]   Here's one fits him!—   170
This was well catch'd, i'faith, son, like a fellow
That rids another country of a plague
And brings it home with him to his own house. [*Knock within.*
Who knocks?
LEAN.   Who's there now? Withdraw you, Bianca;
Thou art a gem no stranger's eye must see,   175
How ev'r thou please now to look dull on me.   [*Exit Bianca.*

Enter Messenger

Y'are welcome, sir: to whom your business, pray?
MESS. To one I see not here now.
LEAN.   Who should that be, sir?
MESS. A young gentlewoman I was sent to.
LEAN. A young gentlewoman?
MESS.   Ay, sir, about sixteen.   180
Why look you wildly, sir?
LEAN.   At your strange error.
Y'have mistook the house, sir. There's none such here,
I assure you.
MESS.   I assure you too:
The man that sent me cannot be mistook.
LEAN. Why, who is't sent you, sir?
MESS.   The Duke.
LEAN.   The Duke?   185
MESS. Yes, he entreats her company at a banquet
At Lady Livia's house.
LEAN.   Troth shall I tell you, sir,
It is the most erroneous business
That e'er your honest pains was abus'd with.
I pray forgive me if I smile a little,   190
I cannot choose, i'faith, sir, at an error
So comical as this—I mean no harm though.
His grace has been most wondrous ill inform'd;
Pray so return it, sir. What should her name be?
MESS. That I shall tell you straight too: Bianca Capella.   195
LEAN. How, sir, Bianca? What do you call th'other?

164   French curtsey] the results of syphilis

MESS. Capella. Sir, it seems you know no such then?
LEAN. Who should this be? I never heard o'th' name.
MESS. Then 'tis a sure mistake.
LEAN.   What if you enquir'd
  In the next street, sir? I saw gallants there   200
  In the new houses that are built of late.
  Ten to one, there you find her.
MESS.   Nay, no matter;
  I will return the mistake, and seek no further.
LEAN. Use your own will and pleasure, sir; y'are welcome.
                                        [*Exit Messenger.*
  What shall I think of first? Come forth, Bianca.   205

                    Enter Bianca

  Thou art betray'd, I fear me.
BIAN.   Betray'd? how, sir?
LEAN. The Duke knows thee.
BIAN.   Knows me! How know you that, sir?
LEAN. Has got thy name.
BIAN. [*Aside*]   Ay, and my good name too;
  That's worse o' th' twain.
LEAN.   How comes this work about?
BIAN. How should the Duke know me? Can you guess, mother? 210
MOTH. Not I, with all my wits. Sure we kept house close.
LEAN. Kept close? Not all the locks in Italy
  Can keep you women so; you have been gadding
  And ventur'd out at twilight, to th' Court-green yonder,
  And met the gallant bowlers coming home—   215
  Without your masks too, both of you, I'll be hang'd else.
  Thou hast been seen, Bianca, by some stranger:
  Never excuse it.
BIAN.   I'll not seek the way, sir.
  Do you think y'have married me to mew me up,
  Not to be seen? What would you make of me?   220
LEAN. A good wife, nothing else.
BIAN.   Why, so are some
  That are seen ev'ry day, else the devil take 'em.
LEAN. No more then. I believe all virtuous in thee
  Without an argument; 'twas but thy hard chance
  To be seen somewhere; there lies all the mischief;   225
  But I have devis'd a riddance.
MOTH.   Now I can tell you, son,
  The time and place.
LEAN.   When? Where?
MOTH.   What wits have I!
  When you last took your leave, if you remember,
  You left us both at window.
LEAN.   Right, I know that.

MOTH. And not the third part of an hour after,   230
    The Duke pass'd by in a great solemnity
    To St. Mark's temple, and to my apprehension
    He look'd up twice to th' window.
LEAN.   O, there quicken'd
    The mischief of this hour!
BIAN. [*Aside*]   If you call't mischief,
    It is a thing I fear I am conceiv'd with.   235
LEAN. Look'd he up twice, and could you take no warning?
MOTH. Why, once may do as much harm, son, as a thousand.
    Do not you know one spark has fir'd an house,
    As well as a whole furnace?
LEAN.   My heart flames for't.
    Yet let's be wise and keep all smother'd closely.   240
    I have bethought a means: is the door fast?
MOTH. I lock'd it myself after him.
LEAN.   You know, mother,
    At the end of the dark parlour there's a place
    So artificially contriv'd for a conveyance,
    No search could ever find it. When my father   245
    Kept in for manslaughter, it was his sanctuary.
    There will I lock my life's best treasure up.
    Bianca!
BIAN.   Would you keep me closer yet?
    Have you the conscience? Y'are best ev'n choke me up, sir.
    You make me fearful of your health and wits,   250
    You cleave to such wild courses. What's the matter?
LEAN. Why, are you so insensible of your danger
    To ask that now? The Duke himself has sent for you
    To Lady Livia's, to a banquet forsooth.
BIAN. Now I beshrew you heartily, has he so?   255
    And you the man would never yet vouchsafe
    To tell me on't till now. You show your loyalty
    And honesty at once, and so farewell, sir.
LEAN. Bianca, whither now?
BIAN.   Why, to the Duke, sir.
    You say he sent for me.
LEAN.   But thou dost not mean   260
    To go, I hope.
BIAN.   No? I shall prove unmannerly,
    Rude and uncivil, mad, and imitate you.
    Come, mother, come; follow his humour no longer;
    We shall be all executed for treason shortly.
MOTH. Not I, i'faith; I'll first obey the Duke   265
    And taste of a good banquet—I'm of thy mind.
    I'll step but up, and fetch two handkerchiefs
    To pocket up some sweet-meats, and o'ertake thee.   [*Exit.*
BIAN. [*Aside*] Why, here's an old wench would trot into a bawd now

For some dry sucket, or a colt in marchpane.   [*Exit*. 270
LEAN. O thou the ripe time of man's misery, wedlock!
    When all his thoughts, like overladen trees,
    Crack with the fruits they bear, in cares, in jealousies.
    Oh, that's a fruit that ripens hastily
    After 'tis knit to marriage; it begins,   275
    As soon as the sun shines upon the bride,
    A little to show colour. Blessed Powers!
    Whence comes this alteration? the distractions,
    The fears and doubts it brings are numberless,
    And yet the cause I know not. What a peace   280
    Has he that never marries! If he knew
    The benefit he enjoy'd, or had the fortune
    To come and speak with me, he should know then
    The infinite wealth he had, and discern rightly
    The greatness of his treasure by my loss: 285
    Nay, what a quietness has he 'bove mine,
    That wears his youth out in a strumpet's arms,
    And never spends more care upon a woman
    Than at the time of lust; but walks away,
    And if he find her dead at his return,   290
    His pity is soon done; he breaks a sigh
    In many parts, and gives her but a piece on't!
    But all the fears, shames, jealousies, costs and troubles,
    And still renew'd cares of a marriage-bed,
    Live in the issue when the wife is dead.   295

Enter Messenger

MESS. A good perfection to your thoughts!
LEAN.   The news, sir?
MESS. Though you were pleas'd of late to pin an error on me,
    You must not shift another in your stead too:
    The Duke has sent me for you.
LEAN.   How, for me, sir?
    [*Aside*] I see then 'tis my theft; w'are both betray'd.   300
    Well I'm not the first has stol'n away a maid;
    My countrymen have us'd it. [*Aloud*] I'll along with you, sir.
                                [*Exeunt*.

[Sc. 2]
    A Banquet prepared: Enter Guardiano and Ward

GUARD. Take you especial note of such a gentlewoman;
    She's here on purpose, I have invited her,
    Her father, and her uncle to this banquet.

270 colt . . . marchpane] marzipan in shape of a colt

Mark her behaviour well, it does concern you;
And what her good parts are, as far as time   5
And place can modestly require a knowledge of,
Shall be laid open to your understanding.
You know I'm both your guardian and your uncle;
My care of you is double, ward and nephew,
And I'll express it here.
WARD.   Faith, I should know her   10
  Now by her mark among a thousand women:
  A little, pretty, deft and tidy thing, you say?
GUARD. Right.
WARD.   With a lusty sprouting sprig in her hair?
GUARD. Thou goest the right way still; take one mark more:
  Thou shalt nev'r find her hand out of her uncle's,   15
  Or else his out of hers, if she be near him.
  The love of kindred never yet stuck closer
  Than their's to one another: he that weds her
  Marries her uncle's heart too.   [*Cornets.*
WARD.   Say you so, sir?
  Then I'll be ask'd i' th' church to both of them.   20
GUARD. Fall back, here comes the Duke.
WARD.   He brings a gentlewoman:
  I should fall forward rather.

        Enter Duke, Bianca, Fabritio, Hippolito, Livia, Mother, Isabella,
                        and Attendants

DUKE.   Come, Bianca!
  Of purpose sent into the world to show
  Perfection once in women; I'll believe
  Henceforward they have ev'ry one a soul too   25
  'Gainst all the uncourteous opinions
  That man's uncivil rudeness ever held of 'em.
  Glory of Florence, light into mine arms!

                        Enter Leantio

BIAN. Yon comes a grudging man will chide you, sir.
  The storm is now in's heart, and would get nearer,   30
  And fall here if it durst; it pours down yonder.
DUKE. If that be he, the weather shall soon clear.
  List, and I'll tell thee how.   [*Whispers to her.*
LEAN. [*Aside*]   A-kissing too?
  I see 'tis plain lust now, adultery bold'ned;
  What will it prove anon, when 'tis stuff'd full   35
  Of wine and sweetmeats, being so impudent fasting?
DUKE. We have heard of your good parts, sir, which we honour
  With our embrace and love. Is not the captainship
  Of Rouans' citadel, since the late deceas'd,
  Suppli'd by any yet?
GENT.   By none, my lord.   40

DUKE. Take it, the place is yours then, [*Leantio kneels*] and as
    faithfulness
  And desert grows, our favour shall grow with't.
  Rise now the captain of our fort at Rouans.
LEAN. The service of whole life give your grace thanks.   [*Rises.*
DUKE. Come sit, Bianca.
LEAN. [*Aside*]   This is some good yet,   45
  And more than ev'r I look'd for, a fine bit
  To stay a cuckold's stomach. All preferment
  That springs from sin and lust, it shoots up quickly,
  As gardeners' crops do in the rotten'st grounds;
  So is all means rais'd from base prostitution,   50
  Ev'n like a sallet growing upon a dunghill.
  I'm like a thing that never yet was heard of,
  Half merry, and half mad; much like a fellow
  That eats his meat with a good appetite
  And wears a plague-sore that would fright a country,   55
  Or rather like the barren harden'd ass,
  That feeds on thistles till he bleeds again;
  And such is the condition of my misery.
LIV. Is that your son, widow?
MOTH.   Yes, did your ladyship
  Never know that till now?
LIV.   No, trust me, did I,   60
  [*Aside*] Nor ever truly felt the power of love,
  And pity to a man, till now I knew him.
  I have enough to buy me my desires
  And yet to spare; that's one good comfort. [*To Leantio*] Hark you!
  Pray let me speak with you, sir, before you go.   65
LEAN. With me, lady? You shall: I am at your service.
  [*Aside*] What will she say now, trow; more goodness yet?
WARD. I see her now, I'm sure; the ape's so little,
  I shall scarce feel her. I have seen almost
  As tall as she sold in the fair for tenpence.   70
  See how she simpers it, as if marmalade
  Would not melt in her mouth; she might have the kindness, i'faith,
  To send me a gilded bull from her own trencher,
  A ram, a goat, or somewhat to be nibbling.
  These women, when they come to sweet things once,   75
  They forget all their friends, they grow so greedy—
  Nay, oftentimes their husbands.
DUKE.   Here's a health now, gallants,
  To the best beauty at this day in Florence.
BIAN. Who'er she be, she shall not go unpledg'd, sir.

73–4 To . . . nibbling] sweets in these shapes. cf. III. i. 268. Barber notes that
    the Ward chooses creatures with horns.

DUKE. Nay, you're excus'd for this.
BIAN.   Who? I, my lord?   80
DUKE. Yes, by the law of Bacchus; plead your benefit;
  You are not bound to pledge your own health, lady.
BIAN. That's a good way, my lord, to keep me dry.
DUKE. Nay, then I will not offend Venus so much:
  Let Bacchus seek his 'mends in another court.   85
  Here's to thyself, Bianca.
BIAN.   Nothing comes
  More welcome to that name than your grace.
LEAN. [Aside]   So, so;
  Here stands the poor thief now that stole the treasure,
  And he's not thought on; ours is near kin now
  To a twin misery born into the world,   90
  First the hard-conscienc'd worldling, he hoards wealth up;
  Then comes the next, and he feasts all upon't;
  One's damn'd for getting, th'other for spending on't.
  O equal Justice, thou hast met my sin
  With a full weight. I'm rightly now oppress'd: 95
  All her friends' heavy hearts lie in my breast.
DUKE. Methinks there is no spirit amongst us gallants
  But what divinely sparkles from the eyes
  Of bright Bianca; we sat all in darkness,
  But for that splendour! Who was't told us lately   100
  Of a match-making rite, a marriage-tender?
GUARD. 'Twas I, my lord.
DUKE.   'Twas you indeed. Where is she?
GUARD. This is the gentlewoman.
FAB.   My lord, my daughter.
DUKE. Why, here's some stirring yet.
FAB.   She's a dear child to me.
DUKE. That must needs be; you say she is your daughter. 105
FAB. Nay, my good lord, dear to my purse I mean,
  Beside my person; I nev'r reckon'd that.
  She has the full qualities of a gentlewoman;
  I have brought her up to music, dancing, what not,
  That may commend her sex and stir her husband.   110
DUKE. And which is he now?
GUARD.   This young heir, my lord.
DUKE. What is he brought up to?
HIP. [Aside]   To cat and trap.
GUARD. My lord, he's a great ward, wealthy but simple;
  His parts consist in acres.
DUKE.   Oh, wise-acres!
GUARD. Y'have spoke him in a word, sir.
BIAN.   'Las, poor gentlewoman! 115

81 plead . . . benefit] claim exemption

She's ill bestead, unless sh'as dealt the wiselier,
And laid in more provision for her youth.
Fools will not keep in summer.

LEAN. [*Aside*]   No, nor such wives
From whores in winter.

DUKE.   Yea, the voice too, sir?

FAB. Ay, and a sweet breast too, my lord, I hope,   120
    Or I have cast away my money wisely;
    She took her prick-song earlier, my lord,
    Than any of her kindred ever did:
    A rare child, though I say't, but I'ld not have
    The baggage hear so much, 'twould make her swell straight;   125
    And maids of all things must not be puff'd up.

DUKE. Let's turn us to a better banquet then,
    For music bids the soul of man to a feast,
    And that's indeed a noble entertainment,
    Worthy Bianca's self; you shall perceive, beauty,   130
    Our Florentine damsels are not brought up idly.

BIAN. They're wiser of themselves it seems, my lord,
    And can take gifts, when goodness offers 'em.

                                  [*Music.*

LEAN. [*Aside*] True, and damnation has taught you that wisdom;
    You can take gifts too. Oh, that music mocks me!   135

LIV. [*Aside*] I am as dumb to any language now,
    But Love's, as one that never learn'd to speak.
    I am not yet so old but he may think of me;
    My own fault, I have been idle a long time;
    But I'll begin the week, and paint tomorrow.   140
    So follow my true labour day by day
    I never thriv'd so well, as when I us'd it.

ISAB. [*Sings*]
    What harder chance can fall to woman,
    Who was born to cleave to some man;
    Than to bestow her time, youth, beauty,   145
    Life's observance, honour, duty,
    On a thing for no use good,
    But to make physic work, or blood
    Force fresh in an old lady's cheek?
    She that would be   150
    Mother of fools, let her compound with me.

WARD. [*During the singing*] Here's a tune indeed: Pish! I had rather
    hear one ballad sung i' th' nose now of the lamentable drowning
    of fat sheep and oxen than all these simpering tunes played upon
    cat's-guts, and sung by little kitlings.   155

---

122   prick-song] Written vocal music, with a sexual quibble. Cf. 'swell'
      (l. 125).
148   make . . . work] i.e. sexual intercourse assists the effect of a laxative.

FAB. How like you her breast now, my lord?

BIAN.   Her breast?
   He talks as if his daughter had given suck
   Before she were married, as her betters have;
   The next he praises, sure, will be her nipples.

DUKE. Methinks now such a voice to such a husband   160
   Is like a jewel of unvalued worth
   Hung at a fool's ear.

FAB.   May it please your grace
   To give her leave to show another quality.

DUKE. Marry, as many good ones as you will, sir;
   The more the better welcome.

LEAN. [*Aside*]   But the less,   165
   The better practis'd. That soul's black indeed
   That cannot commend virtue; but who keeps it?
   The extortioner will say to a sick beggar
   'Heaven comfort thee', though he give none himself.
   This good is common.

FAB.   Will it please you now, sir,   170
   To entreat your ward to take her by the hand,
   And lead her in a dance before the Duke?

GUARD. That will I, sir; 'tis needful. Hark you, nephew.

FAB. Nay, you shall see, young heir, what y'have for your money,
   Without fraud or imposture.

WARD.   Dance with her!   175
   Not I, sweet guardiner; do not urge my heart to't:
   'Tis clean against my blood. Dance with a stranger!
   Let who's will do't, I'll not begin first with her.

HIP. [*Aside*] No fear't not, fool; sh'as took a better order.

GUARD. Who shall take her then?

WARD.   Some other gentleman.   180
   Look, there's her uncle, a fine-timber'd reveller;
   Perhaps he knows the manner of her dancing too.
   I'll have him do't before me, I have sworn, guardiner,
   Then may I learn the better.

GUARD.   Thou'lt be an ass still.

WARD. Ay, all that, uncle, shall not fool me out.   185
   Pish, I stick closer to myself than so.

GUARD. I must entreat you, sir, to take your niece
   And dance with her; my ward's a little wilful:
   He would have you shew him the way.

HIP.   Me, sir?
   He shall command it at all hours, pray tell him so.   190

GUARD. I thank you for him, he has not wit himself, sir.

HIP. [*Aside to Isabella*) Come, my life's peace, I have a strange
      office on't here:

178 who's] whoso

'Tis some man's luck to keep the joys he likes
Conceal'd for his own bosom; but my fortune
To set 'em out now for another's liking,   195
Like the mad misery of necessitous man,
That parts from his good horse with many praises,
And goes on foot himself. Need must be obey'd
In ev'ry action; it mars man and maid.

                                              [*Music.*

A dance, making honours to the Duke and curtsy to themselves,
both before and after

DUKE. Signior Fabritio, y'are a happy father: 200
   Your cares and pains are fortunate, you see;
   Your cost bears noble fruits. Hippolito, thanks.
FAB. Here's some amends for all my charges yet.
   She wins both prick and praise, where'er she comes.
DUKE. How lik'st, Bianca?
BIAN.   All things well, my lord,   205
   But this poor gentlewoman's fortune; that's the worst.
DUKE. There is no doubt, Bianca, she'll find leisure
   To make that good enough; he's rich and simple.
BIAN. She has the better hope o'th' upper hand indeed,
   Which women strive for most.
GUARD.   Do't when I bid you, sir.   210
WARD. I'll venture but a horn-pipe with her, guardiner,
   Or some such married man's dance.
GUARD.   Well, venture something, sir.
WARD. I have rhyme for what I do.
GUARD.   But little reason, I think.
WARD. Plain men dance the measures, the cinquepace the gay;
   Cuckolds dance the horn-pipe, and farmers dance the hay; 215
   Your soldiers dance the round, and maidens that grow big;
   Your drunkards the canaries; your whore and bawd, the jig.
   Here's your eight kind of dancers—he that finds the ninth,
   Let him pay the minstrels.
DUKE. Oh, here he appears once in his own person;   220
   I thought he would have married her by attorney,
   And lain with her so too.
BIAN.   Nay, my kind lord,
   There's very seldom any found so foolish
   To give away his part there.
LEAN. [*Aside*]   Bitter scoff!
   Yet I must do't. With what a cruel pride   225
   The glory of her sin strikes by my afflictions!

Music. The Ward and Isabella dance; he ridiculously imitates Hippolito

213   rhyme] See Ward's next speech.

DUKE. This thing will make shift, sirs, to make a husband,
    For aught I see in him; how think'st, Bianca?
BIAN. 'Faith, an ill-favour'd shift, my lord, methinks.
    If he would take some voyage when he's married,   230
    Dangerous, or long enough, and scarce be seen
    Once in nine year together, a wife then
    Might make indifferent shift to be content with him.
DUKE. A kiss! That wit deserves to be made much on.
    Come, our caroche!
GUARD.   Stands ready for your grace.   235
DUKE. My thanks to all your loves! Come, fair Bianca,
    We have took special care of you, and provided
    Your lodging near us now.
BIAN.   Your love is great, my lord.
DUKE. Once more our thanks to all.
OMNES.   All blest honours guard you.
        [*Exeunt all but Leantio and Livia. Cornets flourish.*
LEAN. [*Aside*] Oh, hast thou left me then, Bianca, utterly?   240
    Bianca! now I miss thee. Oh, return!
    And save the faith of woman. I nev'r felt
    The loss of thee till now; 'tis an affliction
    Of greater weight than youth was made to bear;
    As if a punishment of after-life   245
    Were fall'n upon man here. So new it is
    To flesh and blood, so strange, so insupportable
    A torment, ev'n mistook, as if a body
    Whose death were drowning must needs therefore suffer it
    In scalding oil.
LIV.   Sweet sir!
LEAN. [*Aside*]   As long as mine eye saw thee,   250
    I half enjoy'd thee.
LIV.   Sir?
LEAN. [*Aside*]   Canst thou forget
    The dear pains my love took; how it has watch'd
    Whole nights together in all weathers for thee,
    Yet stood in heart more merry than the tempests
    That sung about mine ears, like dangerous flatterers   255
    That can set all their mischief to sweet tunes;
    And then receiv'd thee from thy father's window
    Into these arms at midnight, when we embrac'd
    As if we had been statues only made for't
    To show art's life, so silent were our comforts,   260
    And kiss'd as if our lips had grown together!
LIV. [*Aside*] This makes me madder to enjoy him now.
LEAN. [*Aside*] Canst thou forget all this? And better joys
    That we met after this, which then new kisses
    Took pride to praise.
LIV. [*Aside*]   I shall grow madder yet. [*To Leantio*] Sir! 265

LEAN. [*Aside*] This cannot be but of some close bawd's working—
   [*To Livia*] Cry mercy, lady. What would you say to me?
   My sorrow makes me so unmannerly,
   So comfort bless me, I had quite forgot you.
LIV. Nothing but ev'n in pity too, that passion   270
   Would give your grief good counsel.
LEAN.   Marry, and welcome, lady,
   It never could come better.
LIV.   Then first, sir,
   To make away all your good thoughts at once of her,
   Know most assuredly, she is a strumpet.
LEAN. Ha! most assuredly? Speak not a thing   275
   So vile so certainly; leave it more doubtful.
LIV. Then I must leave all truth, and spare my knowledge,
   A sin which I too lately found and wept for.
LEAN. Found you it?
LIV.   Ay, with wet eyes.
LEAN.   Oh, perjurious friendship!
LIV. You miss'd your fortunes when you met with her, sir.   280
   Young gentlemen, that only love for beauty,
   They love not wisely; such a marriage rather
   Proves the destruction of affection;
   It brings on want, and want's the key of whoredom.
   I think y'had small means with her?
LEAN.   Oh, not any, lady!   285
LIV. Alas, poor gentleman? What meant'st thou, sir,
   Quite to undo thyself with thine own kind heart?
   Thou art too good and pitiful to woman.
   Marry, sir, thank thy stars for this blest fortune
   That rids the summer of thy youth so well   290
   From many beggars that had lain a-sunning
   In thy beams only else, till thou had'st wasted
   The whole days of thy life in heat and labour.
   What would you say now to a creature found
   As pitiful to you, and as it were   295
   Ev'n sent on purpose from the whole sex general
   To requite all that kindness you have shown to't?
LEAN. What's that, madam?
LIV.   Nay, a gentlewoman,
   And one able to reward good things, ay, and bears
   A conscience to't; couldst thou love such a one   300
   That—blow all fortunes—would never see thee want?
   Nay more, maintain thee to thine enemies' envy,
   And shalt not spend a care for't, stir a thought,
   Nor break a sleep; unless love's music wak'd thee,

267   Cry mercy, lady] Leantio does not know she is the bawd.

No storm of fortune should. Look upon me   305
And know that woman.

LEAN.   Oh my life's wealth, Bianca!

LIV. [*Aside*] Still with her name? Will nothing wear it out?
[*Aloud*] That deep sigh went but for a strumpet, sir.

LEAN. It can go for no other that loves me.

LIV. [*Aside*] He's vex'd in mind; I came too soon to him.   310
Where's my discretion now, my skill, my judgement?
I'm cunning in all arts but my own love.
'Tis as unseasonable to tempt him now
So soon, as a widow to be courted
Following her husband's corse, or to make bargain   315
By the graveside, and take a young man there.
Her strange departure stands like a hearse yet
Before his eyes; which time will take down shortly.   [*Exit.*

LEAN. Is she my wife till death, yet no more mine?
That's a hard measure; then what's marriage good for?   320
Methinks by right I should not now be living,
And then 'twere all well. What a happiness
Had I been made of, had I never seen her!
For nothing makes man's loss grievous to him
But knowledge of the worth of what he loses;   325
For what he never had, he never misses.
She's gone for ever, utterly; there is
As much redemption of a soul from hell
As a fair woman's body from his palace.
Why should my love last longer than her truth?   330
What is there good in woman to be lov'd,
When only that which makes her so has left her?
I cannot love her now, but I must like
Her sin, and my own shame too, and be guilty
Of law's breach with her, and mine own abusing—   335
All which were monstrous. Then my safest course,
For health of mind and body is to turn
My heart, and hate her, most extremely hate her.
I have no other way. Those virtuous powers,
Which were chaste witnesses of both our troths,   340
Can witness she breaks first, and I'm rewarded
With captainship o' th' fort—a place of credit,
I must confess, but poor; my factorship
Shall not exchange means with't. He that died last in 't,
He was no drunkard, yet he died a beggar   345
For all his thrift; besides, the place not fits me,
It suits my resolution, not my breeding.

Enter Livia

LIV. [*Aside*] I have tried all ways I can, and have not power
To keep from sight of him. [*Aloud*] How are you now, sir?

LEAN. I feel a better ease, madam.
LIV.   Thanks to blessedness!   350
    You will do well, I warrant you, fear it not, sir.
    Join but your own good will to't; he's not wise
    That loves his pain or sickness, or grows fond
    Of a disease whose property is to vex him,
    And spitefully drink his blood up. Out upon't, sir,   355
    Youth knows no greater loss. I pray let's walk, sir.
    You never saw the beauty of my house yet,
    Nor how abundantly fortune has bless'd me
    In worldly treasure. Trust me, I have enough, sir,
    To make my friend a rich man in my life,   360
    A great man at my death: yourself will say so.
    If you want anything, and spare to speak,
    Troth, I'll condemn you for a willful man, sir.
LEAN. Why, sure this can be but the flattery of some dream.
LIV. Now by this kiss, my love, my soul and riches,   365
    'Tis all true substance.
    Come, you shall see my wealth, take what you list.
    The gallanter you go, the more you please me.
    I will allow you too your page and footman,
    Your race horses, or any various pleasure   370
    Exercis'd youth delights in; but to me,
    Only, sir, wear your heart of constant stuff:
    Do but you love enough, I'll give enough.
LEAN. Troth then, I'll love enough, and take enough.
LIV. Then we are both pleas'd enough.   375
                                        [*Exeunt.*

[Sc. 3]

*Enter Guardiano and Isabella at one door, and the Ward and Sordido
                        at   another*

GUARD. Now nephew, here's the gentlewoman again.
WARD. Mass, here she's come again: mark her now, Sordido.
GUARD. This is the maid my love and care has chose
    Out for your wife, and so I tender her to you.
    Yourself has been eyewitness of some qualities   5
    That speak a courtly breeding, and are costly.
    I bring you both to talk together now;
    'Tis time you grew familiar in your tongues;
    Tomorrow you join hands, and one ring ties you,
    And one bed holds you—if you like the choice.   10
    Her father and her friends are i' th' next room,
    And stay to see the contract ere they part.
    Therefore dispatch, good ward, be sweet and short:

Like her, or like her not, there's but two ways;
And one your body, th'other your purse pays.   15

WARD. I warrant you, guardiner, I'll not stand all day thrumming,
But quickly shoot my bolt at your next coming.

GUARD. Well said! Good fortune to your birding then.   [*Exit*.

WARD. I never miss'd mark yet.

SORD. Troth, I think, master, if the truth were known,   20
You never shot at any but the kitchen-wench,
And that was a she-woodcock, a mere innocent,
That was oft lost, and cried at eight and twenty.

WARD. No more of that meat, Sordido! Here's eggs o' th' spit now;
We must turn gingerly, draw out the catalogue   25
Of all the faults of women.

SORD. How! all the faults! Have you so little reason to think so
much paper will lie in my breeches? Why, ten carts will not carry it,
if you set down but the bawds! All the faults? Pray let's be content
with a few of 'em; and if they were less, you would find 'em enough,   30
I warrant you. Look you, sir.

ISAB. [*Aside*] But that I have th'advantage of the fool,
As much as woman's heart can wish and joy at,
What an infernal torment 'twere to be
Thus bought and sold, and turn'd and pried into; when, alas,   35
The worst bit is too good for him? and the comfort is
H'as but a cater's place on't, and provides
All for another's table; yet how curious
The ass is, like some nice professor on't,
That buys up all the daintiest food i' th' markets,   40
And seldom licks his lips after a taste on't!

SORD. Now to her, now y'have scann'd all her parts over.

WARD. But at which end shall I begin now, Sordido?

SORD. Oh, ever at a woman's lip! While you live, sir, do you ask
that question?   45

WARD. Methinks, Sordido, sh'as but a crabbed face to begin with.

SORD. A crabbed face? that will save money.

WARD. How! save money, Sordido?

SORD. Ay, sir. For, having a crabbed face of her own, she'll eat the
less verjuice with her mutton; 'twill save verjuice at year's end, sir.   50

WARD. Nay, and your jests begin to be saucy once,
I'll make you eat your meat without mustard.

SORD. And that in some kind is a punishment.

WARD. Gentlewoman, they say 'tis your pleasure to be my wife,
and you shall know shortly whether it be mine or no to be your   55

15   th'other . . . pays] because he would be fined if he refused to marry his
      guardian's choice
22–3 And . . . twenty] an easy mark, and so half-witted that she was often lost
      and cried by the town-crier
24   eggs . . . spit] delicate task in hand
50   verjuice sauce] made of crab-apple.

husband; and thereupon thus I first enter upon you. [*Kisses her*]
Oh most delicious scent! Methinks it tasted as if a man had stepped
into a comfit-maker's shop to let a cart go by, all the while I
kiss'd her. It is reported, gentlewoman, you'll run mad for me, if
you should have me not.   60

ISAB. I should be in great danger of my wits, sir,
  [*Aside*] For being so forward, should this ass kick backward now.

WARD. Alas, poor soul! And is that hair your own?

ISAB. Mine own? Yes sure, sir; I owe nothing for't.

WARD. 'Tis a good hearing; I shall have the less to pay when I have   65
  married you. Look, does her eyes stand well?

SORD. They cannot stand better than in her head, I think. Where
  would you have them? And for her nose, 'tis of a very good last.

WARD. I have known as good as that has not lasted a year though.

SORD. That's in the using of a thing. Will not any strong bridge fall 70
  down in time, if we do nothing but beat at the bottom? A nose of
  buff would not last always, sir, especially if it came into th' camp
  once.

WARD. But Sordido, how shall we do to make her laugh, that I may
  see what teeth she has; for I'll not bate her a tooth, nor take a   75
  black one into th' bargain.

SORD. Why, do but you fall in talk with her, you cannot choose but
  one time or other make her laugh, sir.

WARD. It shall go hard but I will. Pray what qualities have you
  beside singing and dancing? Can you play at shittlecock forsooth?   80

ISAB. Ay, and at stool-ball too, sir, I have great luck at it.

WARD. Why, can you catch a ball well?

ISAB. I have catch'd two in my lap at one game.

WARD. What! Have you, woman? I must have you learn to play at
  trap too, then y'are full and whole.   85

ISAB. Anything that you please to bring me up to, I shall take pains
  to practise.

WARD. 'Twill not do, Sordido; we shall never get her mouth open'd
  wide enough.

SORD. No, sir; that's strange! then here's a trick for your learning. 90
  [*He yawns*] Look now, look now; quick, quick there. [*Isabella
  yawns*]

WARD. Pox of that scurvy mannerly trick with handkerchief!
  It hinder'd me a little, but I am satisfied.
  When a fair woman gapes, and stops her mouth so,
  It shows like a cloth-stopple in a cream-pot.   95
  I have fair hope of her teeth now, Sordido.

SORD. Why, then, y'have all well, sir; for aught I see she's right and
  straight enough now as she stands. They'll commonly lie crooked,

---

62 kick backward] refuse to marry
70 bridge] which was attacked by syphilis
83 I . . . game] i.e. to sleep with

that's no matter; wise gamesters never find fault with that, let 'em
lie still so.   100

WARD. I'ld fain mark how she goes, and then I have all; for of all
creatures I cannot abide a splay-footed woman: she's an unlucky
thing to meet in a morning; her heels keep together so, as if she
were beginning an Irish dance still, and the wriggling of her bum
playing the tune to't. But I have bethought a cleanly shift to find it.   105
Dab down as you see me and peep of one side, when her back's
toward you; I'll show you the way.

SORD. And you shall find me apt enough to peeping;
    I have been one of them has seen mad sights
    Under your scaffolds.

WARD. [To Isabella] Will it please you walk, forsooth,   110
    A turn or two by yourself? You are so pleasing to me,
    I take delight to view you on both sides.

ISAB. I shall be glad to fetch a walk to your love, sir:
    'Twill get affection a good stomach, sir—
    [Aside] Which I had need have, to fall to such coarse victuals.   115

WARD. Now go thy ways for a clean-treading wench
    As ever man in modesty peep'd under.

SORD. I see the sweetest sight to please my master.
    Never went Frenchman righter upon ropes,
    Than she on Florentine rushes.

WARD.   'Tis enough, forsooth.   120

ISAB. And how do you like me now, sir?

WARD.   Faith, so well,
    I never mean to part with thee, sweetheart,
    Under some sixteen children, and all boys.

ISAB. You'll be at simple pains, if you prove kind,
    And breed 'em all in your teeth.

WARD.   Nay, by my faith,   125
    What serves your belly for? 'twould make my cheeks
    Look like blown bagpipes.

Enter Guardiano

GUARD.   How now, ward and nephew,
    Gentlewoman and niece? Speak, is it so or not?

WARD. 'Tis so, we are both agreed, sir.

GUARD.   Into your kindred then:
    There's friends and wine and music waits to welcome you.   130

WARD. Then I'll be drunk for joy.

SORD.   And I for company.
    I cannot break my nose in a better action.

                                                          [*Exeunt.*

119   Never . . . ropes] presumably an acrobat
125   And . . . teeth] husbands of wives in labour suffered from sympathetic
      toothache.

ACT IV

[Sc. 1]

Enter Bianca, attended by two Ladies

BIAN. How goes your watches, ladies? What's a-clock now?
1 LADY. By mine full nine.
2 LADY.   By mine a quarter past.
1 LADY. I set mine by St. Mark's.
2 LADY.   St. Anthony's,
  They say, goes truer.
1 LADY.   That's but your opinion, madam,
  Because you love a gentleman o' th' name.   5
2 LADY. He's a true gentleman then.
1 LADY.   So may he be
  That comes to me tonight, for aught you know.
BIAN. I'll end this strife straight: I set mine by the sun;
  I love to set by th' best, one shall not then
  Be troubled to set often.
2 LADY.   You do wisely in't.   10
BIAN. If I should set my watch as some girls do
  By ev'ry clock i' th' town, 'twould nev'r go true;
  And too much turning of the dial's point
  Or tamp'ring with the spring might in small time
  Spoil the whole work too. Here it wants of nine now.   15
1 LADY. It does indeed, forsooth; mine's nearest truth yet.
2 LADY. Yet I have found her lying with an advocate,
  Which show'd like two false clocks together in one parish.
BIAN. So now I thank you, ladies; I desire
  Awhile to be alone.
1 LADY.   And I am nobody,   20
  Methinks unless I have one or other with me.
  'Faith, my desire and hers will nev'r be sisters.
                                            [*Exeunt Ladies.*
BIAN. How strangely woman's fortune comes about!
  This was the farthest way to come to me,
  All would have judg'd, that knew me born in Venice,   25
  And there with many jealous eyes brought up,
  That never thought they had me sure enough
  But when they were upon me, yet my hap
  To meet it here, so far off from my birth-place,
  My friends, or kindred. 'Tis not good in sadness   30
  To keep a maid so strict in her young days.
  Restraint breeds wand'ring thoughts, as many fasting days

---

8   sun] i.e. the Duke
12 By . . . town] implying promiscuity
13 dial's point] see *R.J.* II. iv. 107–8.

A great desire to see flesh stirring again.
I'll nev'r use any girl of mine so strictly:
Howev'r they're kept, their fortunes find 'em out— 35
I see't in me. If they be got in court,
I'll never forbid 'em the country, nor the court,
Though they be born i' th' country. They will come to't,
And fetch their falls a thousand mile about
Where one would little think on't. 40

Enter Leantio

LEAN. I long to see how my despiser looks,
Now she's come here to court; these are her lodgings;
She's simply now advanc'd. I took her out
Of no such window, I remember, first;
That was a great deal lower, and less carv'd. 45
BIAN. How now! What silkworm's this, i' th' name of pride?
What, is it he?
LEAN.   A bow i' th' ham to your greatness!
You must have now three legs, I take it, must you not?
BIAN. Then I must take another: I shall want else
The service I should have; you have but two there. 50
LEAN. Y'are richly plac'd.
BIAN.   Methinks y'are wond'rous brave, sir.
LEAN. A sumptuous lodging!
BIAN.   Y'have an excellent suit there.
LEAN. A chair of velvet!
BIAN.   Is your cloak lin'd through, sir?
LEAN. Y'are very stately here.
BIAN.   'Faith, something proud, sir.
LEAN. Stay, stay, let's see your cloth-of-silver slippers. 55
BIAN. Who's your shoemaker? H'as made you a neat boot.
LEAN. Will you have a pair? The Duke will lend you spurs.
BIAN. Yes, when I ride.
LEAN.   'Tis a brave life you lead.
BIAN. I could nev'r see you in such good clothes
In my time.
LEAN.   In your time?
BIAN.   Sure, I think, sir, 60
We both thrive best asunder.
LEAN.   Y'are a whore.
BIAN. Fear nothing, sir.
LEAN.   An impudent spiteful strumpet.

39 falls] See *R.J.* I. iii. 43.
48 legs] bows
50 service] (a) attendance (b) sexual satisfaction
   two there] i.e. he is impotent.
57 The . . . spurs] Riding frequently has a sexual meaning.
62 Fear . . . sir] Possibly Leantio expects a blow after his insult.

BIAN. O sir, you give me thanks for your captainship;
  I thought you had forgot all your good manners.
LEAN. And to spite thee as much, look there, there read;   65
                             [Shows her a letter.
  Vex, gnaw, thou shalt find there I am not love-starv'd.
  The world was never yet so cold or pitiless
  But there was ever still more charity found out
  Than at one proud fool's door; and 'twere hard, 'faith,
  If I could not pass that—Read to thy shame there;   70
  A cheerful and a beauteous benefactor too,
  As ev'r erected the good works of love.
BIAN. Lady Livia!
  [*Aside*] Is't possible? her worship was my pandress.
  She dote, and send and give, and all to him!   75
  Why, here's a bawd plagu'd home! [*Aloud*] Y'are simply happy, sir,
  Yet I'll not envy you.
LEAN.   No, court-saint, not thou!
  You keep some friend of a new fashion;
  There's no harm in your devil, he's a suckling,
  But he will breed teeth shortly, will he not?   80
BIAN. Take heed you play not then too long with him.
LEAN. Yes, and the great one too. I shall find time
  To play a hot religious bout with some of you,
  And perhaps drive you and your course of sins
  To their eternal kennels. I speak softly now;   85
  'Tis manners in a noble woman's lodgings,
  And I well know all my degrees of duty.
  But come I to your everlasting parting once,
  Thunder shall seem soft music to that tempest.
BIAN. 'Twas said last week there would be change of weather,   90
  When the moon hung so, and belike you heard it?
LEAN. Why here's sin made, and nev'r a conscience put to't;
  A monster with all forehead, and no eyes.
  Why do I talk to thee of sense or virtue,
  That art as dark as death? and as much madness   95
  To set light before thee, as to lead blind folks
  To see the monuments, which they may smell as soon
  As they behold; marry, ofttimes their heads,
  For want of light, may feel the hardness of 'em.
  So shall thy blind pride my revenge and anger,   100
  That canst not see it now; and it may fall
  At such an hour, when thou least seest of all.
  So to an ignorance darker than thy womb
  I leave thy perjur'd soul. A plague will come.   [*Exit.*
BIAN. Get you gone first, and then I fear no greater;   105

82–5 Yes . . . kennels] He is threatening to avenge himself on the Duke.
91 When . . . so] The horned moon, signifying cuckold.

Nor thee will I fear long; I'll have this sauciness
Soon banish'd from these lodgings, and the rooms
Perfum'd well after the corrupt air it leaves:
His breath has made me almost sick in troth.
A poor base start-up! Life! because h'as got 110
Fair clothes by foul means, comes to rail, and show 'em.

Enter the Duke

DUKE. Who's that?
BIAN.   Cry you mercy, sir.
DUKE.   Prithee, who's that?
BIAN. The former thing, my lord, to whom you gave
   The captainship: he eats his meat with grudging still.
DUKE. Still!
BIAN.   He comes vaunting here of his new love, 115
   And the new clothes she gave him—Lady Livia.
   Who but she now his mistress?
DUKE.   Lady Livia?
   Be sure of what you say.
BIAN.   He show'd me her name, sir,
   In perfum'd paper, her vows, her letter,
   With an intent to spite me. So his heart said, 120
   And his threats made it good: they were as spiteful
   As ever malice utter'd, and as dangerous,
   Should his hand follow the copy.
DUKE.   But that must not.
   Do not vex your mind; prithee to bed, go.
   All shall be well and quiet.
BIAN.   I love peace, sir. 125
DUKE. And so do all that love; take you no care for't;
   It shall be still provided to your hand.

                                        [*Exit Bianca.*

Who's near us there?

Enter Messenger

MESS.   My lord?
DUKE.   Seek out Hippolito,
   Brother to Lady Livia, with all speed.
MESS. He was the last man I saw, my lord.
DUKE.   Make haste. 130
                                        [*Exit Messenger.*
He is a blood soon stirr'd; and as he's quick
To apprehend a wrong, he's bold and sudden
In bringing forth a ruin. I know likewise
The reputation of his sister's honour's
As dear to him as life-blood to his heart; 135
Beside, I'll flatter him with a goodness to her,
Which I now thought on, but nev'r meant to practise

Because I know her base; and that wind drives him.
The ulcerous reputation feels the poise
Of lightest wrongs, as sores are vex'd with flies.   140
He comes.

Enter Hippolito

        Hippolito, welcome.
HIP.   My lov'd lord.
DUKE. How does that lusty widow, thy kind sister?
  Is she not sped yet of a second husband?
  A bed-fellow she has, I ask not that:
  I know she's sped of him.
HIP.   Of him, my lord?   145
DUKE. Yes, of a bed-fellow. Is the news so strange to you?
HIP. I hope 'tis so to all.
DUKE.   I wish it were, sir.
  But 'tis confess'd too fast; her ignorant pleasures
  Only by lust instructed, have receiv'd
  Into their services an impudent boaster,   150
  One that does raise his glory from her shame,
  And tells the midday sun what's done in darkness;
  Yet blinded with her appetite, wastes her wealth,
  Buys her disgraces at a dearer rate
  Than bounteous house-keepers purchase their honour.   155
  Nothing sads me so much as that, in love
  To thee, and to thy blood, I had pick'd out
  A worthy match for her—the great Vincentio,
  High in our favour, and in all men's thoughts.
HIP. Oh, thou destruction of all happy fortunes,   160
  Unsated blood! Know you the name, my lord,
  Of her abuser?
DUKE   One Leantio.
HIP. He's a factor.
DUKE.   He nev'r made so brave a voyage,
  By his own talk.
HIP.   The poor old widow's son!
  I humbly take my leave.
DUKE [*Aside*]   I see 'tis done.   165
  [*Aloud*] Give her good counsel, make her see her error;
  I know she'll hearken to you.
HIP.   Yes, my lord,
  I make no doubt as I shall take the course
  Which she shall never know till it be acted;
  And when she wakes to honour, then she'll thank me for't.   170

---

138   Because . . . base] she has been a bawd to him.
155   bounteous . . . honour] It was a mark of honour to indulge in generous
   hospitality.

I'll imitate the pities of old surgeons
To this lost limb, who, ere they show their art,
Cast one asleep, then cut the diseas'd part.
So out of love to her I pity most,
She shall not feel him going till he's lost: 175
Then she'll commend the cure.   [*Exit.*

DUKE.   The great cure's past;
I count this done already; his wrath's sure,
And speaks an injury deep; farewell, Leantio.
This place will never hear thee murmur more.

Enter Lord Cardinal, attended

Our noble brother, welcome!
CARD.   Set those lights down: 180
Depart till you be call'd.

[*Exit Servant.*

DUKE. [*Aside*]   There's serious business
Fix'd in his look, nay, it inclines a little
To the dark colour of a discontentment.
[*Aloud*] Brother, what is't commands your eye so powerfully?
Speak, you seem lost.
CARD.   The thing I look on seems so—   185
To my eyes lost for ever.
DUKE.   You look on me.
CARD. What a grief 'tis to a religious feeling
To think a man should have a friend so goodly,
So wise, so noble, nay, a Duke, a brother,
And all this certainly damn'd!
DUKE.   How?
CARD.   'Tis no wonder,   190
If your great sin can do't. Dare you look up
For thinking of a vengeance? Dare you sleep
For fear of never waking but to death,
And dedicate unto a strumpet's love
The strength of your affections, zeal and health?   195
Here you stand now: can you assure your pleasures
You shall once more enjoy her, but once more?
Alas! you cannot. What a misery 'tis then
To be more certain of eternal death
Than of a next embrace! Nay, shall I show you   200
How more unfortunate you stand in sin
Than the low private man? All his offences,
Like enclos'd grounds, keep but about himself,
And seldom stretch beyond his own soul's bounds;
And when a man grows miserable, 'tis some comfort   205
When he's no further charg'd than with himself—
'Tis a sweet ease to wretchedness; but, great man,

Ev'ry sin thou commit'st shows like a flame
Upon a mountain; 'tis seen far about,
And, with a big wind made of popular breath,   210
The sparkles fly through cities: here one takes,
Another catches there, and in short time
Waste all to cinders. But remember still
What burnt the valleys first came from the hill.
Ev'ry offence draws his particular pain,   215
But 'tis example proves the great man's bane.
The sins of mean men lie like scatter'd parcels
Of an unperfect bill; but, when such fall,
Then comes example, and that sums up all:
And this your reason grants. If men of good lives,   220
Who by their virtuous actions stir up others
To noble and religious imitation,
Receive the greater glory after death,
As sin must needs confess, what may they feel
In height of torments and in weight of vengeance,   225
Not only they themselves not doing well,
But sets a light up to show men to hell?
DUKE. If you have done, I have: no more, sweet brother.
CARD. I know time spent in goodness is too tedious;
This had not been a moment's space in lust now.   230
How dare you venture on eternal pain
That cannot bear a minute's reprehension?
Methinks you should endure to hear that talk'd of
Which you so strive to suffer. Oh my brother!
What were you, if you were taken now?   235
My heart weeps blood to think on't. 'Tis a work
Of infinite mercy you can never merit
That yet you are not death-struck, no not yet.
I dare not stay you long, for fear you should not
Have time enough allow'd you to repent in.   240
There's but this wall betwixt you and destruction,
When y'are at strongest, and but poor thin clay.
Think upon't, brother. Can you come so near it
For a fair strumpet's love, and fall into
A torment that knows neither end nor bottom   245
For beauty but the deepness of a skin,—
And that not of their own neither? Is she a thing
Whom sickness dare not visit, or age look on,
Or death resist? Does the worm shun her grave?
If not—as your soul knows it—why should lust   250
Bring man to lasting pain for rotten dust?
DUKE. Brother of spotless honour, let me weep
The first of my repentance in thy bosom,

241 wall] i.e. his body

And show the blest fruits of a thankful spirit;
And if I e'er keep woman more unlawfully,   255
May I want penitence at my greatest need!
And wise men know there is no barren place
Threatens more famine than a dearth in grace.
CARD. Why, here's a conversion is at this time, brother,
Sung for a hymn in heaven, and at this instant   260
The powers of darkness groan, makes all hell sorry.
First, I praise Heaven; then in my work I glory.
Who's there attends without?

Enter Servants

1 SERV.   My lord?
CARD. Take up those lights; there was a thicker darkness
When they came first. The peace of a fair soul   265
Keep with my noble brother.
DUKE.   Joys be with you, sir.
                    [*Exit Cardinal, with Servants.*
She lies alone tonight for't, and must still,
Though it be hard to conquer; but I have vow'd
Never to know her as a strumpet more,
And I must save my oath. If fury fail not,   270
Her husband dies tonight, or at the most
Lives not to see the morning spent tomorrow.
Then will I make her lawfully mine own,
Without this sin and horror. Now I'm chidden
For what I shall enjoy then unforbidden,   275
And I'll not freeze in stoves. 'Tis but a while;
Live like a hopeful bridegroom, chaste from flesh,
And pleasure then will seem new, fair and fresh.   [*Exit.*

[Sc. 2]

Enter Hippolito

HIP. The morning so far wasted, yet his baseness
So impudent? See if the very sun
Do not blush at him!
Dare he do thus much, and know me alive?
Put case one must be vicious—as I know my self   5
Monstrously guilty—there's a blind time made for't;
He might use only that, 'twere conscionable.
Art, silence, closeness, subtlety and darkness
Are fit for such a business; but there's no pity
To be bestow'd on an apparent sinner,   10
An impudent daylight lecher. The great zeal

276   freeze in stoves] be lacking in sexual ardour (?)

I bear to her advancement in this match
With Lord Vincentio, as the Duke has wrought it
To the perpetual honour of our house,
Puts fire into my blood, to purge the air   15
Of this corruption, fear it spread too far,
And poison the whole hopes of this fair fortune.
I love her good so dearly, that no brother
Shall venture farther for a sister's glory
Than I for her preferment.

                    Enter Leantio and a Page

LEAN.   Once again   20
I'll see that glitt'ring whore, shines like a serpent
Now the court sun's upon her. Page!
PAGE.   Anon, sir!
LEAN. I'll go in state too. See the coach be ready.   [*Exit Page.*
I'll hurry away presently.
HIP.   Yes, you shall hurry,
And the devil after you; take that at setting forth.   25
                                        [*Strikes him.*
Now, and you'll draw, we are upon equal terms, sir.
Thou took'st advantage of my name in honour
Upon my sister: I nev'r saw the stroke
Come, till I found my reputation bleeding;
And therefore count it I no sin to valour   30
To serve thy lust so. Now we are of even hand,
Take your best course against me. You must die.
LEAN. How close sticks envy to man's happiness!
When I was poor and little car'd for life,
I had no such means offer'd me to die,   35
No man's wrath minded me. Slave, I turn this to thee
To call thee to account, for a wound lately
Of a base stamp upon me.
HIP.   'Twas most fit
For a base metal. Come and fetch one now
More noble, then: for I will use thee fairer   40
Than thou hast done thine own soul, or our honour;
                                        [*They fight.*
And there I think 'tis for thee.   [*Wounds Leantio.*
VOICES [*within*]   Help, help, oh, part 'em.
LEAN. False wife! I feel now th'hast pray'd heartily for me.
Rise, strumpet, by my fall; thy lust may reign now;
My heart-string and the marriage-knot that tied thee   45
Breaks both together.   [*Dies.*
HIP.   There I heard the sound on't,

16 fear] for fear
43 pray'd] i.e. for his murder

And never lik'd string better.

Enter Guardiano, Livia, Isabella, Ward and Sordido

LIV.   'Tis my brother.
  Are you hurt, sir?
HIP.   Not anything.
LIV.   Blessed fortune!
  Shift for thyself. What is he thou hast killed?
HIP. Our honour's enemy.
GUARD.   Know you this man, lady?   50
LIV. Leantio! My love's joy! [*To Hippolito*] Wounds stick upon thee
  As deadly as thy sins! art thou not hurt?
  The devil take that fortune, and he dead!
  Drop plagues into thy bowels without voice,
  Secret, and fearful! Run for officers!   55
  Let him be apprehended with all speed
  For fear he scape away; lay hands on him.
  We cannot be too sure, 'tis wilful murder;
  You do Heaven's vengeance, and the law just service.
  You know him not as I do; he's a villain,   60
  As monstrous as a prodigy, and as dreadful.
HIP. Will you but entertain a noble patience,
  Till you but hear the reason, worthy sister?
LIV. The reason! That's a jest hell falls a-laughing at.
  Is there a reason found for the destruction   65
  Of our more lawful loves? and was there none
  To kill the black lust, twixt thy niece and thee,
  That has kept close so long?
GUARD.   How's that, good madam?
LIV. Too true, sir; there she stands; let her deny't.
  The deed cries shortly in the midwife's arms,   70
  Unless the parents' sins strike it still-born;
  And if you be not deaf and ignorant
  You'll hear strange notes ere long. Look upon me, wench!
  'Twas I betray'd thy honour subtly to him
  Under a false tale. It lights upon me now: 75
  His arm has paid me home upon thy breast,
  My sweet belov'd Leantio!
GUARD.   Was my judgment
  And care in choice so devilishly abus'd,
  So beyond shamefully?—All the world will grin at me.
WARD. Oh Sordido, Sordido, I'm damn'd, I'm damn'd.   80
SORD. Damn'd? Why, sir?
WARD. One of the wicked! Dost not see't? A cuckold, a plain
  reprobate cuckold.
SORD. Nay, and you be damn'd for that, be of good cheer, sir:
  y'have gallant company of all professions. I'll have a wife next   85
  Sunday too, because I'll along with you myself.

WARD. That will be some comfort yet.

LIV. You, sir, that bear your load of injuries,
   As I of sorrows, lend me your griev'd strength
   To this sad burthen, who in life wore actions,   90
   Flames were not nimbler. We will talk of things
   May have the luck to break our hearts together.

GUARD. I'll list to nothing but revenge and anger,
   Whose counsels I will follow.
           [Exeunt Livia and Guardiano with Leantio's body.

SORD. A wife, quotha! Here's a sweet plum-tree of your Guardiner's   95
   graffing!

WARD. Nay, there's a worse name belongs to this fruit yet, and you
   could hit on't, a more open one: for he that marries a whore looks
   like a fellow bound all his life time to a medlar-tree; and that's
   good stuff, 'tis no sooner ripe but it looks rotten; and so do some   100
   queans at nineteen. A pox on't! I thought there was some knavery
   a-broach, for something stirr'd in her belly the first night I lay with
   her.

SORD. What, what, sir!

WARD. This is she brought up so courtly: can sing, and dance, and   105
   tumble too, methinks; I'll never marry wife again, that has so many
   qualities.

SORD. Indeed they are seldom good, master; for likely when they are
   taught so many, they will have one trick more of their own finding
   out. Well, give me a wench but with one good quality, to lie with   110
   none but her husband, and that's bringing up enough for any
   woman breathing.

WARD. This was the fault when she was tender'd to me; you never
   look'd to this.

SORD. Alas, how would you have me see through a great farthingale,   115
   sir? I cannot peep through a millstone, or in the going to see
   what's done i' th' bottom.

WARD. Her father prais'd her breast; sh'ad the voice forsooth;
   I marvell'd she sung so small indeed, being no maid.
   Now I perceive there's a young chorister in her belly: 120
   This breeds a singing in my head, I'm sure.

SORD. 'Tis but the tune of your wife's cinquepace
   Danced in a featherbed. 'Faith, go lie down, master.
   But take heed your horns do not make holes in the pillowberes.
   I would not batter brows with him for a hogshead of angels;   125
   he would prick my skull as full of holes as a scrivener's sand-box.
                 [Exeunt Ward and Sordido.

ISAB. *[Aside]* Was ever maid so cruelly beguil'd,
   To the confusion of life, soul and honour,

---

95   plum-tree] female pudenda
99   medlar-tree] (a) female pudenda (b) whore
121 singing . . . head] thought to be the sign of cuckoldry

All of one woman's murd'ring! I'ld fain bring
Her name no nearer to my blood than woman,   130
And 'tis too much of that. Oh shame and horror!
In that small distance from yon man to me
Lies sin enough to make a whole world perish.
[*Aloud*] 'Tis time we parted, sir, and left the sight
Of one another; nothing can be worse   135
To hurt repentance; for our very eyes
Are far more poisonous to religion
Than basilisks to them. If any goodness
Rest in you, hope of comforts, fear of judgements,
My request is I nev'r may see you more;   140
And so I turn me from you everlastingly,
So is my hope to miss you; but for her
That durst so dally with a sin so dangerous
And lay a snare so spitefully for my youth,
If the least means but favour my revenge,   145
That I may practise the like cruel cunning
Upon her life, as she has on mine honour,
I'll act it without pity.
HIP. [*Aside*]   Here's a care
Of reputation and a sister's fortune,
Sweetly rewarded by her. Would a silence   150
As great as that which keeps among the graves,
Had everlastingly chain'd up her tongue!
My love to her has made mine miserable.

Enter Guardiano and Livia

GUARD. [*To Livia*] If you can but dissemble your heart's griefs now;
   Be but a woman so far,
LIV.   Peace! I'll strive, sir.   155
GUARD. As I can wear my injuries in a smile.
   Here's an occasion offer'd, that gives anger
   Both liberty and safety to perform
   Things worth the fire it holds, without the fear
   Of danger, or of law; for mischiefs, acted   160
   Under the privilege of a marriage triumph
   At the Duke's hasty nuptials, will be thought
   Things merely accidental, all by chance,
   Not got of their own natures.
LIV.   I conceive you, sir,
   Even to a longing for performance on't;   165
   And here behold some fruits. [*Kneels to Isabella and Hippolito.*
                     Forgive me both:
   What I am now, return'd to sense and judgment,

153   My . . . miserable] My love of Livia has made Isabella miserable.
163   accidental, all] Sherman conj.; accidental; all's 1657

Is not the same rage and distraction
Presented lately to you: that rude form
Is gone for ever. I am now myself,   170
That speaks all peace and friendship; and these tears
Are the true springs of hearty, penitent sorrow
For those foul wrongs which my forgetful fury
Sland'red your virtues with. This gentleman
Is well resolv'd now.
GUARD.   I was never otherways.   175
I knew, alas, 'twas but your anger spake it,
And I nev'r thought on't more.
HIP.   Pray rise, good sister.
ISAB. [Aside] Here's ev'n as sweet amends made for a wrong now
As one that gives a wound, and pays the surgeon;
All the smart's nothing, the great loss of blood,   180
Or time of hundrance. Well, I had a mother;
I can dissemble too. [To Livia] What wrongs have slipp'd
Through anger's ignorance, Aunt, my heart forgives.
GUARD. Why, this is tuneful now!
HIP.   And what I did, sister,
Was all for honour's cause, which time to come   185
Will approve to you.
LIV.   Being awak'd to goodness,
I understand so much, sir, and praise now
The fortune of your arm, and of your safety;
For by his death y'have rid me of a sin
As costly as ev'r woman doted on.   190
'T has pleased the Duke so well too, that—behold, sir—
Has sent you here your pardon, which I kiss'd
With most affectionate comfort. When 'twas brought
Then was my fit just past: it came so well methought
To glad my heart.
HIP.   I see his Grace thinks on me.   195
LIV. There's no talk now but of the preparation
For the great marriage.
HIP.   Does he marry her then?
LIV. With all speed, suddenly, as fast as cost
Can be laid on with many thousand hands.
This gentleman and I had once a purpose   200
To have honour'd the first marriage of the Duke
With an invention of his own; 'twas ready,
The pains well past, most of the charge bestow'd on't;
Then came the death of your good mother, niece,
And turned the glory of it all to black.   205
'Tis a device would fit these times so well too,
Art's treasury not better; if you'll join,
It shall be done; the cost shall all be mine.
HIP. Y'have my voice first: 'twill well approve my thankfulness

For the Duke's love and favour.

LIV.   What say you, niece?   210
ISAB. I am content to make one.
GUARD.   The plot's full then.
    Your pages, madam, will make shift for Cupids.
LIV. That will they, sir.
GUARD.   You'll play your old part still?
LIV. What is't? good troth, I have ev'n forgot it.
GUARD. Why Juno Pronuba, the marriage goddess.   215
LIV. 'Tis right indeed.
GUARD.   And you shall play the nymph
    That offers sacrifice to appease her wrath.
ISAB. Sacrifice, good sir?
LIV.   Must I be appeas'd, then?
GUARD. That's as you list yourself, as you see cause.
LIV. Methinks 'twould show the more state in her deity   220
    To be incens'd.
ISAB.   'Twould, but my sacrifice
    Shall take a course to appease you, or I'll fail in't,
    [Aside] And teach a sinful bawd to play a goddess.
GUARD. For our parts, we'll not be ambitious, sir.
    Please you walk in and see the project drawn,   225
    Then take your choice.
HIP.   I weigh not, so I have one.
                           [Exeunt all, except Livia.
LIV. How much ado have I to restrain fury
    From breaking into curses! Oh, how painful 'tis
    To keep great sorrow smother'd! Sure I think
    'Tis harder to dissemble grief than love!   230
    Leantio, here the weight of thy loss lies,
    Which nothing but destruction can suffice.   [Exit.

[Sc. 3]

*Hoboys. Enter in great state the Duke and Bianca, richly attired, with
Lords, Cardinals, Ladies, and other Attendants. They pass solemnly
over the stage. Enter the Lord Cardinal in a rage, seeming to break off
the ceremony.*

CARD. Cease, cease! Religious honours done to sin
    Disparage Virtue's reverence, and will pull
    Heaven's thunder upon Florence: holy ceremonies
    Were made for sacred uses, not for sinful.
    Are these the fruits of your repentance, brother?   5
    Better it had been you had never sorrow'd
    Than to abuse the benefit, and return

221 incens'd] (a) offered incense (b) made angry

To worse than where sin left you.
Vow'd you then never to keep strumpet more,
And are you now so swift in your desires   10
To knit your honours and your life fast to her?
Is not sin sure enough to wretched man,
But he must bind himself in chains to't? Worse!
Must marriage, that immaculate robe of honour,
That renders virtue glorious, fair and fruitful   15
To her great master, be now made the garment
Of leprosy and foulness? Is this penitence,
To sanctify hot lust? What is it otherways
Than worship done to devils? Is this the best
Amends that sin can make after her riots?   20
As if a drunkard, to appease Heaven's wrath,
Should offer up his surfeit for a sacrifice:
If that be comely, then lust's offerings are
On wedlock's sacred altar.
DUKE.   Here y'are bitter
Without cause, brother. What I vow'd, I keep,   25
As safe as you your conscience, and this needs not.
I taste more wrath in't than I do religion,
And envy more than goodness. The path now
I tread, is honest, leads to lawful love,
Which virtue in her strictness would not check.   30
I vow'd no more to keep a sensual woman;
'Tis done: I mean to make a lawful wife of her.
CARD. He that taught you that craft,
Call him not master long: he will undo you.
Grow not too cunning for your soul, good brother.   35
Is it enough to use adulterous thefts,
And then take sanctuary in marriage?
I grant, so long as an offender keeps
Close in a privileg'd temple, his life's safe;
But if he ever venture to come out,   40
And so be taken, then he surely dies for't:
So now y'are safe; but when you leave this body,
Man's only privileg'd temple upon earth,
In which the guilty soul takes sanctuary,
Then you'll perceive what wrongs chaste vows endure,   45
When lust usurps the bed that should be pure.
BIAN. Sir, I have read you over all this while
In silence, and I find great knowledge in you
And severe learning, yet 'mongst all your virtues
I see not charity written, which some call   50
The first-born of religion, and I wonder
I cannot see't in yours. Believe it, sir,
There is no virtue can be sooner miss'd,
Or later welcom'd; it begins the rest,

And sets 'em all in order. Heaven and angels 55
Take great delight in a converted sinner.
Why should you then, a servant and professor,
Differ so much from them? If every woman
That commits evil should be therefore kept
Back in desires of goodness, how should virtue 60
Be known and honour'd? From a man that's blind,
To take a burning taper, 'tis no wrong—
He never misses it: but to take light
From one that sees, that's injury and spite.
Pray, whether is religion better serv'd 65
When lives that are licentious are made honest,
Than when they still run through a sinful blood?
'Tis nothing virtue's temples to deface:
But build the ruins, there's a work of grace,
DUKE. I kiss thee for that spirit: thou hast prais'd thy wit 70
A modest way. On, on there! [*Hoboys.*
CARD.   Lust is bold,
And will have vengeance speak, ere't be controll'd.

[*Exeunt.*

ACT V

[Sc. 1.]

Enter Guardiano and Ward

GUARD. Speak, hast thou any sense of thy abuse?
Dost thou know what wrong's done thee?
WARD.   I were an ass else.
I cannot wash my face but I am feeling on't.
GUARD. Here, take this caltrop, then; convey it secretly
Into the place I show'd you. Look you, sir, 5
This is the trap-door to't.
WARD.   I know't of old, uncle,
Since the last triumph: here rose up a devil
With one eye, I remember, with a company
Of fire-works at's tail.
GUARD. Prithee leave squibbing now. Mark me and fail not, 10
But when thou hear'st me give a stamp, down with't:
The villain's caught then.
WARD.   If I miss you, hang me.
I love to catch a villain and your stamp shall go current, I warrant
you. But how shall I rise up and let him down too? All at one
hole? That will be a horrible puzzle. You know I have a part in't: 15
I play Slander.
GUARD. True, but never make you ready for't.

WARD. No? My clothes are bought and all, and a foul fiend's head
    with a long contumelious tongue i' th' chaps on't, a very fit shape
    for Slander i' th' out-parishes.   20
GUARD. It shall not come so far: thou understand'st it not.
WARD. Oh, oh?
GUARD. He shall lie deep enough ere that time,
    And stick first upon those.
WARD.   Now I conceive you, guardiner.
GUARD. Away, list to the privy stamp: that's all thy part.   25
WARD. Stamp my horns in a mortar if I miss you, and give the
    powder in white wine to sick cuckolds—a very present remedy
    for the head-ache.   [*Exit.*
GUARD. If this should any way miscarry now—
    As if the fool be nimble enough, 'tis certain—   30
    The pages that present the swift-wing'd Cupids
    Are taught to hit him with their shafts of love,
    Fitting his part, which I have cunningly poison'd.
    He cannot 'scape my fury; and those ills
    Will be laid all on fortune, not our wills—   35
    That's all the sport on't! For who will imagine
    That at the celebration of this night
    Any mischance that haps can flow from spite?   [*Exit.*

[Sc. 2]

*Flourish. Enter above Duke, Bianca, Lord Cardinal, Fabritio, and
other Cardinals, Lord and Ladies in state.*

DUKE. Now our fair duchess, your delight shall witness
    How y'are belov'd and honour'd: all the glories
    Bestow'd upon the gladness of this night
    Are done for your bright sake.
BIAN.   I am the more
    In debt, my lord, to loves and courtesies   5
    That offer up themselves so bounteously
    To do me honour'd grace, without my merit.
DUKE. A goodness set in greatness! how it sparkles
    Afar off, like pure diamonds set in gold!
    How perfect my desires were, might I witness   10
    But a fair noble peace 'twixt your two spirits!
    The reconcilement would be more sweet to me
    Than longer life to him that fears to die.
    Good sir!
CARD.   I profess peace, and am content.

20 out-parishes] parishes outside the city limits, where moralities were being
    performed in Middleton's lifetime.
14 am content] The Cardinal's change of attitude is left unexplained.

DUKE. I'll see the seal upon't, and then 'tis firm.   15
CARD. You shall have all you wish.   [*Kisses Bianca.*
DUKE.   I have all indeed now.
BIAN. [*Aside*] But I have made surer work; this shall not blind me.
  He that begins so early to reprove,
  Quickly rid him, or look for little love:
  Beware a brother's envy—he's next heir too,   20
  Cardinal, you die this night; the plot's laid surely;
  In time of sports death may steal in securely.
  Then 'tis least thought on:
  For he that's most religious, holy friend,
  Does not at all hours think upon his end;   25
  He has his times of frailty, and his thoughts
  Their transportations too, through flesh and blood,
  For all his zeal, his learning, and his light,
  As well as we poor souls that sin by night.
DUKE. What's this, Fabritio?
FAB. [*Offers scroll*]   Marry, my lord, the model   30
  Of what's presented.
DUKE.   Oh, we thank their loves.
  Sweet duchess, take your seat; list to the argument.
  [*Reads*] 'There is a nymph that haunts the woods and springs
  In love with two at once, and they with her;
  Equal it runs; but to decide these things,   35
  The cause to mighty Juno they refer,
  She being the marriage-goddess. The two lovers,
  They offer sighs; the nymph, a sacrifice;
  All to please Juno, who by signs discovers
  How the event shall be, so that strife dies.   40
  Then springs a second; for the man refus'd
  Grows discontent, and out of love abus'd
  He raises Slander up, like a black fiend,
  To disgrace th'other, which pays him i'th'end.'
BIAN. In troth, my lord, a pretty, pleasing argument,   45
  And fits th'occasion well: envy and slander
  Are things soon rais'd against two faithful lovers;
  But comfort is, they are not long unrewarded.   [*Music.*
DUKE. This music shows they're upon entrance now.
BIAN. Then enter all my wishes!   50

  *Enter Hymen in yellow, Ganymede in a blue robe powdered with stars,
  and Hebe in a white robe with golden stars, with covered cups in their
  hands. They dance a short dance, then bowing to the Duke etc., Hymen
  speaks:*

HYMEN. To thee, fair bride, Hymen offers up
  Of nuptial joys this the celestial cup;

20 next heir] Bianca is clearly motive-hunting.

Taste it, and thou shalt ever find
Love in thy bed, peace in thy mind.

BIAN. We'll taste you, sure; 'twere pity to disgrace   55
So pretty a beginning.

DUKE.   'Twas spoke nobly.

GANYMEDE. Two cups of nectar have we begged from Jove;
Hebe, give that to Innocence; I this to Love.

        [*Hebe gives a cup to the Cardinal, Ganymede one
                      to the Duke; both drink.*

Take heed of stumbling more, look to your way;
Remember still the *Via Lactea*.   60

HEBE. Well Ganymede, you have more faults, though not so known:
I spill'd one cup, but you have filch'd many a one.

HYMEN. No more, forbear for Hymen's sake;
In love we met, and so let's parting take.

                  [*Exeunt Masquers.*

DUKE. But soft! here's no such persons in the argument   65
As these three, Hymen, Hebe, Ganymede;
The actors that this model here discovers
Are only four—Juno, a nymph, two lovers.

BIAN. This is some antemasque belike, my lord,
To entertain time;—now my peace is perfect.   70
Let sports come on apace; now is their time, my lord,   [*Music.*
Hark you, you hear from 'em.

DUKE.   The nymph indeed!

*Enter two dressed like nymphs, bearing two tapers lighted; then Isabella
dressed with flowers and garlands, bearing a censer with fire in it. They
set the censer and tapers on Juno's altar with much reverence, this ditty
being sung in parts.*

Ditty

Junu, nuptial goddess,
Thou that rul'st o'er coupled bodies,
Ti'st man to woman, never to forsake her;   75
Thou only powerful marriage-maker;
Pity this amaz'd affection:
I love both and both love me;
Nor know I where to give rejection,
My heart likes so equally,   80
Till thou set'st right my peace of life,
And with thy power conclude this strife.

ISAB. Now with my thanks depart, you to the springs,
I to these wells of love.

                [*Exeunt the two nymphs.*

60   *Via Lactea*] The Milky Way. Hebe stumbled and upset 'the wyne or mylke,
      that was in the cuppe', thus colouring part of the heavens. (William Fulke,
      cited by Mulryne).

64   parting take] Gill; part 1657

Thou sacred goddess,
And queen of nuptials, daughter to great Saturn,   85
Sister and wife to Jove, imperial Juno!
Pity this passionate conflict in my breast,
This tedious war 'twixt two affections;
Crown one with victory, and my heart's at peace.

Enter Hippolito and Guardiano like Shepherds

HIP. Make me that happy man, thou mighty goddess.   90
GUARD. But I live most in hope, if truest love
Merit the greatest comfort.
ISAB.   I love both
With such an even and fair affection,
I know not which to speak for, which to wish for,
Till thou, great arbitress 'twixt lovers' hearts,   95
By thy auspicious grace, design the man:
Which pity I implore.
HIP. and GUARD.   We all implore it.
ISAB. And after sighs, contrition's truest odours,
                              [*Livia descends like Juno.*

I offer to thy powerful deity
This precious incense; may it ascend peacefully.   100
[*Aside*] And if it keep true touch, my good aunt Juno,
'Twill try your immortality ere't be long;
I fear you'll never get so nigh Heaven again,
When you're once down.
LIV.   Though you and your affections
Seem all as dark to our illustrious brightness   105
As night's inheritance, hell, we pity you,
And your requests are granted. You ask signs:
They shall be given you; we'll be gracious to you.
He of those twain which we determine for you,
Love's arrows shall wound twice; the later wound   110
Betokens love in age: for so are all
Whose love continues firmly all their lifetime,
Twice wounded at their marriage, else affection
Dies when youth ends.—This savour overcomes me!
—Now for a sign of wealth and golden days,   115
Bright-ey'd prosperity which all couples love,
Ay, and makes love—take that!
                    [*Throws flaming gold upon Isabella who falls dead.*
                              Our brother Jove
Never denies us of his burning treasure
T'express bounty.
DUKE.   She falls down upon't;

89   one] Mulryne; me 1657.
101   keep true touch] acts as it should
114   saviour] Dyce; favor 1657.

What's the conceit of that?

FAB.   As over-joy'd, belike: 120
  Too much prosperity overjoys us all,
  And she has her lapful, it seems, my lord.

DUKE. This swerves a little from the argument, though.
  Look you, my lords.

GUARD. All's fast; now comes my part to toll him hither;   125
  Then, with a stamp given, he's dispatch'd as cunningly.

      The trapdoor opens and Guardiano himself falls through it.
           Hippolito bends over Isabella's body.

HIP. Stark dead! Oh treachery!—cruelly made away! how's that?

FAB. Look, there's one of the lovers dropp'd away too.

DUKE. Why sure, this plot's drawn false; here's no such thing.

LIV. Oh, I am sick to th' death! let me down quickly.   130
  This fume is deadly. Oh, 't has poison'd me!
  My subtlety is sped; her art has quitted me.
  My own ambition pulls me down to ruin.   [*Dies.*

HIP. Nay, then I kiss thy cold lips, and applaud
  This thy revenge in death.   [*Kisses Isabella.*
              [*Cupids shoot at Hippolito.*

FAB.   Look, Juno's down too!   135
  What makes she there? her pride should keep aloft.
  She was wont to scorn the earth in other shows.
  Methinks her peacocks' feathers are much pull'd.

HIP. Oh, death runs through my blood in a wild flame too!
  Plague of those Cupids! some lay hold on 'em.   140
  Let 'em not 'scape, they have spoil'd me; the shaft's deadly.

DUKE. I have lost myself in this quite.

HIP. My great lords, we are all confounded.

DUKE.   How!

HIP. Dead; and I worse.

FAB.   Dead? my girl dead? I hope
  My sister Juno has not serv'd me so.   145

HIP. Lust and forgetfulness has been amongst us,
  And we are brought to nothing. Some blest charity
  Lend me the speeding pity of his sword
  To quench this fire in blood! Leantio's death
  Has brought all this upon us—now I taste it—   150
  And made us lay plots to confound each other;
  The event so proves it; and man's understanding
  Is riper at his fall than all his lifetime.
  She, in a madness for her lover's death,
  Reveal'd a fearful lust in our near bloods,   155
  For which I am punish'd dreadfully and unlook'd for;

126 S.D.] Presumably the Ward hears a noise and thinks Guardiano has
    stamped, before Hippolito has been lured to the trap-door.

Prov'd her own ruin too: vengeance met vengeance
Like a set match, as if the plagues of sin
Had been agreed to meet here all together.
But how her fawning partner fell, I reach not,   160
Unless caught by some springe of his own setting—
For, on my pain, he never dream'd of dying;
The plot was all his own, and he had cunning
Enough to save himself; but 'tis the property
Of guilty deeds to draw your wise men downward;   165
Therefore the wonder ceases.—Oh this torment!
SUKE. Our guard below there!

Enter a Lord with a Guard

LORD.   My lord?
HIP.   Run and meet death then,
And cut off time and pain.   [*Runs on sword.*
LORD.   Behold, my lord,
H'as run his breast upon a weapon's point.
DUKE. Upon the first night of our nuptial honours   170
Destruction plays her triumph, and great mischiefs
Mask in expected pleasures! 'tis prodigious!
They're things most fearfully ominous: I like 'em not.
Remove these ruin'd bodies from our eyes.
                            [*The bodies are taken off.*
BIAN. [*Aside*] Not yet? no change? when falls he to the earth?   175
LORD. Please but your Excellence to peruse that paper,
Which is a brief confession from the heart
Of him that fell first, ere his soul departed;
And there the darkness of these deeds speaks plainly:
'Tis the full scope, the manner and intent.   180
His ward, that ignorantly let him down,
Fear put to present flight at the voice of him.
BIAN. [*Aside*] Nor yet?
DUKE.   Read, read; for I am lost in sight and strength.
CARD. My noble brother!
BIAN.   Oh the curse of wretchedness!
My deadly hand is fall'n upon my lord.   185
Destruction take me to thee, give me way—
The pains and plagues of a lost soul upon him
That hinders me a moment!
DUKE. My heart swells bigger yet; help here, break't ope!
My breast flies open next.
BIAN.   Oh, with the poison   190
That was prepar'd for thee, thee, Cardinal!
'Twas meant for thee!
CARD.   Poor prince!
BIAN.   Accursed error!
Give me thy last breath, thou infected bosom,

And wrap two spirits in one poison'd vapour.
Thus, thus, reward thy murderer, and turn death   195
Into a parting kiss! [*Duke dies*] My soul stands ready at my lips,
Ev'n vex'd to stay one minute after thee.
CARD. The greatest sorrow and astonishment
  That ever struck the general peace of Florence
  Dwells in this hour.
BIAN.   So my desires are satisfied,   200
  I feel death's power within me!
  Thou hast prevail'd in something, cursed poison,
  Though thy chief force was spent in my lord's bosom.
  But my deformity in spirit's more foul:
  A blemish'd face best fits a leprous soul.   205
  What make I here? these are all strangers to me,
  Not known but by their malice, now th'art gone,
  Nor do I seek their pities.
CARD.   Oh, restrain
  Her ignorant, wilful hand!
               [*Bianca drinks from the poisoned cup.*
BIAN.   Now do; 'tis done.
  Leantio, now I feel the breach of marriage   210
  At my heart-breaking! Oh the deadly snares
  That women set for women—without pity
  Either to soul or honour! Learn by me
  To know your foes. In this belief I die:
  Like our own sex, we have no enemy,   215
  No enemy!
LORD.   See, my lord,
  What shift sh'as made to be her own destruction.
BIAN. Pride, greatness, honours, beauty, youth, ambition—
  You must all down together, there's no help for't.
  Yet this my gladness is, that I remove,   220
  Tasting the same death in a cup of love.   [*Dies.*
CARD. Sin, what thou art, these ruins show too piteously!
  Two kings on one throne cannot sit together,
  But one must needs down, for his title's wrong:
  So where lust reigns, that prince cannot reign long.   225
                          [*Exeunt.*

205   A ... soul] Her face is burnt by the poison. Cf. II. ii. 425.

THE
CHANGELING:

As it was Acted (with great Applause)
at the Privat house in D r u r y ʃ L a n e,
and *Salisbury Court*.

Written by {
THOMAS MIDLETON,
and
WILLIAM ROWLEY.
} Gent᾿..

Never Printed before.

L O N D O N,

Printed for H u m p h r e y M o s e l e y, and are to
be sold at his shop at the sign of the *Princes-Arms*
in St *Pauls* Church-yard, 1 6 5 3.

NOTE

The Changeling was written in 1622 and performed in the same year by the Lady Elizabeth's Servants at the Phoenix theatre. It was published in 1653. The main source of the plot is to be found in John Reynolds's *The Triumph of Gods Revenge against the Crying and Execrable Sinne of Wilful and Premeditated Murder* (1621). Some details are taken from Leonard Digges's *Gerardo the Unfortunate Spaniard* (1622), translated from the Spanish. The standard edition is by N. W. Bawcutt (1958), but I have also used those of George Walton Williams (1967), Patricia Thomson (1964) and Richard C. Harrier (1963). A facsimile of the 1653 edition has just been issued by the Scolar Press (1973).

DRAMATIS PERSONAE

VERMANDERO
TOMAZO DE PIRACQUO, a noble lord
ALONZO DE PIRACQUO, his brother, suitor to Beatrice
ALSEMERO, a nobleman
JASPERINO, his friend
ALIBIUS, a jealous doctor
LOLLIO, his servant
PEDRO, friend to Antonio
ANTONIO, the changeling (a counterfeit fool)
FRANCISCUS, a counterfeit madman
DEFLORES, servant to Vermandero
   Madmen, Fools, Servants

BEATRICE JOANNA, Vermandero's daughter
DIAPHANTA, her waiting-woman
ISABELLA, wife to Alibius

The Scene: Allegant

Deflores] Most editors emend to De Flores

151

THE CHANGELING

ACT I

[Sc. 1]

Enter Alsemero

ALS. 'Twas in the temple where I first beheld her,
  And now again the same. What omen yet
  Follows of that? None but imaginary.
  Why should my hopes or fate be timorous?
  The place is holy, so is my intent: 5
  I love her beauties to the holy purpose,
  And that, methinks, admits comparison
  With man's first creation, the place blest,
  And is his right home back—if he achieve it.
  The Church hath first begun our interview,   10
  And that's the place must join us into one,
  So there's beginning and perfection too.

Enter Jasperino

JASP. O sir, are you here? Come, the wind's fair with you.
  Y'are like to have a swift and pleasant passage.
ALS. Sure, y'are deceived, friend; 'tis contrary   15
  In my best judgement.
JASP.   What, for Malta?
  If you could buy a gale amongst the witches,
  They could not serve you such a lucky pennyworth
  As comes a' God's name.
ALS.   Even now I observ'd
  The temple's vane to turn full in my face;   20
  I know 'tis against me.
JASP.   Against you?
  Then you know not where you are.
ALS.   Not well indeed.
JASP. Are you not well, sir?
ALS.   Yes, Jasperino;
  Unless there be some hidden malady
  Within me, that I understand not.
JASP.   And that   25
  I begin to doubt, sir; I never knew
  Your inclinations to travels at a pause
  With any cause to hinder it till now.
  Ashore you were wont to call your servants up
  And help to trap your horses for the speed.   30

At sea I have seen you weigh the anchor with 'em,
Hoist sails for fear to lose the foremost breath,
Be in continual prayers for fair winds—
And have you chang'd your orisons?

ALS.   No, friend,
I keep the same church, same devotion.   35

JASP. Lover I'm sure y'are none; the stoic was
Found in you long ago; your mother nor
Best friends, who have set snares of beauty, ay,
And choice ones too, could never trap you that way.
What might be the cause?

ALS.   Lord, how violent   40
Thou art; I was but meditating of
Somewhat I heard within the temple.

JASP. Is this violence? 'Tis but idleness
Compar'd with your haste yesterday.

ALS. I'm all this while a-going, man.   45

Enter Servants

JASP. Backwards, I think, sir. Look, your servants!

1 SERV. The seamen call. Shall we board your trunks?

ALS. No, not today.

JASP   'Tis the critical day, it seems;
And the sign in Aquarius.

2 SERV.   We must not to sea
Today: this smoke will bring forth fire.   50

ALS. Keep all on shore! I do not know the end—
Which needs I must do—of an affair in hand,
Ere I can go to sea.

1 SERV.   Well, your pleasure!

2 SERV. Let him e'en take his leisure too, we are safer on land.

Exeunt Servants. Enter Beatrice, Diaphanta, and Servants

ASP. [*Aside*] How now! The laws of the Medes are changed sure.   55
Salute a woman! He kisses too: wonderful! Where learnt he
this? And does it perfectly too! In my conscience he ne'er re-
hears'd it before. Nay, go on! This will be stranger and better
news at Valencia than if he had ransom'd half Greece from the
Turk.   60

BEAT. You are a scholar, sir.

ALS.   A weak one, lady.

BEAT. Which of the sciences is this love you speak of?

ALS. From your tongue I take it to be music.

BEAT. You are skillful in't, can sing at first sight.

ALS. And I have show'd you all my skill at once.   65

49 Aquarius] The sign of the zodiac propitious for sea voyages.
50 this . . . fire] There's no smoke without fire, i.e. there's a good reason for
    not sailing.

I want more words to express me further,
And must be forc'd to repetition:
I love you dearly.
BEAT.   Be better advis'd, sir.
  Our eyes are sentinels unto our judgements,
  And should give certain judgement what they see;   70
  But they are rash sometimes, and tell us wonders
  Of common things, which when our judgements find,
  They can then check the eyes, and call them blind.
ALS. But I am further, lady; yesterday
  Was mine eyes' employment, and hither now   75
  They brought my judgement, where are both agreed.
  Both houses then consenting, 'tis agreed,
  Only there wants the confirmation.
  By the hand royal: that's your part, lady.
BEAT. Oh, there's one above me, sir! [Aside] For five days past   80
  To be recall'd! Sure, mine eyes were mistaken:
  This was the man was meant me. That he should come
  So near his time, and miss it!
JASP. [Aside]   We might have come
  By the carriers from Valencia, I see,
  And sav'd all our sea-provision: we are at farthest   85
  Sure; methinks I should do something too;
  I meant to be a venturer in this voyage.
  Yonder's another vessel. I'll board her.
  If she be lawful prize, down goes her top-sail!
                                        [Approaches Diaphanta.

                    Enter Deflores

DEF. Lady, your father—
BEAT.   Is in health, I hope.   90
DEF. Your eye shall instantly instruct you, lady;
  He's coming hitherward.
BEAT.   What needed then
  Your duteous preface? I had rather
  He had come unexpected; you must stall
  A good presence with unnecessary blabbing: 95
  And how welcome for your part you are,
  I'm sure you know.
DEF. [Aside]   Will't never mend this scorn
  One side nor other? Must I be enjoin'd
  To follow still whilst she flies from me? Well,
  Fates do your worst, I'll please myself with sight   100
  Of her, at all opportunities,
  If but to spite her anger. I know she had
  Rather see me dead than living, and yet
  She knows no cause for't, but a peevish will.
ALS. You seem'd displeased, lady, on the sudden.   105

BEAT. Your pardon, sir, 'tis my infirmity,
  Nor can I other reason render you
  Than his or hers, of some particular thing
  They must abandon as a deadly poison,
  Which to a thousand other tastes were wholesome: 110
  Such to mine eyes is that same fellow there,
  The same that report speaks of the basilisk.
ALS. This is a frequent frailty in our nature;
  There's scarce a man amongst a thousand found,
  But hath his imperfection; one distastes   115
  The scent of roses, which to infinites
  Most pleasing is, and odoriferous;
  One oil, the enemy of poison;
  Another wine, the cheerer of the heart,
  And lively refresher of the countenance.   120
  Indeed this fault—if so it be—is general:
  There's scarce a thing but is both lov'd and loath'd.
  Myself, I must confess, have the same frailty.
BEAT. And what may be your poison, sir? I am bold with you.
ALS. What might be your desire—perhaps a cherry.   125
BEAT. I am no enemy to any creature
  My memory has, but yonder gentleman.
ALS. He does ill to tempt your sight, if he knew it.
BEAT. He cannot be ignorant of that, sir.
  I have not spar'd to tell him so, and I want   130
  To help myself, since he's a gentleman
  In good respect with my father, and follows him.
ALS. He's out of his place then now.
                        [They continue their conversation.
JASP. I am a mad wag, wench.
DIA. So methinks; but for your comfort I can tell you, we have a   135
  doctor in the city that undertakes the cure of such.
JASP. Tush! I know what physic is best for the state of mine own
  body.
DIA. 'Tis scarce a well govern'd state, I believe.
JASP. I could show thee such a thing with an ingredient that we two   140
  would compound together; and if it did not tame the maddest
  blood i' th' town for two hours after, I'll ne'er profess physic
  again.
DIA. A little poppy, sir, were good to cause you sleep.
JASP. Poppy! I'll give thee a pop i' th' lips for that first, and begin   145
  there [*kisses her*]. Poppy is one simple indeed, and cuckoo—what
  you call't—another. I'll discover no more now. Another time I'll
  show thee all.

Enter Vermandero and Servants

114   found] sound Q.
147   cuckoo . . . call't] cuckoo pintle-root, which is shaped like a phallus.

BEAT. My father, sir.

VER.   Oh, Joanna, I came to meet thee.
  Your devotion's ended?

BEAT.   For this time, sir.   150
  [*Aside*] I shall change my saint, I fear me. I find
  A giddy turning in me. Sir, this while
  I am beholding to this gentleman
  Who left his own way to keep me company,
  And in discourse I find him much desirous   155
  To see your castle. He hath deserv'd it, sir,
  If ye please to grant it.

VER.   With all my heart, sir.
  Yet there's an article between; I must know
  Your country. We use not to give survey
  Of our chief strengths to strangers; our citadels   160
  Are plac'd conspicuous to outward view
  On promonts' tops; but within are secrets.

ALS. A Valencian, sir.

VER.   A Valencian?
  That's native, sir. Of what name, I beseech you?

ALS. Alsemero, sir.

VER.   Alsemero? Not the son   165
  Of John de Alsemero?

ALS.   The same, sir

VER. My best love bids you welcome.

BEAT. [*Aside*]   He was wont
  To call me so, and then he speaks a most
  Unfeigned truth.

VER.   Oh, sir, I knew your father.
  We two were in acquaintance long ago   170
  Before our chins were worth Iulan down
  And so continued till the stamp of time
  Had coin'd us into silver. Well, he's gone:
  A good soldier went with him.

ALS.   You went together
  In that, sir.

VER.   No, by Saint Jaques, I came behind him.   175
  Yet I have done somewhat too. An unhappy day
  Swallowed him at last at Gibraltar
  In fight with those rebellious Hollanders—
  Was it not so?

ALS.   Whose death I had reveng'd,
  Or followed him in fate, had not the late league   180
  Prevented me.

VER.   Ay, ay, 'twas time to breathe.

---

151   change] implying that Beatrice is a kind of changeling.
171   Iulan down] the first growth of beard, from Iulus Ascanius (*Aeneid*, I. 267).

Oh, Joanna, I should ha' told thee news.
I saw Piracquo lately.
BEAT. [*Aside*]   That's ill news.
VER. He's hot preparing for this day of triumph:
Thou must be a bride within this sevennight.
ALS. [*Aside*]   Ha!   185
BEAT. Nay, good sir, be not so violent; with speed
I cannot render satisfaction
Unto the dear companion of my soul,
Virginity, whom I thus long have liv'd with,
And part with it so rude and suddenly.   190
Can such friends divide never to meet again
Without a solemn farewell?
VER.   Tush, tush, there's a toy!
ALS. [*Aside*] I must now part, and never meet again
With any joy on earth.—Sir, your pardon:
My affairs call on me.
VER.   How, sir? By no means!   195
Not chang'd so soon, I hope. You must see my castle
And her best entertainment ere we part,
I shall think myself unkindly us'd else.
Come, come, let's on; I had good hope your stay
Had been a while with us in Alligant,   200
I might have bid you to my daughter's wedding.
ALS. [*Aside*] He means to feast me, and poisons me beforehand.
I should be dearly glad to be there, sir,
Did my occasions suit as I could wish.
BEAT. I shall be sorry if you be not there,   205
When it is done, sir, but not so suddenly.
VER. I tell you, sir, the gentleman's complete,
A courtier and a gallant, enrich'd
With many fair and noble ornaments.
I would not change him for a son-in-law   210
For any he in Spain, the proudest he,
And we have great ones—that you know.
ALS.   He's much
Bound to you, sir.
VER.   He shall be bound to me
As fast as this tie can hold him: I'll want
My will else.
BEAT. [*Aside*] I shall want mine if you do it.   215
VER. But come; by the way, I'll tell you more of him.
ALS. [*Aside*] How shall I dare to venture in his castle,
When he discharges murderers at the gate?
But I must on, for back I cannot go.

---

218   murderers] (a) small cannon (b) perhaps an unconscious reference to
      Beatrice and Deflores (c) conversation about his rival

BEAT. [*Aside*] Not this serpent gone yet? [*Drops her glove.*
VER.   Look girl, thy glove's fall'n. 220
                 [*Alsemero goes to pick it up.*
  Stay, stay. Deflores, help a little.
      [*Exeunt Vermandero, Alsemero, Jasperino and Servants.*
DEF. [*Offering the glove*]   Here, Lady.
BEAT. Mischief on your officious forwardness!
  Who bade you stoop? They touch my hand no more.
  There, for t'other's sake I part with this:
  Take 'um and draw thine own skin off with 'um.   225
             [*Exeunt Beatrice and Diaphanta.*
DEF. Here's a favour come, with a mischief!
  Now I know she had rather wear my pelt
  Tann'd in a pair of dancing pumps than I
  Should thrust my fingers into her sockets here.
  I know she hates me, yet cannot choose but love her.   230
  No matter; if but to vex her, I'll haunt her still;
  Though I get nothing else, I'll have my will.   [*Exit.*

[Sc. 2]

Enter Alibius and Lollio

ALIB. Lollio, I must trust thee with a secret,
  But thou must keep it.
LOL.   I was ever close to a secret, sir.
ALIB. The diligence that I have found in thee,
  The care and industry already past,
  Assures me of thy good continuance.   5
  Lollio, I have a wife.
LOL. Fie, sir, 'tis too late to keep her secret; she's known to be
  married all the town and country over.
ALIB. Thou goest too fast, my Lollio; that knowledge
  I allow no man can be barr'd it; but there is a knowledge   10
  Which is nearer, deeper and sweeter, Lollio.
LOL. Well, sir, let us handle that between you and I.
ALIB. 'Tis that I go about, man. Lollio,
  My wife is young.
LOL. So much the worse to be kept secret, sir.   15
ALIB. Why, now thou meet'st the substance of the point:
  I am old, Lollio.
LOL.   No, sir; 'tis I am old Lollio.
ALIB. Yet why may not this concord and sympathize?
  Old trees and young plants often grow together,
  Well enough agreeing.   20
LOL. Ay, sir, but the old trees raise themselves higher and broader
  than the young plants.

ALIB. Shrewd application! There's the fear, man.
  I would wear my ring on my own finger;
  Whilst it is borrow'd it is none of mine,   25
  But his that useth it.
LOL. You must keep it on still then; if it but lie by,
  One or other will be thrusting into't.
ALIB. Thou conceiv'st me, Lollio; here thy watchful eye
  Must have employment; I cannot always be at home.   30
LOL. I dare swear you cannot.
ALIB.   I must look out.
LOL. I know't, you must look out: 'tis every man's case.
ALIB. Here I do say must thy employment be:
  To watch her treadings, and in my absence
  Supply my place.   35
LOL. I'll do my best, sir, yet surely I cannot see who you should have
  cause to be jealous of.
ALIB. Thy reason for that, Lollio? 'Tis a comfortable question.
LOL. We have but two sorts of people in the house, and both under
  the whip—that's fools and madmen; the one has not wit enough   40
  to be knaves, and the other not knavery enough to be fools.
ALIB. Ay, those are all my patients, Lollio.
  I do profess the cure of either sort:
  My trade, my living 'tis, I thrive by it.
  But here's the care that mixes with my thrift.   45
  The daily visitants that come to see
  My brainsick patients, I would not have
  To see my wife. Gallants I do observe
  Of quick-enticing eyes, rich in habits,
  Of stature and proportion very comely.   50
  These are most shrewd temptations, Lollio.
LOL. They may be easily answered, sir; if they come to see the fools
  and madmen, you and I may serve the turn, and let my mistress
  alone; she's of neither sort.
ALIB. 'Tis a good ward; indeed they come to see   55
  Our madmen or our fools. Let 'um see no more
  Than what they come for; by that consequent
  They must not see her: I'm sure she's no fool.
LOL. And I'm sure she's no madman.
ALIB. Hold that buckler fast, Lollio; my trust   60
  Is on thee, and I account it firm and strong.
  What hour is't, Lollio?
LOL. Towards belly-hour, sir.
ALIB. Dinner time? Thou mean'st twelve o'clock.
LOL. Yes, sir, for every part has his hour. We wake at six and look   65
  about us, that's eye-hour; at seven we should pray, that's knee-
  hour; at eight walk, that's leg-hour; at nine gather flowers, and

24 ring] cf. *M.V.* V. i. 307.

pluck a rose, that's nose-hour; at ten we drink, that's mouth-hour;
at eleven lay about us for victuals, that's hand-hour; at twelve go
to dinner, that's belly-hour.   70

ALIB. Profoundly, Lollio! It will be long
Ere all thy scholars learn this lesson, and
I did look to have a new one enter'd—stay!
I think my expectation is come home.

Enter Pedro and Antonio, like an idiot

PED. Save you, sir; my business speaks itself: 75
This sight takes off the labour of my tongue.

ALIB. Ay, ay, sir,
'Tis plain enough: you mean him for my patient.

PED. And if your pains prove but commodious, to give but some
little strength to his sick and weak part of nature in him, these are   80
but patterns to show you of the whole pieces that will follow to you
[*gives money*], beside the charge of diet, washing, and other neces-
saries fully defrayed.

ALIB. Believe it, sir, there shall no care be wanting.

LOL. Sir, an officer in this place may deserve something; the trouble   85
will pass through my hands.

PED. 'Tis fit something should come to your hands then, sir.
                                                      [*Gives money.*

LOL. Yes, sir, 'tis I must keep him sweet, and read to him. What is
his name?

PED. His name is Antonio; marry, we use but half to him, only Tony.   90

LOL. Tony, Tony, 'tis enough, and a very good name for a fool.
What's your name, Tony?

ANT. He, he, he! Well, I thank you, cousin; he, he, he!

LOL. Good boy! Hold up your head. He can laugh:
I perceive by that he is no beast.

PED.   Well, sir,   95
If you can raise him but to any height,
Any degree of wit, might he attain—
As I might say—to creep but on all four
Towards the chair of wit, or walk on crutches,
'Twould add an honour to your worthy pains,   100
And a great family might pray for you,
To which he should be heir, had he discretion
To claim and guide his own. Assure you, sir,
He is a gentleman.

LOL. Nay, there's nobody doubted that; at first sight I knew him   105
for a gentleman; he looks no other yet.

PED. Let him have good attendance and sweet lodging,

LOL. As good as my mistress lies in, sir; and as you allow us time

---

98   all four] obs. form of 'all fours'

and means, we can raise him to the higher degree of discretion.

PED. Nay, there shall no cost want, sir.   110

LOL. He will hardly be stretch'd up to the wit of a Magnifico.

PED. Oh no, that's not to be expected; far shorter will be enough.

LOL. I'll warrant you I make him fit to bear office in five weeks.
I'll undertake to wind him up to the wit of constable,

PED. If it be lower than that it might serve his turn.   115

LOL. No, fie! to level him with a headborough, beadle or watchman
were but little better than he is; constable I'll able him: if he do
come to be a Justice afterwards, let him thank the keeper. Or I'll
go further with you; say I do bring him up to my own pitch, say I
make him as wise as myself?   120

PED. Why, there I would have it.

LOL. Well, go to, either I'll be as arrant a fool as he, or he shall be as
wise as I, and then I think 'twill serve his turn.

PED. Nay, I do like thy wit passing well.

LOL. Yes, you may; yet if I had not been a fool, I had had more wit   125
than I have too; remember what state you find me in.

PED. I will, and so leave you: your best cares, I beseech you.

ALIB. Take you none with you; leave 'um all with us.

[Exit Pedro.

ANT. Oh, my cousin's gone! cousin, cousin, oh!

LOL. Peace, peace, Tony; you must not cry, child; you must be   130
whipp'd if you do; your cousin is here still; I am your cousin,
Tony.

ANT. He, he! then I'll not cry, if thou be'st my cousin, he, he, he!

LOL. I were best try his wit a little, that I may know what form to
place him in.   135

ALIB. Ay, do Lollio, do.

LOL. I must ask him easy questions at first. Tony, how many true
fingers has a tailor on his right hand?

ANT. As many as on his left, cousin.

LOL. Good! and how many on both?   140

ANT. Two less than a deuce, cousin.

LOL. Very well answered! I come to you again, cousin Tony. How
many fools goes to a wise man?

ANT. Forty in a day sometimes, cousin.

LOL. Forty in a day? How prove you that?   145

ANT. All that fall out amongst themselves and go to a lawyer to be
made friends.

LOL. A parlous fool! He must sit in the fourth form at least, I perceive that. I come again, Tony. How many knaves make an honest
man?   150

ANT. I know not that, cousin.

108   As . . . in] hinting that he may share her bed
137–8   true fingers] tailors had a reputation for dishonesty.

LOL. No, the question is too hard for you. I'll tell you, cousin, there's three knaves may make an honest man—a sergeant, a jailor, and a beadle. The sergeant catches him, the jailor holds him, and the beadle lashes him; and if he be not honest then, the hangman   155
must cure him.

ANT. Ha, ha, ha! that's fine sport, cousin.

ALIB. That was too deep a question for the fool, Lollio.

LOL. Yes, this might have serv'd yourself, though I say't.
   Once more, and you shall go play, Tony.   160

ANT. Ay, play at push-pin, cousin, ha, he!

LOL. So thou shalt. Say how many fools are here.

ANT. Two, cousin; thou and I.

LOL. Nay, y'are too forward there, Tony. Mark my question: how many fools and knaves are here? A fool before a knave, a fool   165
behind a knave, between every two fools a knave—how many fools, how many knaves?

ANT. I never learnt so far, cousin.

ALIB. Thou put'st too hard questions to him, Lollio.

LOL. I'll make him understand it easily. Cousin, stand there.   170

ANT. Ay, cousin.

LOL. Master, stand you next the fool.

ALIB. Well, Lollio.

LOL. Here's my place. Mark now, Tony, there's a fool before a knave.   175

ANT. That's I, cousin.

LOL. Here's a fool behind a knave, that's I; and between us two fools there's a knave, that's my master; 'tis but we three, that's all.

ANT. We three, we three, cousin.

> *[Noise of madmen within.*

1 MAD. [*Within*] Put's head i'th' pillory, the bread's too little.   180

2 MAD. [*Within*] Fly, fly, and he catches the swallow.

3 MAD. [*Within*] Give her more onion, or the devil put the rope about her crag.

LOL. You may hear what time of day it is; the chimes of Bedlam goes.   185

ALIB. Peace, peace, or the wire comes!

3 MAD. [*Within*] Cat-whore, cat-whore, her permasant, her permasant.

ALIB. Peace, I say; their hour's come; they must be fed, Lollio.

LOL. There's no hope of recovery of that Welsh madman; was undone by a mouse, that spoil'd him a permasant; lost his wits for't.   190

---

161 push-pin] a game in which the players push one pin across another—with a sexual innuendo
178 we three] alluding to pictures of two donkeys, the spectator making the third
186 wire] whip
187 cat-whore] the cat is called names for not protecting the cheese from mice. 'Her' is stage-Welsh for 'my' (Sampson *apud* Bawcutt).

ALIB. Go to your charge, Lollio, I'll to mine.

LOL. Go to your madmen's ward, let me alone with your fools.

ALIB. And remember my last charge, Lollio.   [*Exit*.

LOL. Of which your patients do you think I am? Come Tony, you
must amongst your school-fellows now; there's pretty scholars   195
amongst 'um; I can tell you there's some of 'em at *stultus, stulta,
stultum*.

ANT. I would see the madmen, cousin, if they would not bite me.

LOL. No, they shall not bite thee, Tony.

ANT. They bite when they are at dinner; do they not, coz?   200

LOL. They bite at dinner indeed, Tony. Well, I hope to get credit by
thee; I like thee the best of all the scholars that ever I brought up,
and thou shalt prove a wise man, or I'll prove a fool myself.

[*Exeunt*.

ACT II

[Sc. 1]

Enter Beatrice and Jasperino severally

BEAT. Oh, sir, I'm ready now for that fair service
Which makes the name of friend sit glorious on you.
Good angels and this conduct be your guide;   [*Gives a letter*]
Fitness of time and place is there set down, sir.

JASP. The joy I shall return rewards my service.   [*Exit*.   5

BEAT. How wise is Alsemero in his friend!
It is a sign he makes his choice with judgment.
Then I appear in nothing more approv'd
Than making choice of him;
For 'tis a principle, he that can choose   10
That bosom well, who of his thoughts partakes,
Proves most discreet in every choice he makes.
Methinks I love now with the eyes of judgment,
And see the way to merit, clearly see it.
A true deserver like a diamond sparkles,   15
In darkness you may see him, that's in absence,
Which is the greatest darkness falls on love;
Yet he is best discern'd then
With intellectual eyesight. What's Piracquo
My father spends his breath for? And his blessing   20
Is only mine as I regard his name,
Else it goes from me, and turns head against me,
Transform'd into a curse; some speedy way
Must be rememb'red; he's so forward too,

So urgent that way, scarce allows me breath   25
To speak to my new comforts.

Enter Deflores

DEF. [*Aside*]   Yonder's she.
Whatever ails me, now alate especially,
I can as well be hang'd as refrain seeing her;
Some twenty times a day, nay, not so little,
Do I force errands, frame ways and excuses   30
To come into her sight, and I have small reason for't,
And less encouragement; for she baits me still
Every time worse than other, does profess herself
The cruellest enemy to my face in town,
At no hand can abide the sight of me,   35
As if danger or ill luck hung in my looks.
I must confess my face is bad enough,
But I know far worse has better fortune,
And not endur'd alone, but doted on;
And yet such pick-hair'd faces, chins like witches',   40
Here and there five hairs whispering in a corner,
As if they grew in fear one of another,
Wrinkles like troughs, where swine-deformity swills
The tears of perjury that lie there like wash
Fallen from the slimy and dishonest eye;   45
Yet such a one pluck'd sweet withouts restraint,
And has the grace of beauty to his sweet.
Though my hard fate has thrust me out to servitude,
I tumbled into th' world a gentleman.
She turns her blessed eye upon me now,   50
And I'll endure all storms before I part with't.
BEAT. [*Aside*] Again!
This ominous ill-fac'd fellow more disturbs me
Than all my other passions.
DEF. [*Aside*]   Now't begins again;
I'll stand this storm of hail though the stones pelt me.   55
BEAT. Thy business? What's thy business?
DEF. [*Aside*]   Soft and fair;
I cannot part so soon now.
BEAT. [*Aside*]   The villain's fix'd—
Thou standing toad-pool!
DEF. [*Aside*]   The shower falls amain now.
BEAT. Who sent thee? What's thy errand? Leave my sight.
DEF. My lord your father charg'd me to deliver   60
A message to you.
BEAT.   What, another since?
Do't and be hang'd then, let me be rid of thee.
DEF. True service merits mercy.
BEAT.   What's thy message?

DEF. Let beauty settle but in patience,
  You shall hear all.
BEAT.   A dallying, trifling torment!   65
DEF. Signior Alonzo de Piracquo, lady,
  Sole brother to Tomazo de Piracquo—
BEAT. Slave, when wilt make an end?
DEF. [*Aside*]   Too soon I shall.
BEAT. What all this while of him?
DEF.   The said Alonzo,
  With the foresaid Tomazo—
BEAT.   Yet again?   70
DEF. Is new alighted.
BEAT.   Vengeance strike the news!
  Thou thing most loath'd, what cause was there in this
  To bring thee to my sight?
DEF.   My lord your father
  Charg'd me to seek you out.
BEAT.   Is there no other
  To send his errand by?
DEF.   It seems 'tis my luck   75
  To be i' th' way still.
BEAT.   Get thee from me.
DEF. [*Aside*]   So!
  Why, am not I an ass to devise ways
  Thus to be rail'd at? I must see her still!
  I shall have a mad qualm within this hour again,
  I know't, and, like a common Garden-bull,   80
  I do but take breath to be lugg'd again.
  What this may bode I know not; I'll despair the less,
  Because there's daily precedents of bad faces
  Belov'd beyond all reason; these foul chops
  May come into favour one day 'mongst his fellows;   85
  Wrangling has prov'd the mistress of good pastime;
  As children cry themselves asleep, I ha' seen
  Women have chid themselves abed to men.   [*Exit Deflores.*
BEAT. I never see this fellow, but I think
  Of some harm towards me; danger's in my mind still;   90
  I scarce leave trembling of an hour after.
  The next good mood I find my father in,
  I'll get him quite discarded. Oh, I was
  Lost in this small disturbance, and forgot
  Affliction's fiercer torrent that now comes   95
  To bear down all my comforts.

                    Enter Vermandero, Alonzo, Tomazo

VER.   Y'are both welcome,

80   common Garden-bull] referring to Paris Garden, Southwark, where bulls
     and bears were baited, with a quibble on 'common or garden'

But an especial one belongs to you, sir,
To whose most noble name our love presents
The addition of a son, our son Alonzo.
ALON. The treasury of honour cannot bring forth   100
A title I should more rejoice in, sir.
VER. You have improv'd it well; daughter, prepare;
The day will steal upon thee suddenly.
BEAT. [*Aside*] Howe'er, I will be sure to keep the night,
If it should come so near me.
                         [*Beatrice and Vermandero talk apart.*
TOM.   Alonzo.
ALON.   Brother?   105
TOM. In troth I see small welcome in her eye.
ALON. Fie, you are too severe a censurer
Of love in all points, there's no bringing on you;
If lovers should mark everything a fault.
Affection would be like an ill-set book,   110
Whose faults might prove as big as half the volume.
BEAT. That's all I do entreat.
VER.   It is but reasonable;
I'll see what my son says to't: son Alonzo,
Here's a motion made but to reprieve
A maidenhead three days longer; the request   115
Is not far out of reason, for indeed
The former time is pinching.
ALON.   Though my joys
Be set back so much time as I could wish
They had been forward, yet since she desires it,
The time is set as pleasing as before,   120
I find no gladness wanting.
VER.   May I ever
Meet it in that point still! Y'are nobly welcome, sirs.
                         [*Exeunt Vermandero and Beatrice.*
TOM. So: did you mark the dulness of her parting now?
ALON. What dulness? Thou art so exceptious still!
TOM. Why, let it go then, I am but a fool   125
To mark your harms so heedfully.
ALON.   Where's the oversight?
TOM. Come, your faith's cozen'd in her, strongly cozen'd;
Unsettle your affection with all speed
Wisdom can bring it to, your peace is ruin'd else.
Think what a torment 'tis to marry one   130
Whose heart is leap'd into another's bosom;
If ever pleasure she receive from thee,
It comes not in thy name, or of thy gift;
She lies but with another in thine arms,
He the half-father unto all thy children   135
In the conception; if he get 'em not,

She helps to get 'em for him, in his passions,
And how dangerous
And shameful her restraint may go in time to,
It is not to be thought on without sufferings. 140
ALON. You speak as if she lov'd some other, then.
TOM. Do you apprehend so slowly?
ALON.   Nay, and that
Be your fear only, I am safe enough.
Preserve your friendship and your counsel, brother,
For times of more distress; I should depart 145
An enemy, a dangerous, deadly one,
To any but thyself, that should but think
She knew the meaning of inconstancy,
Much less the use and practice; yet w'are friends;
Pray, let no more be urg'd; I can endure 150
Much, till I meet an injury to her,
Then I am not myself. Farewell, sweet brother;
How much w'are bound to heaven to depart lovingly. [*Exit.*
TOM. Why, here is love's tame madness; thus a man
Quickly steals into his vexation. [*Exit.* 155

[Sc. 2]

Enter Diaphanta and Alsemero

DIAP. The place is my charge, you have kept your hour,
And the reward of a just meeting bless you.
I hear my lady coming; complete gentleman,
I dare not be too busy with my praises,
Th'are dangerous things to deal with. [*Exit.*
ALS.   This goes well; 5
These women are the ladies' cabinets,
Things of most precious trust are lock'd into 'em.

Enter Beatrice

BEAT. I have within mine eye all my desires;
Requests that holy prayers ascend heaven for,
And brings 'em down to furnish our defects, 10
Come not more sweet to our necessities
Than thou unto my wishes.
ALS.   W'are so like
In our expressions, lady, that unless I borrow
The same words, I shall never find their equals.
BEAT. How happy were this meeting, this embrace, 15
If it were free from envy! This poor kiss,

___

137 in his passions] most editors omit; but the compositor probably omitted
some words from the beginning of l. 138.

It has an enemy, a hateful one,
That wishes poison to't; how well were I now
If there were none such name known as Piracquo,
Nor no such tie as the command of parents!   20
I should be but too much blessed.
ALS.   One good service
Would strike off both your fears, and I'll go near it too,
Since you are so distress'd; remove the cause,
The command ceases, so there's two fears blown out
With one and the same blast.
BEAT.   Pray, let me find you, sir.   25
What might that service be so strangely happy?
ALS. The honourablest piece 'bout man, valour.
I'll send a challenge to Piracquo instantly.
BEAT. How? Call you that extinguishing of fear,
When 'tis the only way to keep it flaming?   30
Are not you ventured in the action,
That's all my joys and comforts? Pray, no more, sir.
Say you prevail'd, y'are danger's and not mine then;
The law would claim you from me, or obscurity
Be made the grave to bury you alive.   35
I'm glad these thoughts come forth; oh, keep not one
Of this condition, sir; here was a course
Found to bring sorrow on her way to death;
The tears would ne'er ha' dried till dust had chok'd 'em.
Blood-guiltiness becomes a fouler visage,   40
[*Aside*]—And now I think on one. I was too blame,
I ha' marr'd so good a market with my scorn;
'T had been done questionless; the ugliest creature
Creation fram'd for some use, yet to see
I could not mark so much where it should be!   45
ALS. Lady,—
BEAT. [*Aside*] Why, men of art make much of poison,
Keep one to expel another; where was my art?
ALS. Lady, you hear not me.
BEAT.   I do especially, sir;
The present times are not so sure of our side
As those hereafter may be; we must use 'em then   50
As thrifty folks their wealth, sparingly now,
Till the time opens.
ALS.   You teach wisdom, lady.
BEAT. Within there! Diaphanta!

Enter Diaphanta

DIAP.   Do you call, madam?
BEAT. Perfect your service, and conduct this gentleman

25 find] understand

The private way you brought him.
DIAP.   I shall, madam.   55
ALS. My love's as firm as love e'er built upon.
                          [*Exeunt Diaphanta and Alsemero.*
                          Enter Deflores

DEF. [*Aside*] I have watch'd this meeting, and do wonder much
    What shall become of t'other; I'm sure both
    Cannot be serv'd unless she transgress; happily
    Then I'll put in for one; for if a woman   60
    Fly from one point, from him she makes a husband,
    She spreads and mounts then like arithmetic,
    One, ten, a hundred, a thousand, ten thousand,
    Proves in time sutler to an army royal.
    Now do I look to be most richly rail'd at,   65
    Yet I must see her.
BEAT. [*Aside*]   Why, put case I loath'd him
    As much as youth and beauty hates a sepulchre,
    Must I needs show it? Cannot I keep that secret
    And serve my turn upon him?—See, he's here.
    Deflores!
DEF. [*Aside*] Ha, I shall run mad with joy!   70
    She call'd me fairly by my name, Deflores,
    And neither rogue nor rascal.
BEAT.   What ha' you done
    To your face alate? Y'have met with some good physician;
    Y'have prun'd yourself, methinks; you were not wont
    To look so amorously.
DEF. [*Aside*]   Not I;   75
    'Tis the same physnomy, to a hair and pimple,
    Which she call'd scurvy scarce an hour ago;
    How is this?
BEAT.   Come hither; nearer, man.
DEF. [*Aside*] I'm up to the chin in heaven!
BEAT.   Turn, let me see;
    Faugh, 'tis but the heat of the liver, I perceive't;   80
    I thought it had been worse.
DEF. [*Aside*]   Her fingers touch'd me!
    She smells all amber.
BEAT. I'll make a water for you shall cleanse this
    Within a fortnight.
DEF.   With your own hands, lady?
BEAT. Yes, mine own, sir; in a work of cure   85
    I'll trust no other.
DEF. [*Aside*] 'Tis half an act of pleasure
    To hear her talk thus to me.
BEAT.   When w'are us'd

66 put case] supposing

To a hard face, 'tis not so unpleasing;
It mends still in opinion, hourly mends,
I see it by experience.

DEF. [*Aside*]   I was bless'd   90
To light upon this minute; I'll make use on't.

BEAT. Hardness becomes the visage of a man well,
It argues service, resolution, manhood,
If cause were of employment.

DEF.   'Twould be soon seen,
If e'er your ladyship had cause to use it.   95
I would but wish the honour of a service
So happy as that mounts to.

BEAT.   We shall try you—
Oh my Deflores!

DEF. [*Aside*]   How's that? She calls me hers
Already, my Deflores!—You were about
To sigh out somewhat, madam?

BEAT.   No, was I?   100
I forgot—Oh!—

DEF.   There 'tis again, the very fellow on't.

BEAT. You are too quick, sir.

DEF. There's no excuse for't now; I heard it twice, madam;
That sigh would fain have utterance, take pity on't,
And lend it a free word; 'las, how it labours   105
For liberty! I hear the murmur yet
Beat at your bosom.

BEAT.   Would creation—

DEF. Ay, well said, that's it.

BEAT.   Had form'd me man!

DEF. Nay, that's not it.

BEAT.   Oh, 'tis the soul of freedom!
I should not then be forc'd to marry one   110
I hate beyond all depths; I should have power
Then to oppose my loathings, nay, remove 'em
For ever from my sight.

DEF. [*Aside*]   O blest occasion!—
Without change to your sex, you have your wishes.
Claim so much man in me.

BEAT.   In thee, Deflores?   115
There's small cause for that.

DEF.   Put it not from me;
It's a service that I kneel for to you.   [*Kneels*]

BEAT. You are too violent to mean faithfully;
There's horror in my service, blood and danger;
Can those be things to sue for?

DEF.   If you knew   120
How sweet it were to me to be employed
In any act of yours, you would say then

I fail'd, and us'd not reverence enough
When I receive the charge on't.
BEAT. [*Aside*]   This is much, methinks;
Belike his wants are greedy, and to such   125
Gold tastes like angel's food.—Rise.
DEF. I'll have the work first.
BEAT. [*Aside*]   Possible his need
Is strong upon him.—There's to encourage thee;
                                        [*Gives him money*]
As thou art forward and thy service dangerous,
Thy reward shall be precious.
DEF.   That I have thought on;   130
I have assur'd myself of that beforehand,
And know it will be precious; the thought ravishes.
BEAT. Then take him to thy fury!
DEF.   I thirst for him.
BEAT. Alonzo de Piracquo!
DEF.   His end's upon him;
He shall be seen no more.
BEAT.   How lovely now   135
Dost thou appear to me! Never was man
Dearlier rewarded.
DEF.   I do think of that.
BEAT. Be wondrous careful in the execution.
DEF. Why, are not both our lives upon the cast?
BEAT. Then I throw all my fears upon thy service.   140
DEF. They ne'er shall rise to hurt you.
BEAT.   When the deed's done,
I'll furnish thee with all things for thy flight;
Thou may'st live bravely in another country.
DEF. Ay, ay, we'll talk of that hereafter.
BEAT. [*Aside*]   I shall rid myself
Of two inveterate loathings at one time,   145
Piracquo, and his dog-face.   [*Exit*.
DEF.   Oh, my blood!
Methinks I feel her in mine arms already,
Her wanton fingers combing out this beard,
And, being pleased, praising this bad face.
Hunger and pleasure, they'll commend sometimes   150
Slovenly dishes, and feed heartily on 'em,
Nay, which is stranger, refuse daintier for 'em.
Some women are odd feeders.—I'm too loud.
Here comes the man goes supperless to bed,
Yet shall not rise tomorrow to his dinner.   155

Enter Alonzo

ALON. Deflores.
DEF.   My kind, honourable lord?

ALON. I am glad I ha' met with thee.

DEF.   Sir?

ALON.   Thou canst show me
  The full strength of the castle?

DEF.   That I can, sir.

ALON. I much desire it.

DEF.   And if the ways and straits
  Of some of the passages be not too tedious for you,   160
  I will assure you, worth your time and sight, my lord.

ALON. Push, that shall be no hindrance.

DEF.   I'm your servant then.
  'Tis now near dinner time; 'gainst your lordship's rising,
  I'll have the keys about me.

ALON.   Thanks, kind Deflores.

DEF. [Aside] He's safely thrust upon me beyond hopes.   165

                                        [Exeunt.

ACT III

[Sc. 1]

Enter Alonzo and Deflores
(In the act-time Deflores hides a naked rapier.)

DEF. Yes, here are all the keys; I was afraid, my 'ord,
  I'd wanted for the postern, this is it.
  I've all, I've all, my lord; this for the sconce.

ALON. 'Tis a most spacious and impregnable fort.

DEF. You'll tell me more, my lord: this descent   5
  Is somewhat narrow, we shall never pass
  Well with our weapons, they'll but trouble us.

ALON. Thou say'st true.

DEF.   Pray let me help your lordship.

ALON. 'Tis done. Thanks, kind Deflores.

DEF.   Here are hooks, my lord,
  To hang such things on purpose.   [He hangs up the swords]

ALON.   Lead, I'll follow thee.   10

                    [Exeunt at one door and enter at the other.

[Sc. 2]

DEF. All this is nothing; you shall see anon
  A place you little dream on.

ALON.   I am glad

         I have this leisure; all your master's house
         Imagine I ha' taken a gondola.
DEF. All but myself, sir,—[*Aside*] which makes up my safety.   5
         My lord, I'll place you at a casement here
         Will show you the full strength of all the castle.
         Look, spend your eye awhile upon that object.
ALON. Here's rich variety, Deflores.
DEF.   Yes, sir.
ALON. Goodly munition.
DEF.   Ay, there's ordnance, sir,   10
         No bastard metal, will ring you a peal like bells
         At great men's funerals; keep your eye straight, my lord;
         Take special notice of that sconce before you,
         There you may dwell awhile.   [*Takes up the rapier*]
ALON.   I am upon't.
DEF. And so am I.   [*Stabs him*]
ALON. Deflores! Oh, Deflores!   15
         Whose malice hast thou put on?
DEF.   Do you question
         A work of secrecy? I must silence you.   [*Stabs him*]
ALON. Oh, oh, oh!
DEF.   I must silence you.   [*Stabs him*]
         So here's an undertaking well accomplish'd.
         This vault serves to good use now.—Ha, what's that   20
         Threw sparkles in my eye? Oh, 'tis a diamond
         He wears upon his finger; it was well found,
         This will approve the work. What, so fast on?
         Not part in death? I'll take a speedy course then,
         Finger and all shall off [*Cuts off the finger*]. So now I'll clear   25
         The passages from all suspect or fear.   [*Exit with body.*

[Sc. 3]

Enter Isabella and Lollio

ISAB. Why, sirrah? Whence have you commission
         To fetter the doors against me? If you
         Keep me in a cage, pray whistle to me,
         Let me be doing something.
LOL. You shall be doing, if it please you; I'll whistle   5
         to you if you'll pipe after.
ISAB. Is it your master's pleasure or your own,
         To keep me in this pinfold?
LOL. 'Tis for my master's pleasure, lest being taken in another
         man's corn, you might be pounded in another place.   10
ISAB. 'Tis very well, and he'll prove very wise.
LOL. He says you have company enough in the house, if you please
         to be sociable, of all sorts of people.
ISAB. Of all sorts? Why, here's none but fools and madmen.

LOL. Very well; and where will you find any other, if you should go   15
    abroad? There's my master and I to boot too.
ISAB. Of either sort one, a madman and a fool.
LOL. I would ev'n participate of both then, if I were as you;
    I know y'are half mad already, be half foolish too.
ISAB. Y'are a brave, saucy rascal! Come on, sir,   20
    Afford me then the pleasure of your bedlam;
    You were commending once today to me
    Your last-come lunatic; what a proper
    Body there was without brains to guide it,
    And what a pitiful delight appear'd   25
    In that defect, as if your wisdom had found
    A mirth in madness; pray, sir, let me partake,
    If there be such a pleasure.
LOL. If I do not show you the handsomest, discreetest madman, one
    that I may call the understanding madman, then say I am a fool.   30
ISAB. Well, a match, I will say so.
LOL. When you have a taste of the madman, you shall, if you please,
    see Fools College, o' th' side; I seldom lock there, 'tis but shooting
    a bolt or two, and you are amongst 'em.   [*Exit. Enter presently*.
    Come on, sir, let me see how handsomely you'll behave yourself   35
    now.

Enter Franciscus

FRAN. How sweetly she looks! Oh, but there's a wrinkle in her
    brow as deep as philosophy. Anacreon, drink to my mistress'
    health, I'll pledge it; stay, stay, there's a spider in the cup! no,
    'tis but a grape-stone; swallow it, fear nothing, poet; so, so, lift   40
    higher.
ISAB. Alack, alack, 'tis too full of pity
    To be laugh'd at. How fell he mad? Canst thou tell?
LOL. For love, mistress; he was a pretty poet too, and that set him
    forwards first; the Muses then forsook him; he ran mad for a   45
    chambermaid, yet she was but a dwarf neither.
FRAN. Hail, bright Titania!
    Why stand'st thou idle on these flow'ry banks?
    Oberon is dancing with his Dryades;
    I'll gather daisies, primrose, violets,   50
    And bind them in a verse of poesie.
LOL. Not too near; you see your danger.   [*Shows the whip*]
FRAN. Oh, hold thy hand, great Diomed!
    Thou feed'st thy horses well, they shall obey thee;
    Get up, Bucephalus kneels.   [*Kneels*]   55

38   Anacreon] who, choked to death on a grape-stone while drinking wine
53   Diomed] Diomedes, who fed his horses with human flesh—not the charac-
    ter who seduced Cressida
55   Bucephalus] Alexander the Great's horse

LOL. You see how I awe my flock; a shepherd has not his dog at
     more obedience.
ISAB. His conscience is unquiet; sure that was
     The cause of this. A proper gentleman.
FRAN. Come hither, Esculapius; hide the poison.   60
LOL. Well, 'tis hid.   [*Hides the whip*]
FRAN. Didst thou never hear of one Tiresias,
     A famous poet?
LOL. Yes, that kept tame wild geese.
FRAN. That's he; I am the man.   65
LOL. No!
FRAN. Yes, but make no words on't; I was a man
     Seven years ago.
LOL. A stripling I think you might.
FRAN. Now I'm a woman, all feminine.   70
LOL. I would I might see that.
FRAN. Juno struck me blind.
LOL. I'll ne'er believe that; for a woman, they say, has an eye more
     than a man.
FRAN. I say she struck me blind.   75
LOL. And Luna made you mad; you have two trades to beg with.
FRAN. Luna is now big-bellied, and there's room
     For both of us to ride with Hecate;
     I'll drag thee up into her silver sphere,
     And there we'll kick the dog, and beat the bush,   80
     That barks against the witches of the night,
     The swift lycanthropi that walks the round,
     We'll tear their wolvish skins and save the sheep.
                                         [*Tries to seize Lollio*]
LOL. Is't come to this? Nay, then my poison comes forth again
     [*Shows the whip*]; mad slave, indeed, abuse your keeper!   85
ISAB. I prithee, hence with him, now he grows dangerous.
FRAN. [*Sings*] Sweet love, pity me.
     Give me leave to lie with thee.
LOL. No, I'll see you wiser first; to your own kennel.
FRAN. No noise, she sleeps, draw all the curtains round,   90
     Let no soft sound molest the pretty soul,
     But love, and love creeps in at a mouse-hole.
LOL. I would you would get into your hole!   [*Exit Franciscus.*
     Now mistress, I will bring you another sort, you shall be
     fool'd another while; Tony, come hither, Tony; look who's   95
     yonder, Tony.

Enter Antonio

60 Esculapius] Greek god of medicine
62 Tiresias . . . poet] a soothsayer, not a poet, who was changed into a woman,
    and struck blind by Juno
76 Luna] the Moon, who makes people lunatic

ANT. Cousin, is it not my aunt?

LOL. Yes, 'tis one of 'um, Tony.

ANT. He, he! How do you, uncle?

LOL. Fear him not, mistress, 'tis a gentle nigget; you may play with   100
him, as safely with him as with his bauble.

ISAB. How long hast thou been a fool?

ANT. Ever since I came hither, cousin.

ISAB. Cousin? I'm none of thy cousins, fool.

LOL. Oh mistress, fools have always so much wit as to claim their   105
kindred.

MADMAN. [*Within*] Bounce, bounce, he falls, he falls!

ISAB. Hark you, your scholars in the upper room
Are out of order.

LOL. Must I come amongst you there? Keep you the fool, mistress;   110
I'll go up and play left-handed Orlando amongst the madmen.
                                                              [*Exit.*

ISAB. Well, sir.

ANT. 'Tis opportuneful now, sweet lady! Nay,
Cast no amazing eye upon this change.

ISAB. Ha!   115

ANT. This shape of folly shrouds your dearest love,
The truest servant to your powerful beauties,
Whose magic had this force thus to transform me.

ISAB. You are a fine fool indeed.

ANT.   Oh, 'tis not strange;
Love has an intellect that runs through all   120
The scrutinous sciences and, like
A cunning poet, catches a quantity
Of every knowledge, yet brings all home
Into one mystery, into one secret
That he proceeds in.

ISAB.   Y'are a parlous fool.   125

ANT. No danger in me; I bring naught but love
And his soft-wounding shafts to strike you with.
Try but one arrow; if it hurt you,
I'll stand you twebty back in recompense.
                                        [*Attempts to kiss her.*]

ISAB. A forward fool too!

ANT.   This was love's teaching.   130
A thousand ways he fashion'd out my way,
And this I found the safest and the nearest
To tread the Galaxia to my star.

ISAB. œrofound, withal! Certain, you dream'd of this;
Love never taught it waking.

ANT.   Take no acquaintance   351

---

111   Orlando] hero of Ariosto's *Orlando Furioso*.
133   Galaxia] The Milky Way.

Of these outward follies; there is within
A gentleman that loves you.

ISAB.   When I see him,
I'll speak with him; so in the meantime keep
Your habit, it becomes you well enough.
As you are a gentleman, I'll not discover you;   140
That's all the favour that you must expect;
When you are weary, you may leave the school,
For all this while you have but play'd the fool.

Enter Lollio

ANT. And must again.—He, he! I thank you, cousin;
I'll be your valentine tomorrow morning.   145

LOL. How do you like the fool, mistress?

ISAB. Passing well, sir.

LOL. Is he not witty, pretty well for a fool?

ISAB. If he hold on as he begins, he is like
To come to something.   150

LOL. Ay, thank a good tutor; you may put him to't; he begins
to answer pretty hard questions. Tony, how many is five times
six?

ANT. Five times six is six times five.

LOL. What arithmetician could have answer'd better? How many is   155
one hundred and seven?

ANT. One hundred and seven is seven hundred and one, cousin.

LOL. This is no wit to speak on; will you be rid of the fool now?

ISAB. By no means, let him stay a little.

MADMAN. [*Within*] Catch there, catch the last couple in hell!   160

LOL. Again! must I come amongst you? Would my master were
come home! I am not able to govern both these wards together.
                                        [*Exit.*

ANT. Why should a minute of love's hour be lost?

ISAB. Fie, out again! I had rather you kept
Your other posture; you become not your tongue   165
When you speak from your clothes.

ANT.   How can he freeze,
Lives near so sweet a warmth? Shall I alone
Walk through the orchard of the Hesperides,
And cowardly not dare to pull an apple?
This with the red cheeks I must venture for.   170

Enter Lollio, above

ISAB. Take heed, there's giants keep 'em.   [*He kisses her.*]

LOL. [*Aside*] How now, fool, are you good at that? Have you read

160   last . . . hell] In the game of Barley-break, two players, a man and a
        woman, in a space called 'Hell' try to catch the others as they run through
        it. See V. iii. 163.

Lipsius? He's past *Ars Amandi*; I believe I must put harder questions to him, I perceive that—

ISAB. You are bold without fear too.

ANT.   What should I fear,   175
Having all joys about me? Do you smile,
And love shall play the wanton on your lip,
Meet and retire, retire and meet again;
Look you but cheerfully, and in your eyes
I shall behold mine own deformity,   180
And dress myself up fairer; I know this shape
Becomes me not, but in those bright mirrors
I shall array me handsomely.

LOL.   Cuckoo, cuckoo!   [*Exit.*

Enter Madmen above, some as birds, others as beasts

ANT. What are these?

ISAB.   Of fear enough to part us;
Yet they are but our schools of lunatics,   185
That act their fantasies in any shapes
Suiting their present thoughts; if sad, they cry;
If mirth be their conceit, they laugh again.
Sometimes they imitate the beasts and birds,
Singing, or howling, braying, barking; all   190
As their wild fancies prompt 'um.

Enter Lollio

ANT.   These are no fears.

ISAB. But here's a large one, my man.

ANT. Ha, he! That's fine sport indeed, cousin.

LOL. I would my master were come home, 'tis too much for one shepherd to govern two of these flocks; nor can I believe that one church-   195
man can instruct two benefices at once; there will be some incurable mad of the one side, and very fools on the other. Come, Tony.

ANT. Prithee, cousin, let me stay here still.

LOL. No, you must to your book now, you have play'd sufficiently.   200

ISAB. Your fool is grown wondrous witty.

LOL. Well, I'll say nothing; but I do not think but he will put you
down one of these days.

                              [*Exeunt Lollio and Antonio.*

ISAB. Here the restrained current might make breach,
Spite of the watchful bankers; would a woman stray,   205
She need not gad abroad to seek her sin,
It would be brought home one ways or other:
The needle's point will to the fixed north;
Such drawing arctics women's beauties are.

173   Lipsius] famous jurist (d. 1606), mentioned for the sake of the quibble on
        'lips'. *Ars Amandi*] The Art of Love.
202–3   put . . . down] (a) outshine you in wit (b) lie with you.

Enter Lollio

LOL. How dost thou, sweet rogue?   210
ISAB. How now?
LOL. Come, there are degrees, one fool may be better than another.
ISAB. What's the matter?
LOL. Nay, if thou giv'st thy mind to fool's-flesh, have at thee!
                                              [*Tries to kiss her*]
ISAB. You bold slave, you!   215
LOL. I could follow now as t'other fool did:
     'What should I fear,
     Having all joys about me? Do you but smile,
     And love shall play the wanton on your lip,
     Meet and retire, retire and meet again;   220
     Look you but cheerfully, and in your eyes
     I shall behold my own deformity,
     And dress myself up fairer; I know this shape
     Becomes me not—'
     and so as it follows, but is not this the more foolish way? 225
     Come, sweet rogue; kiss me, my little Lacedemonian. Let me feel
     how thy pulses beat; thou hast a thing about thee would do a man
     pleasure, I'll lay my hand on't.
ISAB. Sirrah, no more! I see you have discovered
     This love's knight-errant, who hath made adventure   230
     For purchase of my love; be silent, mute,
     Mute as a statue, or his injunction
     For me enjoying, shall be to cut thy throat;
     I'll do it, though for no other purpose,
     And be sure he'll not refuse it.   235
LOL. My share, that's all; I'll have my fool's part with you.
ISAB. No more! Your master.

Enter Alibius

ALIB.   Sweet, how dost thou?
ISAB. Your bounden servant, sir.
ALIB.   Fie, fie, sweetheart,
     No more of that.
ISAB.   You were best lock me up.
ALIB. In my arms and bosom, my sweet Isabella,   240
     I'll lock thee up most nearly. Lollio,
     We have employment, we have task in hand;
     At noble Vermandero's, our castle captain,
     There is a nuptial to be solemniz'd—
     Beatrice-Joanna, his fair daughter, bride,—   245
     For which the gentleman hath bespoke our pains,
     A mixture of our madmen and our fools,
     To finish, as it were, and make the fag
     Of all the revels, the third night from the first;
     Only an unexpected passage over,   250

To make a frightful pleasure, that is all,
But not the all I aim at; could we so act it,
To teach it in a wild, distracted measure;
Though out of form and figure, breaking time's head,
It were no matter, 'twould be heal'd again   255
In one age or other, if not in this.
This, this, Lollio; there's a good reward begun,
And will beget a bounty be it known.

LOL. This is easy, sir, I'll warrant you; you have about you fools and
madmen that can dance very well, and 'tis no wonder, your best   260
dancers are not the wisest men; the reason is, with often jumping
they jolt their brains down into their feet, that their wits lie more in
their heels than in their heads.

ALIB. Honest Lollio, thou giv'st me a good reason
And a comfort in it.

ISAB.   Y'have a fine trade on't;   265
Madmen and fools are a staple commodity.

ALIB. Oh wife, we must eat, wear clothes, and live;
Just at the lawyer's haven we arrive,
By madmen and by fools we both do thrive.

                                        [*Exeunt.*

[Sc. 4]
          Enter Vermandero, Alsemero, Jasperino and Beatrice

VER. Valencia speaks so nobly of you, sir,
I wish I had a daughter now for you.

ALS. The fellow of this creature were a partner
For a king's love.

VER.   I had her fellow once, sir,
But Heaven has married her to joys eternal;   5
'Twere sin to wish her in this vale again.
Come, sir, your friend and you shall see the pleasures
Which my health chiefly joys in.

ALS. I hear the beauty of this seat largely.

VER. It falls much short of that.
                              [*Exeunt. Manet Beatrice.*
BEAT.   So, here's one step   10
Into my father's favour; time will fix him.
I have got him now the liberty of the house;
So wisdom by degrees works out her freedom;
And if that eye be dark'ned that offends me—
I wait but that eclipse—this gentleman   15
Shall soon shine glorious in my father's liking,
Through the refulgent virtue of my love.

                         Enter Deflores

258 be] let it be

DEF. [*Aside*] My thoughts are at a banquet; for the deed,
  I feel no weight in't, 'tis but light and cheap
  For the sweet recompense that I set down for't.   20
BEAT. Deflores.
DEF.   Lady?
BEAT.   Thy looks promise cheerfully.
DEF. All things are answerable, time, circumstance,
  Your wishes, and my service.
BEAT.   Is it done then?
DEF. Piracquo is no more.
BEAT. My joys start at mine eyes; our sweet'st delights   25
  Are evermore born weeping.
DEF.   I've a token for you.
BEAT. For me?
DEF.   But it was sent somewhat unwillingly,
  I could not get the ring without the finger. [*Shows her the finger*]
BEAT. Bless me! What hast thou done?
DEF.   Why, is that more
  Than killing the whole man? I cut his heart-strings.   30
  A greedy hand thrust in a dish at court
  In a mistake hath had as much as this.   ·
BEAT. 'Tis the first token my father made me send him.
DEF. And I have made him send it back again
  For his last token; I was loath to leave it,   35
  And I'm sure dead men have no use of jewels.
  He was as loath to part with't, for it stuck
  As if the flesh and it were both one substance.
BEAT. At the stag's fall the keeper has his fees;
  'Tis soon applied, all dead men's fees are yours, sir.   40
  I pray, bury the finger, but the stone
  You may make use on shortly; the true value,
  Take't of my truth, is near three hundred ducats.
DEF. 'Twill hardly buy a capcase for one's conscience, though,
  To keep it from the worm, as fine as 'tis.   45
  Well, being my fees, I'll take it;
  Great men have taught me that, or else my merit
  Would scorn the way on't.
BEAT.   It might justly, sir;
  Why, thou mistak'st, Deflores, 'tis not given
  In state of recompense.
DEF.   No, I hope so, lady,   50
  You should soon witness my contempt to't then.
BEAT. Prithee, thou look'st as if thou wert offended.
DEF. That were strange, lady; 'tis not possible
  My service should draw such a cause from you.
  Offended? Could you think so? That were much   55

32–3 A . . . this] i.e. cut accidentally by another diner's knife

   For one of my performance, and so warm
   Yet in my service.
BEAT. 'Twere misery in me to give you cause, sir.
DEF. I know so much, it were so, misery
   In her most sharp condition.
BEAT.   'Tis resolv'd then;   60
   Look you, sir, here's three thousand golden florins;
   I have not meanly thought upon thy merit.
DEF. What, salary? Now you move me.
BEAT.   How, Deflores?
DEF. Do you place me in the rank of verminous fellows,
   To destroy things for wages? Offer gold?   65
   The life blood of a man! Is anything
   Valued too precious for my recompense?
BEAT. I understand thee not.
DEF.   I could ha' hir'd
   A journeyman in murder at this rate,
   And mine own conscience might have slept at ease,   70
   And have had the work brought home.
BEAT. [*Aside*]   I'm in a labyrinth;
   What will content him? I would fain be rid of him.—
   I'll double the sum, sir.
DEF.   You take a course
   To double my vexation, that's the good you do.
BEAT. [*Aside*] Bless me! I am now in worse plight than I was;   75
   I know not what will please him.—For my fear's sake,
   I prithee make away with all speed possible;
   And if thou be'st so modest not to name
   The sum that will content thee, paper blushes not;
   Send thy demand in writing, it shall follow thee,   80
   But prithee take thy flight.
DEF.   You must fly too then.
BEAT. I?
DEF.   I'll not stir a foot else.
BEAT.   What's your meaning?
DEF. Why, are not you as guilty? In, I'm sure,
   As deep as I? And we should stick together.
   Come, your fears counsel you but ill; my absence   85
   Would draw suspect upon you instantly;
   There were no rescue for you.
BEAT. [*Aside*]   He speaks home.
DEF. Nor is it fit we two engag'd so jointly,
   Should part and live asunder.   [*Tries to kiss her*]
BEAT.   How, now, sir?

69–71 A . . . home] given the job to a professional cut-throat, who would be
     paid piece-rates
70 slept . . . ease] Dyce's completion of an unfinished line

This shows not well.

DEF.   What makes your lip so strange?   90

This must not be betwixt us.

BEAT. [*Aside*]   The man talks wildly.

DEF. Come, kiss me with a zeal now.

BEAT. [*Aside*]   Heaven, I doubt him!

DEF. I will not stand so long to beg 'em shortly.

BEAT. Take heed, Deflores, of forgetfulness,

    'Twill soon betray us.

DEF.   Take you heed first;   95

    Faith, y'are grown much forgetful, y'are too blame in't.

BEAT. [*Aside*] He's bold, and I am blam'd for't!

DEF.   I have eas'd

    You of your trouble, think on't; I'm in pain,

    And must be eas'd of you; 'tis a charity.

    Justice invites your blood to understand me.   100

BEAT. I dare not.

DEF.   Quickly!

BEAT.   Oh, I never shall!

    Speak it yet further off that I may lose

    What has been spoken, and no sound remain on't.

    I would not hear so much offence again

    For such another deed.

DEF.   Soft, lady, soft;   105

    The last is not yet paid for. Oh, this act

    Has put me into spirit; I was as greedy on't

    As the parch'd earth of moisture, when the clouds weep.

    Did you not mark, I wrought myself into't,

    Nay, sued and kneel'd for't? Why was all that pains took?   110

    You see I have thrown contempt upon your gold,

    Not that I want it not, for I do piteously;

    In order I will come unto't, and make use on't,

    But 'twas not held so precious to begin with;

    For I place wealth after the heels of pleasure,   115

    And were I not resolv'd in my belief

    That thy virginity were perfect in thee,

    I should but take my recompense with grudging,

    As if I had but half my hopes I agreed for.

BEAT. Why, 'tis impossible thou canst be so wicked,   120

    Or shelter such a cunning cruelty,

    To make his death the murderer of my honour!

    Thy language is so bold and vicious,

    I cannot see which way I can forgive it

    With any modesty.

DEF.   Push! You forget yourself!   125

    A woman dipp'd in blood, and talk of modesty!

113   In order] in due course

BEAT. Oh, misery of sin! Would I had been bound
    Perpetually unto my living hate
    In that Piracquo, than to hear these words.
    Think but upon the distance that creation   130
    Set betwixt thy blood and mine, and keep thee there.
DEF. Look but into your conscience, read me there,
    'Tis a true book, you'll find me there your equal.
    Push! Fly not to your birth, but settle you
    In what the act has made you, y'are no more now.   135
    You must forget your parentage to me:
    Y'are the deed's creature; by that name
    You lose your first condition, and I challenge you,
    As peace and innocency has turn'd you out,
    And made you one with me.
BEAT.   With thee, foul villain?   140
DEF. Yes, my fair murd'ress; do you urge me?
    Though thou writ'st maid, thou whore in thy affection,
    'Twas chang'd from thy first love, and that's a kind
    Of whoredom in thy heart; and he's chang'd now,
    To bring thy second on, thy Alsemero,   145
    Whom (by all sweets that ever darkness tasted)
    If I enjoy thee not, thou ne'er enjoy'st;
    I'll blast the hopes and joys of marriage,
    I'll confess all; my life I rate at nothing.
BEAT. Deflores!
DEF.   I shall rest from all lovers' plagues then;   150
    I live in pain now; that shooting eye
    Will burn my heart to cinders.
BEAT.   Oh, sir, hear me.
DEF. She that in life and love refuses me,
    In death and shame my partner she shall be.
BEAT. [Kneels] Stay, hear me once for all; I make thee master   155
    Of all the wealth I have in gold and jewels;
    Let me go poor unto my bed with honour,
    And I am rich in all things.
DEF.   Let this silence thee:
    The wealth of all Valencia shall not buy
    My pleasure from me;   160
    Can you weep Fate from its determin'd purpose?
    So soon may you weep me.
BEAT.   Vengeance begins;
    Murder, I see, is followed by more sins.
    Was my creation in the womb so curs'd,
    It must engender with a viper first?   165
DEF. Come, rise, and shroud your blushes in my bosom;
                                        [Raises her]

144 chang'd] i.e. to a corpse

Silence is one of pleasure's best receipts;
Thy peace is wrought for ever in this yielding.
'Las, how the turtle pants! Thou'lt love anon
What thou so fear'st and faint'st to venture on.   170

[Exeunt.

ACT IV

[Sc. 1]

[Dumb Show]

*Enter Gentlemen, Vermandero meeting them with action of wonderment at
the flight of Piracquo. Enter Alsemero, with Jasperino and Gallants;
Vermandero points to him, the Gentlemen seeming to applaud the choice.*

*[Exeunt] Alsemero, Jasperino, and Gentlemen; Beatrice the bride following
in great state, accompanied with Diaphanta, Isabella, and other Gentlewomen; Deflores after all, smiling at the accident; Alonzo's ghost appears to
Deflores in the midst of his smile, startles him, showing him the hand whose
finger he had cut off. They pass over in great solemnity.*

Enter Beatrice

BEAT. This fellow has undone me endlessly,
Never was bride so fearfully distress'd;
The more I think upon th' ensuing night,
And whom I am to cope with in embraces,
One who's ennobled both in blood and mind,   5
So clear in understanding,—that's my plague now—
Before whose judgement will my fault appear
Like malefactors' crimes before tribunals;
There is no hiding on't, the more I dive
Into my own distress; how a wise man   10
Stands for a great calamity! There's no venturing
Into his bed, what course soe'er I light upon,
Without my shame, which may grow up to danger;
He cannot but in justice strangle me
As I lie by him, as a cheater use me;   15
'Tis a precious craft to play with a false die
Before a cunning gamester. Here's his closet,
The key left in't, and he abroad i'th' park.
Sure 'twas forgot; I'll be so bold as look in't.   *[Opens closet]*
Bless me! A right physician's closet 'tis,   20
Set round with vials, every one her mark too.
Sure he does practise physic for his own use,
Which may be safely call'd your great man's wisdom.
What manuscript lies here? 'The Book of Experiment,

Call'd Secrets in Nature'; so 'tis, 'tis so;   25
'How to know whether a woman be with child or no';
I hope I am not yet; if he should try though!
Let me see, folio forty-five. Here 'tis;
The leaf ruck'd down upon't, the place suspicious:
'If you would know whether a woman be with child or not, give   30
her two spoonfuls of the white water in glass C'—
Where's that glass C? Oh, yonder, I see't now—'and if she be with
child she sleeps full twelve hours after; if not, not.'
None of that water comes into my belly.
I'll know you from a hundred; I could break you now,   35
Or turn you into milk, and so beguile
The master of the mystery, but I'll look to you.
Ha. That which is next is ten times worse:
'How to know whether a woman be a maid or not.'
If that should be appli'd, what would become of me?   40
Belike he has a strong faith of my purity,
That never yet made proof; but this he calls
'A merry sleight, but true experiment, the author Antonius
Mizaldus. Give the party you suspect the quantity of a spoonful
of the water in the glass M, which, upon her that is a maid, makes   45
three several effects: 'twill make her incontinently gape, then fall
into a sudden sneezing, last into a violent laughing; else dull,
heavy, and lumpish.'
Where had I been?
I fear it, yet 'tis seven hours to bedtime.   50

Enter Diaphanta

DIAP. Cuds, madam, are you here?
BEAT. [*Aside*]   Seeing that wench now,
   A trick comes in my mind; 'tis a nice piece
   Gold cannot purchase.—I come hither, wench,
   To look my lord.
DIAP. [*Aside*]   Would I had such a cause
   To look him too!—Why, he's i'th' park, madam.   55
BEAT. There let him be.
DIAP.   Ay, madam, let him compass
   Whole parks and forests, as great rangers do;
   At roosting time a little lodge can hold 'em.
   Earth-conquering Alexander, that thought the world
   Too narrow for him, in the end had but his pit-hole.   60
BEAT. I fear thou art not modest, Diaphanta.
DIAP. Your thoughts are so unwilling to be known, madam;
   'Tis ever the bride's fashion towards bed-time

25 Secrets . . . Nature] Although this book by Antonius Mizaldus (1520–78)
    does not contain pregnancy tests, another book of his does.
61 not modest] because her last remark has a bawdy secondary meaning

    To set light by her joys, as if she ow'd 'em not.
BEAT. Her joys? Her fears, thou would'st say.
DIAP.   Fear of what?   65
BEAT. Art thou a maid, and talk'st so to a maid?
    You leave a blushing business behind,
    Beshrew your heart for't!
DIAP.   Do you mean good sooth, madam?
BEAT. Well, if I'd thought upon the fear at first,
    Man should have been unknown.
DIAP.   Is't possible?   70
BEAT. I will give a thousand ducats to that woman
    Would try what my fear were, and tell me true
    Tomorrow, when she gets from't; as she likes,
    I might perhaps be drawn to't.
DIAP.   Are you in earnest?
BEAT. Do you get the woman, then challenge me,   75
    And see if I'll fly from't; but I must tell you
    This by the way, she must be a true maid,
    Else there's no trial, my fears are not hers else.
DIAP. Nay, she that I would put into your hands, madam,
    Shall be a maid.
BEAT.   You know I should be sham'd else,   80
    Because she lies for me.
DIAP.   'Tis a strange humour;
    But are you serious still? Would you resign
    Your first night's pleasure, and give money too?
BEAT. As willingly as live;—[*aside*] alas, the gold
    Is but a by-bet to wedge in the honour.   85
DIAP. I do not know how the world goes abroad
    For faith or honesty, there's both requir'd in this.
    Madam, what say you to me, and stray no further?
    I've a good mind, in troth, to earn your money.
BEAT. Y'are too quick, I fear, to be a maid.   90
DIAP. How? Not a maid? Nay, then you urge me, madam;
    Your honourable self is not a truer
    With all your fears upon you—
BEAT. [*Aside*]   Bad enough then.
DIAP. Than I with all my lightsome joys about me.
BEAT. I'm glad to hear't; then you dare put your honesty   95
    Upon an easy trial?
DIAP.   Easy? Anything.
BEAT. I'll come to you straight.   [*Goes to the closet*]
DIAP. [*Aside*]   She will not search me, will she,
    Like the forewoman of a female jury?
BEAT. Glass M; ay, this is it; look, Diaphanta,
    You take no worse than I do.   [*Drinks*]
DIAP.   And in so doing,   100
    I will not question what 'tis, but take it.   [*Drinks*]

BEAT. [*Aside*] Now if the experiment be true, 'twill praise itself,
  And give me noble ease:—Begins already;

                       [*Diaphanta gapes*]

  There's the first symptom; and what haste it makes
  To fall into the second, there by this time!   105

                    [*Diaphanta sneezes*]

  Most admirable secret! On the contrary,
  It stirs not me a whit, which most concerns it.
DIAP. Ha, ha, ha!
BEAT. [*Aside*]   Just in all things and in order,
  As if 'twere circumscrib'd; one accident
  Gives way unto another.
DIAP.   Ha, ha, ha!   110
BEAT. How now, wench?
DIAP.   Ha, ha, ha! I am so, so light
  At heart—ha, ha, ha!—so pleasurable.
  But one swig more, sweet madam.
BEAT.   Ay, tomorrow;
  We shall have time to sit by't.
DIAP.   Now I'm sad again.
BEAT. [*Aside*] It lays itself so gently, too!—Come, wench,   115
  Most honest Diaphanta I dare call thee now.
DIAP. Pray tell me, madam, what trick call you this?
BEAT. I'll tell thee all hereafter; we must study
  The carriage of this business.
DIAP. [*Aside*]   I shall carry't well,
  Because I love the burthen.
BEAT.   About midnight   120
  You must not fail to steal forth gently.
  That I may use the place.
DIAP.   Oh, fear not, madam,
  I shall be cool by that time;—the bride's place,
  And with a thousand ducats! I'm for a justice now,
  I bring a portion with me; I scorn small fools.   125

                       [*Exeunt.*

[Sc. 2]

Enter Vermandero and Servant

VER. I tell thee, knave, mine honour is in question,
  A thing till now free from suspicion,
  Nor ever was there cause; who of my gentlemen
  Are absent? Tell me and truly how many and who.
SERV. Antonio, sir, and Franciscus.   5
VER. When did they leave the castle?
SERV. Some ten days since, sir, the one intending to Briamata,
  th'other for Valencia.

VER. The time accuses 'em; a charge of murder
　　Is brought within my castle gate, Piracquo's murder;　　　　　10
　　I dare not answer faithfully their absence;
　　A strict command of apprehension
　　Shall pursue 'em suddenly, and either wipe
　　The stain off clear, or openly discover it.
　　Provide me winged warrants for the purpose.　　　　　　15
　　　　　　　　　　　　　　　　　　　　　　[*Exit Servant.*

　　See, I am set on again.

　　　　　　　　　　　Enter Tomazo

TOM. I claim a brother of you.
VER.　　　　　　　　　Y'are too hot,
　　Seek him not here.
TOM.　　　　　　　Yes, 'mongst your dearest bloods,
　　If my peace find no fairer satisfaction;
　　This is the place must uield account for him,　　　　　20
　　For here I left him, and the hasty tie
　　Of this snatch'd marriage gives strong testimony
　　Of his most certain ruin.
VER.　　　　　　　　Certain falsehood!
　　This is the place indeed; his breach of faith
　　Has too much marr'd both my abused love,　　　　　25
　　The honourable love I reserv'd for gim,
　　And mock'd my daughter's joy; the prepar'd morning
　　Blush'd at his infidelity; he left
　　Contempt and scorn to throw upon those friends
　　Whose belief hurt 'em; oh, 'twas most ignoble　　　　　30
　　To take his flight so unexpectedly,
　　And throw such public wrongs on those that lov'd him.
TOM. Then this is all your answer?
VER.　　　　　　　　　　'Tis too fair
　　For one of his alliance; and I warn you
　　That this place no more see you.　　　　　　　[*Exit.*

　　　　　　　　　　　Enter Deflores

TOM.　　　　　　　　　The best is,　　　　　35
　　There is more ground to meet a man's revenge on—
　　Honest Deflores?
DEF.　　　　　　That's my name, indeed.
　　Saw you the bride? Good sweet sir, which way took she?
TOM. I have bless'd mine eyes from seeing such a false one.
DEF. [*Aside*] I'd fain get off, this man's not for my company,　　　40
　　I smell his brother's blood when I come near him.
TOM. Come hither, kind and true one; I remember
　　My brother lov'd thee well.
DEF.　　　　　　　　Oh, purely, dear sir!
　　[*Aside*]—Methinks I am now again a-killing on him,

He brings it so fresh to me.

TOM.   Thou canst guess, sirrah,—   45
One honest friend has an instinct of jealousy—
At some foul guilty person?

DEF.   'Las, sir,
I am so charitable I think none
Worse than myself.—You did not see the bride then?

TOM. I prithee name her not. Is she not wicked?   50

DEF. No, no, a pretty, easy, round-pack'd sinner,
As your most ladies are, else you might think
I flatter'd her; but, sir, at no hand wicked,
Till th'are so old their chins and noses meet,
And they salute witches. I am call'd, I think, sir.   55
[Aside]—His company ev'n o'erlays my conscience.   [Exit.

TOM. That Deflores has a wondrous honest heart;
He'll bring it out in time, I'm assur'd on't.
Oh, here's the glorious master of the day's joy;
'Twill not be long till he and I do reckon.   60

                    Enter Alsemero

Sir!

ALS. You are most welcome.

TOM.   You may call that word back;
I do not think I am, nor wish to be.

ALS. 'Tis strange you found the way to this house then.

TOM. Would I'd ne'er known the cause! I'm none of those, sir, 65
That come to give you joy and swill your wine;
'Tis a more precious liquor that must lay
The fiery thirst I bring.

ALS.   Your words and you
Appear to me great strangers.

TOM.   Time and our swords
May make us more acquainted; this the business: 70
I should have a brother in your place;
How treachery and malice have dispos'd of him,
I'm bound to enquire of him which holds his right,
Which never could come fairly.

ALS.   You must look
To answer for that word, sir.

TOM.   Fear you not,   75
I'll have it ready drawn at our next meeting.
Keep your day solemn. Farewell, I disturb it not;
I'll bear the smart with patience for a time.   [Exit.

ALS. 'Tis somewhat ominous this, a quarrel enter'd
Upon this day; my innocence relieves me,   80

                    Enter Jasperino

I should be wondrous sad else. Jasperino,
I have news to tell thee, strange news.

JASP.   I ha' some too,
I think as strange as yours; would I might keep
Mine, so my faith and friendship might be kept in't!
Faith, sir, dispense a little with my zeal,   85
And let it cool in this.
ALS.   This puts me on,
And blames thee for thy slowness.
JASP.   All may prove nothing,
Only a friendly fear that leapt from me, sir.
ALS. No question it may prove nothing; let's partake it, though.
JASP. 'Twas Diaphanta's chance (for to that wench   90
I pretend honest love, and she deserves it)
To leave me in a back part of the house,
A place we chose for private conference;
She was no sooner gone, but instantly
I heard your bride's voice in the next room to me,   95
And, lending more attention, found Deflores
Louder than she.
ALS.   Deflores? Thou art out now.
JASP. You'll tell me more anon.
ALS.   Still I'll prevent thee;
The very sight of him is poison to her.
JASP. That made me stagger too, but Diaphanta   100
At her return confirm'd it.
ALS.   Diaphanta!
JASP. Then fell we both to listen, and words pass'd
Like those that challenge interest in a woman.
ALS. Peace! quench thy zeal; 'tis dangerous to thy bosom.
JASP. Then truth is full of peril.
ALS.   Such truths are,   105
—Oh, were she the sole glory of the earth,
Had eyes that could shoot fire into kings' breasts,
And touch'd, she sleeps not here! Yet I have time,
Though night be near, to be resolv'd hereof;
And, prithee, do not weigh me by my passions.   110
JASP. I never weigh'd friend so.
ALS.   Done charitably!
That key will lead thee to a pretty secret,
By a Chaldean taught me, and I have
My study upon some. Bring from my closet
A glass inscrib'd there with the letter M,   115
And question not my purpose.
JASP.   It shall be done, sir.   [*Exit.*
ALS. How can this hang together? Not an hour since,
Her woman came pleading her lady's fears,
Deliver'd her for the most timorous virgin

86 puts ... on] spurs me

That ever shrunk at man's name, and so modest,   120
She charg'd her weep out her request to me
That she might come obscurely to my bosom.
Enter Beatrice
BEAT. (*Aside*) All things go well; my woman's preparing yonder
For her sweet voyage, which grieves me to lose;
Necessity compels it; I lose all else.   125
ALS. [*Aside*] Push! Modesty's shrine is set in yonder forehead,
I cannot be too sure though.—My Joanna!
BEAT. Sir, I was bold to weep a message to you;
Pardon my modest fears.
ALS. [*Aside*]   The dove's not meeker;
She's abus'd, questionless.

Enter Jasperino

                    —Oh, are you come, sir?   130
BEAT. [*Aside*] The glass, upon my life! I see the letter.
JASP. Sir, this is M.
ALS.   'Tis it.
BEAT. [*Aside*]   I am suspected.
ALS. How fitly our bride comes to partake with us!
BEAT. What is't, my lord?
ALS.   No hurt.
BEAT.   Sir, pardon me,
I seldom taste of any composition.   135
ALS. But this, upon my warrant, you shall venture on.
BEAT. I fear 'twill make me ill.
ALS.   Heaven forbid that!
BEAT. [*Aside*] I'm put now to my cunning; th' effects I know,
If I can now but feign 'em handsomely.   [*Drinks*]
ALS. [*to Jasperino*] It has that secret virtue it ne'er miss'd, sir,   140
Upon a virgin.
JASP.   Treble qualitied?
                    [*Beatrice gapes, then sneezes*]
ALS. By all that's virtuous, it takes there, proceeds!
JASP. This is the strangest trick to know a maid by.
BEAT. Ha, ha, ha!
You have given me joy of heart to drink, my lord.   145
ALS. No, thou hast given me such joy of heart,
That never can be blasted.
BEAT.   What's the matter, sir?
ALS. [*to Jasperino*] See, now 'tis settled in a melancholy,
Keeps both the time and method.—My Joanna,
Chaste as the breath of Heaven, or morning's womb   150
That brings the day forth, thus my love encloses thee.
                              [*Exeunt.*

[Sc. 3]

Enter Isabella, reading a letter, and Lollio

ISAB. O heaven! Is this the waxing moon?
　　Does love turn fool, run mad, and all at once?
　　Sirrah, here's a madman, akin to the fool too,
　　A lunatic lover.
LOL. No, no, not he I brought the letter from?　　　　　　5
ISAB. Compare his inside with his out, and tell me.
LOL. The out's mad, I'm sure of that; I had a taste on't.
　　'To the bright Andromeda, chief chambermaid to the Knight of
　　the Sun, at the sign of Scorpio, in the middle region, sent by the
　　bellows-mender of Æolus. Pay the post.' This is stark madness.　10
ISAB. Now mark the inside. [*Reads*] 'Sweet lady, having now cast
　　off this counterfeit cover of a madman, I appear to your best
　　judgment a true and faithful lover of your beauty.'
LOL. He is mad still.
ISAB. 'If any fault you find, chide those perfections in you which　15
　　have made me imperfect; 'tis the same sun that causeth to grow
　　and enforceth to wither,—'
LOL. Oh rogue!
ISAB. '—Shapes and transhapes, destroys and builds again; I come
　　in winter to you dismantled of my proper ornaments; by the sweet　20
　　splendour of your cheerful smiles, I spring and live a lover.'
LOL. Mad rascal still!
ISAB. 'Tread him not under foot; that shall appear an honour to
　　your bounties. I remain—mad till I speak with you, from whom I
　　expect my cure—Yours all, or one beside himself, Franciscus.'　25
LOL. You are like to have a fine time on't; my master and I may give
　　over our professions, I do not think but you can cure fools and
　　madmen faster than we, with little pains too.
ISAB. Very likely.
LOL. One thing I must tell you, mistress: you perceive that I am privy　30
　　to your skill; if I find you minister once and set up the trade, I put
　　in for my thirds, I shall be mad or fool else.
ISAB. The first place is thine, believe it, Lollio,
　　If I do fall—
LOL. I fall upon you.　　　　　　　　　　　　　　　　　35
ISAB. So.
LOL. Well, I stand to my venture.
ISAB. But thy counsel now, how shall I deal with 'em?
LOL. Why, do you mean to deal with 'em?
ISAB. Nay, the fair understanding, how to use 'em.　　　　40

1　waxing] *Williams*; waiting Q.
32　thirds] a third share in Isabella's favours, the other sharers being her
　　husband, Franciscus or Antonio
40　fair understanding] Lollio has assumed that 'deal' has a sexual meaning.

LOL. Abuse 'em! That's the way to mad the fool, and make a fool of
the madman, and then you use 'em kindly.

ISAB. 'Tis easy, I'll practise; do thou observe it;
The key of thy wardrobe.

LOL. There; fit yourself for 'em, and I'll fit 'em both for you.   45
[*Gives her the key*]

ISAB. Take thou no further notice than the outside.   [*Exit.*

LOL. Not an inch; I'll put you to the inside.

Enter Alibius

ALIB. Lollio, art there? Will all be perfect, think'st thou?
Tomorrow night, as if to close up the solemnity,
Vermandero expects us.   50

LOL. I mistrust the madmen most: the fools will do well enough;
I have taken pains with them.

ALIB. Tush, they cannot miss; the more absurdity,
The more commends it, so no rough behaviours
Affright the ladies; they are nice things, thou know'st.   55

LOL. You need not fear, sir; so long as we are there with our com-
manding pizzles, they'll be as tame as the ladies themselves.

ALIB. I will see them once more rehearse before they go.

LOL. I was about it, sir; look you to the madmen's morris, and let
me alone with the other; there is one or two that I mistrust their   60
fooling; I'll instruct them, and then they shall rehearse the whole
measure.

ALIB. Do so; I'll see the music prepar'd; but, Lollio,
By the way, how does my wife brook her restraint?
Does she not grudge at it?   65

LOL. So, so; she takes some pleasure in the house, she would abroad
else; you must allow her a little more length, she's kept too short.

ALIB. She shall along to Vermandero's with us;
That will serve her for a month's liberty.

LOL. What's that on your face, sir?   70

ALIB. Where, Lollio? I see nothing.

LOL. Cry you mercy, sir, 'tis your nose; it showed like the trunk of a
young elephant.

ALIB. Away, rascal! I'll prepare the music, Lollio.   [*Exit Alibius.*

LOL. Do, sir, and I'll dance the whilst. Tony, where art thou, Tony?   75

Enter Antonio

ANT. Here, cousin; where art thou?

LOL. Come, Tony, the footmanship I taught you.

ANT. I had rather ride, cousin.

LOL. Ay, a whip take you; but I'll keep you out.
Vault in; look you, Tony: fa, la, la la, la.   [*Dances*]   80

ANT. Fa, la, la, la, la.   [*Dances*]

LOL. There, an honour.

ANT. Is this an honour, coz? [*Bows*]

42   kindly] (a) according to their kind (b) gently

LOL. Yes, and it please your worship.

ANT. Does honour bend in the hams, coz?   85

LOL. Marry, does it, as low as worship, squireship, nay yeomandry
   itself sometimes, from whence it first stiffened; there, rise, a caper.

ANT. Caper after an honour, coz?

LOL. Very proper; for honour is but a caper, rises as fast and high,
   has a knee or two, and falls to th'ground again. You can remember   90
   your figure, Tony?

ANT. Yes, cousin; when I see thy figure, I can remember mine.

Enter Isabella (dressed like a madwoman)

ISAB. Hey, how he treads the air! Shough, shough, t'other way!
   He burns his wings else; here's wax enough below,
   Icarus, more than will be cancelled these eighteen moons;   95
   He's down, he's down! What a terrible fall he had!
   Stand up, thou son of Cretan Dedalus,
   And let us tread the lower labyrinth;
   I'll bring thee to the clue.

ANT. Prithee, coz, let me alone.   100

ISAB. Art thou not drown'd?
   About thy head I saw a heap of clouds,
   Wrapp'd like a Turkish turban; on thy back
   A crook'd chameleon-colour'd rainbow hung
   Like a tiara down unto thy hams.   105
   Let me suck out those billows in thy belly;
   Hark how they roar and rumble in the straits!
   Bless thee from the pirates.

ANT. Pox upon you; let me alone!

ISAB. Why shouldst thou mount so high as Mercury,   110
   Unless thou hadst reversion of his place?
   Stay in the moon with me, Endymion,
   And we will rule these wild, rebellious waves,
   That would have drown'd my love.

ANT. I'll kick thee if again thou touch me,   115
   Thou wild unshapen antic; I am no fool,
   You bedlam!

ISAB.   But you are, as sure as I am, mad.
   Have I put on this habit of a frantic,
   With love as full of fury, to beguile
   The nimble eye of watchful jealousy,   120
   And am I thus rewarded?   *[Reveals herself]*

ANT.   Ha, dearest beauty!

ISAB. No, I have no beauty now,
   Nor never had, but what was in my garments.
   You, a quick-sighted lover? Come not near me!
   Keep your caparisons, y'are aptly clad;   125
   I came a feigner to return stark mad.   *[Exit.*

Enter Lollio

ANT. Stay, or I shall change condition,
  And become as you are.
LOL. Why, Tony, whither now? Why, fool?
ANT. Whose fool, usher of idiots? You coxcomb!   130
  I have fool'd too much.
LOL. You were best be mad another while then.
ANT. So I am, stark mad; I have cause enough;
  And I could throw the full effects on thee,
  And beat thee like a fury.   135
LOL. Do not, do not; I shall not forbear the gentleman under the
  fool, if you do; alas, I saw through your fox-skin before now!
  Come, I can give you comfort; my mistress loves you, and there is
  as arrant a madman i' th' house as you are a fool, your rival, whom
  she loves not; if after the masque we can rid her of him, you earn   140
  her love, she says, and the fool shall ride her.
ANT. May I believe thee?
LOL. Yes, or you may choose whether you will or no.
ANT. She's eas'd of him; I have a good quarrel on't.
LOL. Well, keep your old station yet, and be quiet.   145
ANT. Tell her I will deserve her love.
LOL. And you are like to have your desire.   [*Exit Antonio.*

Enter Franciscus

FRAN. [*Sings*] 'Down, down down a-down a-down' and then with a
  horse-trick
  To kick Latona's forehead, and break her bowstring.
LOL. This is t'other counterfeit; I'll put him out of his humour.   150
  [*Takes out letter and reads*] 'Sweet lady, having now cast off this
  counterfeit cover of a madman, I appear to your best judgment a
  true and faithful lover of your beauty.' This is pretty well for a
  madman.
FRAN. Ha! What's that?   155
LOL. 'Chide those perfections in you which have made me imperfect.'
FRAN. I am discover'd to the fool.
LOL. I hope to discover the fool in you, ere I have done with you.
  'Yours all, or one beside himself, Franciscus.' This madman will
  mend sure.   160
FRAN. What do you read, sirrah?
LOL. Your destiny, sir; you'll be hang'd for this trick, and another
  that I know.
FRAN. Art thou of counsel with thy mistress?
LOL. Next her apron-strings.   165
FRAN. Give me thy hand.
LOL. Stay, let me put yours in my pocket first [*puts away the letter*];
  your hand is true, is it not? It will not pick? I partly fear it, because
  I think it does lie.

144   eas'd] Cf. III. iv. 99.
149   Latona] Diana's mother in fact, but here used for Diana herself

FRAN. Not in a syllable.   170

LOL. So; if you love my mistress so well as you have handled the
matter here, you are like to be cur'd of your madness.

FRAN. And none but she can cure it.

LOL. Well, I'll give you over then, and she shall cast your water next.

FRAN. Take for thy pains past.   [*Gives him money*]   175

LOL. I shall deserve more, sir, I hope; my mistress loves you, but
must have some proof of your love to her.

FRAN. There I meet my wishes.

LOL. That will not serve, you must meet her enemy and yours.

FRAN. He's dead already!   180

LOL. Will you tell me that, and I parted but now with him?

FRAN. Show me the man.

LOL. Ay, that's a right course now; see him before you kill him
in any case, and yet it needs not go so far neither; 'tis but a fool
that haunts the house and my mistress in the shape of an idiot;   185
bang but his fool's coat well-favouredly, and 'tis well.

FRAN. Soundly, soundly!

LOL. Only reserve him till the masque be past; and if you find him
not now in the dance yourself, I'll show you. In, in! My master!

FRAN. He handles him like a feather. Hey!   [*Exit dancing.*   190

Enter Alibius

ALIB. Well said; in a readiness, Lollio?

LOL. Yes, sir.

ALIB. Away then, and guide them in, Lollio;
Entreat your mistress to see this sight.
Hark, is there not one incurable fool   195
That might be begg'd? I have friends.

LOL. I have him for you, one that shall deserve it too.   [*Exit.*

ALIB. Good boy, Lollio.

Enter Isabella, then Lollio with Madmen and Fools.
The Madmen and Fools dance.

'Tis perfect; well, fit but once these strains,
We shall have coin and credit for our pains.   200

[*Exeunt.*

ACT V

[Sc. 1]

Enter Beatrice. A clock strikes one.

BEAT. One struck, and yet she lies by't!—Oh, my fears!
This strumpet serves her own ends, 'tis apparent now,

190 He . . . feather] he dances as light as a feather
195–6 fool . . . begg'd] so that, as guardian, he could get control of his estate

Devours the pleasure with a greedy appetite,
And never minds my honour or my peace,
Makes havoc of my right; but she pays dearly for't: 5
No trusting of her life with such a secret,
That cannot rule her blood to keep her promise.
Beside, I have some suspicion of her faith to me,
Because I was suspected of my lord,
And it must come from her. Hark! By my horrors, 10
Another clock strikes two! [*Strikes two*]

Enter Deflores

DEF.   Pist, where are you?
BEAT. Deflores?
DEF.   Ay; is she not come from him yet?
BEAT. As I am a living soul, not.
DEF.   Sure the devil
  Hath sow'd his itch within her! Who'd trust
  A waiting-woman?
BEAT.   I must trust somebody. 15
DEF. Push! They are termagants,
  Especially when they fall upon their masters,
  And have their ladies' first-fruits; th'are mad whelps,
  You cannot stave 'em off from game royal; then
  You are so harsh and hardy, ask no counsel, 20
  And I could have help'd you to an apothecary's daughter,
  Would have fall'n off before eleven, and thank'd you too.
BEAT. O me, not yet? This whore forgets herself.
DEF. The rascal fares so well; look, y'are undone,
  The day-star, by this hand! See Phosphorus plain yonder. 25
BEAT. Advise me now to fall upon some ruin,
  There is no counsel safe else.
DEF.   Peace, I ha't now;
  For we must force a rising, there's no remedy.
BEAT. How? Take heed of that.
DEF. Tush, be you quiet, or else give over all. 30
BEAT. Prithee, I ha' done then.
DEF.   This is my reach: I'll set
  Some part afire of Diaphanta's chamber.
BEAT. How? Fire, sir? That may endanger the whole house.
DEF. You talk of danger when your fame's on fire?
BEAT. That's true; do what thou wilt now.
DEF.   Push! I aim 35
  At a most rich success, strikes all dead sure;
  The chimney being afire, and some light parcels
  Of the least danger in her chamber only,
  If Diaphanta should be met by chance then,

26   fall . . . ruin] hit upon some desperate solution

Far from her lodging—which is now suspicious—   40
It would be thought her fears and affrights then
Drove her to seek for succour; if not seen
Or met at all, as that's the likeliest,
For her own shame she'll hasten towards her lodging;
I will be ready with a piece high-charg'd,   45
As 'twere to cleanse the chimney; there 'tis proper now,
But she shall be the mark.
BEAT.   I'm forc'd to love thee now,
'Cause thou provid'st so carefully for my honour.
DEF. 'Slid, it concerns the safety of us both,
Our pleasure and continuance.
BEAT.   One word now, prithee;   50
How for the servants?
DEF.   I'll despatch them
Some one way, some another in the hurry,
For buckets, hooks, ladders; fear not you;
The deed shall find its time; and I've thought since
Upon a safe conveyance for the body too.   55
How this fire purifies wit! Watch you your minute.
BEAT. Fear keeps my soul upon't, I cannot stray from't.

Enter Alonzo's ghost

DEF. Ha! What art thou that tak'st away the light
'Twixt that star and me? I dread thee not.
'Twas but a mist of conscience—all's clear again.   [*Exit.*   60
BEAT. Who's that, Deflores? Bless me! It slides by;

[*Exit Ghost.*

Some ill thing haunts the house; 't has left behind it
A shivering sweat upon me; I'm afraid now;
This night hath been so tedious. Oh, this strumpet!
Had she a thousand lives, he should not leave her   65
Till he had destroy'd the last.—List! Oh, my terrors!
Three struck by Saint Sebastian's!—   [*Struck three o'clock*]
WITHIN. Fire, fire, fire!
BEAT. Already! How rare is that man's speed!
How heartily he serves me! His face loathes one,   70
But look upon his care, who would not love him?
The east is not more beauteous than his service.
WITHIN. Fire, fire, fire!
Enter Deflores; Servants pass over, ring a bell
DEF. Away, despatch! Hooks, buckets, ladders! That's well said;
The fire-bell rings, the chimney works; my charge;   75
The piece is ready.   [*Exit.*
BEAT.   Here's a man worth loving—
Enter Diaphanta

74   That's . . . said] That's a good idea

Oh, y'are a jewel!
DIAP.   Pardon frailty, madam;
  In troth I was so well, I ev'n forgot myself.
BEAT. Y'have made trim work.
DIAP.   What?
BEAT.   Hie quickly to your chamber;
  Your reward follows you.
DIAP.   I never made   80
  So sweet a bargain.   [*Exit.*

Enter Alsemero

ALS.   O my dear Joanna,
  Alas, art thou risen too? I was coming,
  My absolute treasure.
BEAT.   When I miss'd you,
  I could not choose but follow.
ALS.   Th'art all sweetness;
  The fire is not so dangerous.
BEAT.   Think you so, sir?   85
ALS. I prithee tremble not; believe me, 'tis not.

Enter Vermandero and Jasperino

VER. Oh, bless my house and me!
ALS.   My lord your father.

Enter Deflores with a piece

VER. Knave, whither goes that piece?
DEF.   To scour the chimney.
                                          [*Exit.*

VER. Oh, well said, well said;
  That fellow's good on all occasions.   90
BEAT. A wondrous necessary man, my lord.
VER. He hath a ready wit, he's worth 'em all, sir;
  Dog at a house of fire; I ha' seen him sing'd ere now.
                          [*The piece goes off*]

  —Ha, there he goes.
BEAT. [*Aside*]   'Tis done.
ALS.   Come, sweet, to bed now;
  Alas, thou wilt get cold.
BEAT.   Alas, the fear keeps that out;   95
  My heart will find no quiet till I hear
  How Diaphanta, my poor woman, fares;
  It is her chamber, sir, her lodging chamber.
VER. How should the fire come there?
BEAT. As good a soul as ever lady countenanc'd,   100
  But in her chamber negligent and heavy;
  She scap'd a mine twice.
VER.   Twice?
BEAT.   Strangely twice, sir.

VER. Those sleepy sluts are dangerous in a house,
  And they be ne'er so good.

Enter Deflores

DEF.   O poor virginity,
  Thou hast paid dearly for't!
VER.   Bless us! What's that?   105
DEF. A thing you all knew once—Diaphanta's burnt.
BEAT. My woman, oh, my woman!
DEF.   Now the flames
  Are greedy of her; burnt, burnt, burnt to death, sir!
BEAT. Oh, my presaging soul!
ALS.   Not a tear more;
  I charge you by the last embrace I gave you   110
  In bed before this rais'd us.
BEAT.   Now you tie me;
  Were it my sister now, she gets no more.

Enter Servant

VER. How now?
SERV.   All danger's past; you may now take
  Your rests, my lords, the fire is throughly quench'd;
  Ah, poor gentlewoman, how soon was she stifled!   115
BEAT. Deflores, what is left of her inter,
  And we as mourners all will follow her;
  I will entreat that honour to my servant,
  Ev'n of my lord himself.
ALS.   Command it, sweetness.
BEAT. Which of you spied the fire first?
DEF.   'Twas I, madam.   120
BEAT. And took such pains in't too? A double goodness!
  'Twere well he were rewarded.
VER.   He shall be;
  Deflores, call upon me.
ALS.   And upon me, sir.
                         [*Exeunt all except Deflores.*
DEF. Rewarded? Precious! Here's a trick beyond me;
  I see in all bouts both of sport and wit,   125
  Always a woman strives for the last hit.   [*Exit.*

[Sc. 2]

Enter Tomazo

TOM. I cannot taste the benefits of life
  With the same relish I was wont to do.
  Man I grow weary of, and hold his fellowship
  A treacherous, bloody friendship; and because

I am ignorant in whom my wrath should settle,   5
I must think all men villains, and the next
I meet, whoe'er he be, the murderer
Of my most worthy brother.—Ha! What's he?

Enter Deflores, passes over the stage

Oh, the fellow that some call honest Deflores;
But methinks honesty was hard bested   10
To come there for a lodging, as if a queen
Should make her palace of a pest-house.
I find a contrariety in nature
Betwixt that face and me; the least occasion
Would give me game upon him; yet he's so foul   15
One would scarce touch him with a sword he lov'd
And made account of; so most deadly venomous,
He would go near to poison any weapon
That should draw blood on him; one must resolve
Never to use that sword again in fight,   20
In way of honest manhood, that strikes him;
Some river must devour't, 'twere not fit
That any man should find it.—What, again?

Enter Deflores

He walks a' purpose by, sure, to choke me up,
To infect my blood.
DEF.   My worthy noble lord!   25
TOM. Dost offer to come near and breathe upon me?
                                              [*Strikes him*]
DEF. A blow!   [*Draws his sword*]
TOM.   Yea, are you so prepar'd?
  I'll rather, like a soldier, die by th' sword   [*Draws*]
  Than like a politician by thy poison.
DEF. Hold, my lord, as you are honourable.   30
TOM. All slaves that kill by poison are still cowards.
DEF. [*Aside*] I cannot strike; I see his brother's wounds
  Fresh bleeding in his eye, as in a crystal.—
  I will not question this; I know y'are noble;
  I take my injury with thanks given, sir,   35
  Like a wise lawyer; and as a favour
  Will wear it for the worthy hand that gave it.—
  [*Aside*] Why this from him that yesterday appear'd
  So strangely loving to me?
  Oh, but instinct is of a subtler strain;   40
  Guilt must not walk so near his lodge again;
  He came near me now.   [*Exit.*
TOM. All league with mankind I renounce for ever,

10   bested] put to it
15   give . . . him] make me challenge him

Till I find this murderer; not so much
As common courtesy, but I'll lock up;   45
For in the state of ignorance I live in,
A brother may salute his brother's murderer,
And wish good speed to th' villain in a greeting.

Enter Vermandero, Alibius and Isabella

VER. Noble Piracquo!

TOM.   Pray keep on your way, sir,
I've nothing to say to you.

VER.   Comforts bless you, sir.   50

TOM. I have forsworn compliment, in troth I have, sir;
As you are merely man, I have not left
A good wish for you, nor any here.

VER. Unless you be so far in love with grief
You will not part from't upon any terms,   55
We bring that news will make a welcome for us.

TOM. What news can that be?

VER.   Throw no scornful smile
Upon the zeal I bring you, 'tis worth more, sir.
Two of the chiefest men I kept about me
I hide not from the law or your just vengeance.   60

TOM. Ha!

VER.   To give your peace more ample satisfaction,
Thank these discoverers.

TOM.   If you bring that calm,
Name but the manner I shall ask forgiveness in
For that contemptuous smile upon you:
I'll perfect it with reverence that belongs   65
Unto a sacred altar.   [*Kneels*]

VER.   Good sir, rise;
Why, now you overdo as much a' this hand
As you fell short a' t'other. Speak, Alibius.

ALIB. 'Twas my wife's fortune, as she is most lucky
At a discovery, to find out lately   70
Within our hospital of fools and madmen
Two counterfeits slipp'd into these disguises;
Their names, Franciscus and Antonio.

VER. Both mine, sir, and I ask no favour for 'em.

ALIB. Now that which draws suspicion to their habits: 75
The time of their disguisings agrees justly
With the day of the murder.

TOM.   O blest revelation!

VER. Nay more, nay more, sir—I'll not spare mine own
In way of justice—they both feign'd a journey
To Briamata, and so wrought out their leaves;   80
My love was so abus'd in't.

TOM.   Time's too precious

To run in waste now; you have brought a peace
The riches of five kingdoms could not purchase.
Be my most happy conduct; I thirst for 'em;
Like subtle lightning will I wind about 'em,   85
And melt their marrow in 'em.

                                        [*Exeunt.*

[Sc. 3]
                    Enter Alsemero and Jasperino

JASP. Your confidence, I'm sure, is now of proof.
   The prospect from the garden has show'd
   Enough for deep suspicion.
ALS.   The black mask
   That so continually was worn upon't
   Condemns the face for ugly ere't be seen;   5
   Her despite of him, and so seeming bottomless.
JASP. Touch it home then; 'tis not a shallow probe
   Can search this ulcer soundly; I fear you'll find it
   Full of corruption; 'tis fit I leave you:
   She meets you opportunely from that walk;   10
   She took the back door at his parting with her.   [*Exit Jasperino.*

ALS. Did my fate wait for this unhappy stroke
   At my first sight of woman?—She's here.
                    Enter Beatrice

BEAT. Alsemero!
ALS.   How do you?
BEAT.   How do I?
   Alas! how do you? You look not well.   15
ALS. You read me well enough. I am not well.
BEAT. Not well, sir? Is't in my power to better you?
ALS. Yes.
BEAT.   Nay, then y'are cur'd again.
ALS. Pray resolve me one question, lady.
BEAT.   If I can.
ALS. None can so sure. Are you honest?   20
BEAT. Ha, ha, ha! That's a broad question, my lord.
ALS. But that's not a modest answer, my lady.
   Do you laugh? My doubts are strong upon me.
BEAT. 'Tis innocence that smiles, and no rough brow
   Can take away the dimple in her cheek.   25
   Say I should strain a tear to fill the vault,
   Which would you give the better faith to?

1   confidence] belief in my story

ALS. 'Twere but hypocrisy of a sadder colour,
　But the same stuff; neither your smiles nor tears
　Shall move or flatter me from my belief: 30
　You are a whore!
BEAT.　　　　　　What a horrid sound it hath!
　It blasts a beauty to deformity;
　Upon what face soever that breath falls,
　It strikes it ugly; oh, you have ruin'd
　What you can ne'er repair again.   35
ALS. I'll all demolish, and seek out truth within you,
　If there be any left; let your sweet tongue
　Prevent your heart's rifling; there I'll ransack
　And tear out my suspicion.
BEAT.　　　　　　　　You may, sir,
　'Tis an easy passage; yet, if you please,   40
　Show me the ground whereon you lost your love;
　My spotless virtue may but tread on that
　Before I perish.
ALS.　　　　Unanswerable!
　A ground you cannot stand on; you fall down
　Beneath all grace and goodness when you set   45
　Your ticklish heel on't; there was a visor
　O'er that cunning face, and that became you;
　Now impudence in triumph rides upon't;
　How comes this tender reconcilement else
　'Twixt you and your despite, your rancorous loathing,   50
　Deflores? He that your eye was sore at sight of,
　He's now become your arm's supporter, your
　Lip's saint!
BEAT.　　Is there the cause?
ALS.　　　　　　　Worse; your lust's devil,
　Your adultery!
BEAT.　　　　Would any but yourself say that,
　'Twould turn him to a villain.
ALS.　　　　　　　　'Twas witness'd   55
　By the counsel of your bosom, Diaphanta.
BEAT. Is your witness dead then?
ALS.　　　　　　　'Tis to be fear'd
　It was the wages of her knowledge; poor soul,
　She liv'd not long after the discovery.
BEAT. Then hear a story of not much less horror   60
　Than this your false suspicion is beguil'd with;
　To your bed's scandal I stand up innocent,
　Which even the guilt of one black other deed
　Will stand for proof of: your love has made me
　A cruel murd'ress.
ALS.　　　Ha!
BEAT.　　　　　A bloody one;   65

I have kiss'd poison for't, strok'd a serpent:
That thing of hate, worthy in my esteem
Of no better employment, and him most worthy
To be so employ'd, I caus'd to murder
That innocent Piracquo, having no   70
Better means than that worst, to assure
Yourself to me.
ALS.   Oh, the place itself e'er since
Has crying been for vengeance, the temple
Where blood and beauty first unlawfully
Fir'd their devotion and quench'd the right one;   75
'Twas in my fears at first, 'twill have it now;
Oh, thou art all deform'd!
BEAT.   Forget not, sir,
It for your sake was done; shall greater dangers
Make the less welcome?
ALS.   Oh, thou shouldst have gone
A thousand leagues about to have avoided   80
This dangerous bridge of blood! Here we are lost.
BEAT. Remember I am true unto your bed.
ALS. The bed itself's a charnel, the sheets shrouds
For murder'd carcasses. It must ask pause
What I must do in this; meantime you shall   85
Be my prisoner only. Enter my closet;
I'll be your keeper yet. [*Exit Beatrice*] Oh, in what part
Of this sad story shall I first begin?—Ha!
This same fellow has put me in—

Enter Deflores

Deflores!
DEF. Noble Alsemero!
ALS.   I can tell you   90
News, sir; my wife has her commended to you.
DEF. That's news indeed, my lord; I think she would
Commend me to the gallows if she could,
She ever lov'd me so well; I thank her.
ALS. What's this blood upon your band, Deflores?   95
DEF. Blood? No, sure, 'twas wash'd since.
ALS.   Since when, man?
DEF. Since t'other day I got a knock
In a sword-and-dagger school; I think 'tis out.
ALS. Yes, 'tis almost out, but 'tis perceiv'd though.
I had forgot my message; this it is: 100
What price goes murder?
DEF.   How sir?
ALS.   I ask you, sir;

89   put me in] suggested to me, put me in mind of

My wife's behindhand with you, she tells me,
For a brave bloody blow you gave for her sake
Upon Piracquo.

DEF.   Upon? 'Twas quite through him, sure;
Has she confess'd it?

ALS.   As sure as death to both of you,   105
And much more than that.

DEF.   It could not be much more:
'Twas but one thing, and that—that she's a whore.

ALS. It could not choose but follow; oh, cunning devils!
How should blind men know you from fair-fac'd saints?

BEAT. [*Within*] He lies, the villain does belie me!   110

DEF. Let me go to her, sir.

ALS.   Nay, you shall to her.
Peace, crying crocodile, your sounds are heard!
Take your prey to you, get you in to her, sir.

                                        [*Exit Deflores.*

I'll be your pander now; rehearse again
Your scene of lust, that you may be perfect   115
When you shall come to act it to the black audience
Where howls and gnashings shall be music to you.
Clip your adult'ress freely, 'tis the pilot
Will guide you to the *Mare Mortuum*,
Where you shall sink to fathoms bottomless.   120

Enter Vermandero, Alibius, Isabella, Tomazo, Franciscus, and Antonio

VER. Oh, Alsemero, I have a wonder for you!

ALS. No, sir, 'tis I, I have a wonder for you.

VER. I have suspicion near as proof itself
For Piracquo's murder.

ALS.   Sir, I have proof
Beyond suspicion for Piracquo's murder.   125

VER. Beseech you, hear me; these two have been disguis'd
E'er since the deed was done.

ALS.   I have two other
That were more close disguis'd than your two could be
E'er since the deed was done.

VER. You'll hear me—these mine own servants—   130

ALS. Hear me: those nearer than your servants,
That shall acquit them and prove them guiltless.

FRAN. That may be done with easy truth, sir.

TOM. How is my cause bandied through your delays!
'Tis urgent in my blood and calls for haste;   135
Give me a brother alive or dead;
Alive, a wife with him; if dead, for both
A recompense for murder and adultery.

107   that—that] conj. Sherman; that Q.

BEAT. [*Within*] Oh, oh, oh!
ALS.   Hark! 'Tis coming to you.
DEF. [*Within*] Nay, I'll along for company.
BEAT. [*Within*]   Oh, oh!   140
VER. What horrid sounds are these?
ALS. Come forth, you twins of mischief.

Enter Deflores, bringing in Beatrice wounded

DEF. Here we are; if you have any more
  To say to us speak quickly; I shall not
  Give you the hearing else; I am so stout yet,   145
  And so, I think, that broken rib of mankind.
VER. An host of enemies enter'd my citadel
  Could not amaze like this: Joanna! Beatrice-Joanna!
BEAT. Oh, come not near me, sir, I shall defile you;
  I am that of your blood was taken from you   150
  For your better health; look no more upon't,
  But cast it to the ground regardlessly,
  Let the common sewer take it from distinction.
  Beneath the stars, upon yon meteor
  Ever hung my fate, 'mongst things corruptible;   155
  I ne'er could pluck it from him; my loathing
  Was prophet to the rest, but ne'er believ'd;
  Mine honour fell with him, and now my life.
  Alsemero, I am a stranger to your bed,
  Your bed was cozen'd on the nuptial night,   160
  For which your false bride died.
ALS.   Diaphanta!
DEF. Yes, and the while I coupled with your mate
  At barley-break; now we are left in hell.
VER. We are all there, it circumscribes us here.
DEF. I lov'd this woman in spite of her heart;   165
  Her love I earn'd out of Piracquo's murder.
TOM. Ha! my brother's murderer?
DEF.   Yes, and her honour's prize
  Was my reward; I thank life for nothing
  But that pleasure; it was so sweet to me
  That I have drunk up all, left none behind   170
  For any man to pledge me.
VER.   Horrid villain!
  Keep life in him for further tortures.
DEF.   No!
  I can prevent you; here's my penknife still;
  It is but one thread more, [*stabs himself*] and now 'tis cut.
  Make haste, Joanna; by that token to thee,   175
  Canst not forget, so lately put in mind;
  I would not go to leave thee far behind.   [*Dies*]
BEAT. Forgive me, Alsemero, all forgive;

'Tis time to die when 'tis a shame to live.   [*Dies*]
VER. Oh, my name is ent'red now in that record,   180
  Where till this fatal hour 'twas never read.
ALS. Let it be blotted out; let your heart lose it,
  And it can never look you in the face,
  Nor tell a tale behind the back of life
  To your dishonour; justice hath so right   185
  The guilty hit that innocence is quit
  By proclamation, and may joy again.
  [*To Tomazo*] Sir, you are sensible of what truth hath done;
  'Tis the best comfort that your grief can find.
TOM. Sir, I am satisfied; my injuries   190
  Lie dead before me; I can exact no more,
  Unless my soul were loose, and could o'ertake
  Those black fugitives that are fled from thence,
  To take a second vengeance; but there are wraths
  Deeper than mine, 'tis to be fear'd, about 'em.   195
ALS. What an opacous body had that moon
  That last chang'd on us! Here's beauty chang'd
  To ugly whoredom; here, servant obedience
  To a master-sin, imperious murder;
  I, a suppos'd husband, chang'd embraces   200
  With wantonness, but that was paid before;
  Your change is come too, from an ignorant wrath
  To knowing friendship. Are there any more on's?
ANT. Yes, sir, I was chang'd too, from a little ass as I was to a great
  fool as I am, and had like to ha' been chang'd to the gallows, but 205
  that you know my innocence always excuses me.
FRAN. I was chang'd from a little wit to be stark mad,
  Almost for the same purpose.
ISAB.   Your change is still behind
  But deserve best your transformation.
  You are a jealous coxcomb, keep schools of folly,   210
  And teach your scholars how to break your own head.
ALIB. I see all apparent, wife, and will change now
  Into a better husband, and never keep
  Scholars that shall be wiser than myself.
ALS. Sir, you have yet a son's duty living,   215
  Please you accept it; let that your sorrow,
  As it goes from your eye, go from your heart;
  Man and his sorrow at the grave must part.

EPILOGUE

ALS. All we can do to comfort one another,
  To stay a brother's sorrow for a brother,
  To dry a child from the kind father's eyes,
  Is to no purpose, it rather multiplies;
  Your only smiles have power to cause relive   5
  The dead again, or in their rooms to give
  Brother a new brother, father a child;
  If these appear, all griefs are reconcil'd.

                         [*Exeunt omnes.*

EPILOGUE] Dyce and Bullen added these lines to Alsemero's last speech, but l. 5 is clearly an appeal to the audience.

GLOSSARY

ABROACH (*a*) give utterance to; (*b*) afoot

ACCIDENT event, sympton

ADDITION title

ALATE of late

ALL'S all as

ALMOND-MILK drink made from sweet almonds and water

AMOROUSLY attractive

AND if

ANGEL gold coin

ANTIC grotesque figure

APPROVE confirm, justify

AQUA COELISTIS strong spirits

AQUA VITAE strong spirits

ARTIFICIALLY skilfully, artfully

AUNT bawd, whore

BAFFLING public disgrace

BAND neck-band

BANKERS men who protect and strengthen river-banks

BANQUET a light repast, with sweetmeats, wine, etc.

BARREN dull, stupid

BATING abating

BEHINDHAND in debt

BLAME blameworthy

BLEAKING-HOUSE brothel

BLOW hang

BLUE-COATS liveried servants

BONE-PICKER one who gets the remains of someone else's dinner

BORD quality, condition

BOUNCE bang

BRACKS flaws

BRANCHED embroidered

BRAVE smart, well dressed

BREAST singing voice

BREED cut (teeth)

BREEDS YOUNG BONES is pregnant

BREVITY sexually inadequate man

BRIDE-HOUSE house of a bride

BUDGELLING ? boggling

BUFF ox-hide leather

BUM-ROLL cushion worn round the hips

BY-BET additional attraction

CALENDAR almanac

CALTROP spikes used to stop cavalry

CANARIES (*a*) sweet wines; (*b*) lively dance

CAPCASE bag, wallet, cover

CAREFUL full of care

CAROCHE kind of coach

CAST arranged

CASTING-BOTTLE bottle for sprinkling perfumed water

CAT piece of wood used in the game of tip-cat; CAT-STICK used in the game of tip-cat

CATES delicacies; CATER man who bought provisions for large household

CAUDLE spiced warm drink made with ale or wine

CHALDRON 32 bushels (dry measure)

CHARGE powder

CHOPPER strapping child; CHOPPING strapping

CHOPS jaws

CINQUE-PACE lively dance

CLAP-FALLEN infected with gonorrhoea

CLEANLY neat

CLIP embrace

CLOTH-STOPPLE plug made of cloth

COADS See cud's

COG cheat; COGGING JOHN cheater

COME CUT AND LONG TAIL all sorts of people

COMELY handsome, decent

COMFIT-MAKER sweet manufacturer

COMFORTABLE comforting

COMMODIOUS beneficial

213

COMPASS due limits

COMPOSITION made-up drink; cocktail

COMPOUND mix

CONCEIT fancy, opinion, meaning

CONDITION character, quality

CONSORTS companions, followers

CONVEYANCE secret passage

COPY (*a*) copyhold tenure; (*b*) passage to be copied by pupil

COURSE (*a*) action; (*b*) pack

COURT-PASSAGE (*a*) gambling game; (*b*) amorous intrigue

COURT-SAINT chaste maid at court

CRAG neck

CUD'S BODKINS God's body!

CURIOUS fastidious

CUTTED bad-tempered

CUT-WORK lace or embroidery

CYPRESS light, transparent material

DAB duck

DEFEND forbid

DESIGN designate

DEVOTION alms

DILDO artificial sexual organ, used for masturbation

DISLIKE offend

DISTINCTION being distinct

DOUBT fear

DUKE rook

DUNKIRKS privateers from Dunkirk

EMBOSSINGS embossed decoration

ENTAILED permanently

EQUAL fair

ERGO therefore

ESCAPES excuses

EWE-MUTTON experienced prostitute

EXPRESS distil

FAG end

FAST certainly

FEAR frighten

'FECTION (AFFECTION) affectation

FETCH . . . ABOUT take a roundabout course

FETCH IN (*a*) bring in; (*b*) deceive

FETCH O'ER trick you, get the better of you

FIDDLE get at, get near

FIGGING dressy

FIGIENT fidgety

FIND understand

FINE-TIMBER'D well built

FIRKIN small cask

FIRST HAND first strike

FITTER piece

FLESH-FLY blow-fly

FOND foolish

FOOTRA obscene oath

FORCE, OF of necessity

FOREHEAD impudence

FRENCH CURTSEY awkward gait (due to effects of pox)

GAMESTER rake

GAUDY-SHOP shop for finery

GEAR affair, trouble

GET UP make up for

GOING passage

GOLLS hands

GOSSIPING christening

GRATED IN having difficulty with

GRISTLES sexual organs

GRUB insignificant creature

HAIR, AGAINST THE against the grain

HANSELL'D given an advance

HAPLY, HAPPILLY by chance

HAY country dance

HEADBOROUGH parish official, similar to a constable

HEARSE framework over coffin in church

HEAT climax

HOBOYS oboes

HOFTE TOFTE an exclamation

HONEST chaste

HONOUR bow

HOPPER-RUMP'D with a rump shaped like a miller's hopper

HORSING (*a*) horsy; (*b*) copulating

HOUSE-KEEPER householder

HOYDA heyday

INCONTINENTLY immediately

INNOCENT fool, half-wit

JACKS fellows

JEALOUS suspicious

JET swagger

JIGGAM-BOB thingammybob, knick-knack

JUGGLE play, deceive; JUGGLING deceiving, trickery

KENNELS lairs
KICKSHAWS fancy dishes
KITLING cub, kitten
KNED kneaded
KNOCKER (a) woman of stunning appearance; (b) one who is expert in bed

LAMBSTONES lamb's testicles
LARGELY far and wide
LAY search
LEAGUE armistice, alliance
LEGS bows
LET prevent
LIBERTY district with its own commission
LIFT blow
LIKE please
LIN leave off
LIVELY lifelike
LONG ON because of
LURCH cheat

MALTMEN maltsters
MARCHPANE marzipan
MARE MORTUUM dead sea
MARK (a) target; (b) coin
MARKET purchase
MEASURE stately dance
MENDS amends
METAL with a quibble on *mettle*
MINE ? disaster
MISTRESS small ball at which bowlers aimed
MOON-CALF lumpish person
MOTIONED OF proposed by
MYSTICAL secret

NARROW-EYED (a) closely observing; (b) difficult to have intercourse with
NICE fastidious; NICELY fastidiously, precisely
NIGGET nidget, idiot
NIGHT-PIECE bed-fellow
NOISE sounds heard before death

OPACOUS opaque
ORDINARY eating-house
OUGHT owed
OUTCRY auction

PAINTS WHITE turns pale
PARBREAKING vomiting
PARLOUS dangerous, cunning
PASS surpass
PASSION sorrow
PERFECT contented
PERMASANT parmesan cheese
PHYSIC laxative
PICK steal
PICK-HAIR'D sparsely bearded (Thomson)
PIECE (a) girl; (b) gun; (c) (master)-piece
PILLOWBERES pillow-cases
PIN bolt
PINK stab
PIPES casks
PIZZLE bull's penis, used as whip
PLEAD . . . BENEFIT claim exemption
PLUM-TREE female pudenda
POINT full stop
POISE weight
POUNDED impounded
PRECEDENTS exemplars
PREPARATIVE something administered before a course of treatment
PRESENTERS performers
PRESENTLY immediately
PRETEND offer
PREVENT forestall
PRICK (a) bull's eye; (b) penis; PRICKER (a) one who aims at a target; (b) a copulator
PRINCIPAL choice
PROCEEDED graduated
PROMONT promontory
PROMOTER informer
PRONE, PRONENESS sexually aroused
PROPER handsome
PRUN'D preened
PURCHASE winning, acquisition
PUSH! Tush!
PUT CASE supposing

QUEAN whore
QUICKNESS liveliness
QUIT requite

RACK neck
REACH plan, understand
RECEIPTS recipes

REFUSE renounce

REMEMBER remind

REPREHENSION reproof

RESPECTIVE FOR attentive to, concerned with

RESTORATIVE medicine or cordial to restore a person's strength

RIGGLE-TAIL with twisted tail

RISING i.e. from sleep

ROPES tight-ropes

ROSA SOLACE ? spelling of *Rosa Solis*; ROSA SOLIS liqueur made of brandy, sugar and spices

ROUND-PACK'D fleshly

RULE WITH prevail upon

RUNLET cask

SACK white Spanish wine; SACK-POSSET drink made from sack and hot milk

SADNESS, IN seriously

SALLET salad, lettuce

SAMPIER samphire

SAND-BOX box for sprinkling sand to blot ink

SCONCE small fort

SCRUTINOUS searching

SCURVY-GRASS cruciferous plant, believed to possess anti-scorbutic properties (*O.E.D.*)

SET UP stable (horses)

SETTER UP one who invests or engages in business

SHOGS jogs

'SHREW curse

SHREWD effective, cunning

SIMPLE foolish, sheer

SIMPLY absolutely

SISTER sister-in-law

SLID God's eyelid

SLIP (*a*) counterfeit coin; (*b*) escaping

SMACK taste, kiss

SMELT-BOAT boat for catching small fish

SNEAKER sneak

SOJOURNER lodger

SOLEMNITY festival, ceremony

SPED rid

SPEED succeed

SPEEDING swift

SPEEDY expeditious, fertile

SPINY lean

SQUAT knock down, crush

STALL forestall

STAND UPON asset or claim respect or credit for (*O.E.D.*)

STARTED startled, awakened

STARTERS wanderers, deserters

STARTING FROM evading

START-UP upstart

STICK hesitate

STIRRING movements

STOMACH (*a*) sexual appetite; (*b*) courage

STOOL-BALL game with stool as wicket

STOP hindrance

STOVE hot air bath, hot room

STRAIT-BODIED frigid

STRANGELY urgently

STRIKE OUT obtain

STROKES streaks

STROSSERS tight drawers

SUBSIDY solid and respectable

SUCCESS what transpires, whether good or bad

SUCKET crystallized fruit

SUGAR-SOPS bits of bread, soaked and sweetened

SUSPECT suspicion

SWEET sweetheart

SWEETLY delicately

SWINGE freedom

TESTER sixpence

THRUM waste time; THRUMMY trifling

TICKLE chastise

TICKLISH lascivious

TIPPING knocking up the 'cat' at tip-cat

TOLL entice

TOUCH'D tainted

TOY trifle

TRAPSTICK stick used in the game of trap

TREADINGS (*a*) steps; (*b*) copulations

TRIUMPH show, pageant

TROLL pass round

TUBS sweating-tubs for the treatment of venereal disease

TUMBLER (*a*) acrobat; (*b*) copulator (Parker)

TUMBLING-CAST throw

TWIGGER prolific breeder, lascivious person

'UM them

UNDERVALUED'ST invaluable

UNKINDLY unnatural

USE (a) are accustomed; (b) interest

VENTURE hazard

VERJUICE juice of sour fruit, including crab-apples

VEX behave contrarily

VILDE vile

VOIDER a receptacle into which the remains of a meal were shovelled

WARD (a) security; (b) fortify; (c) section of prison

WARDED locked

WARDEN member of governing body of a city company

WASH lotion

WATER-HOUSE reservoir

WHILOM once

WOODCOCK simpleton

ZOUNS, ZOUNDS God's wounds!